(Cover) Clouds Reflect into Chinook Bay, Little Redfish Lake - Sawtooths

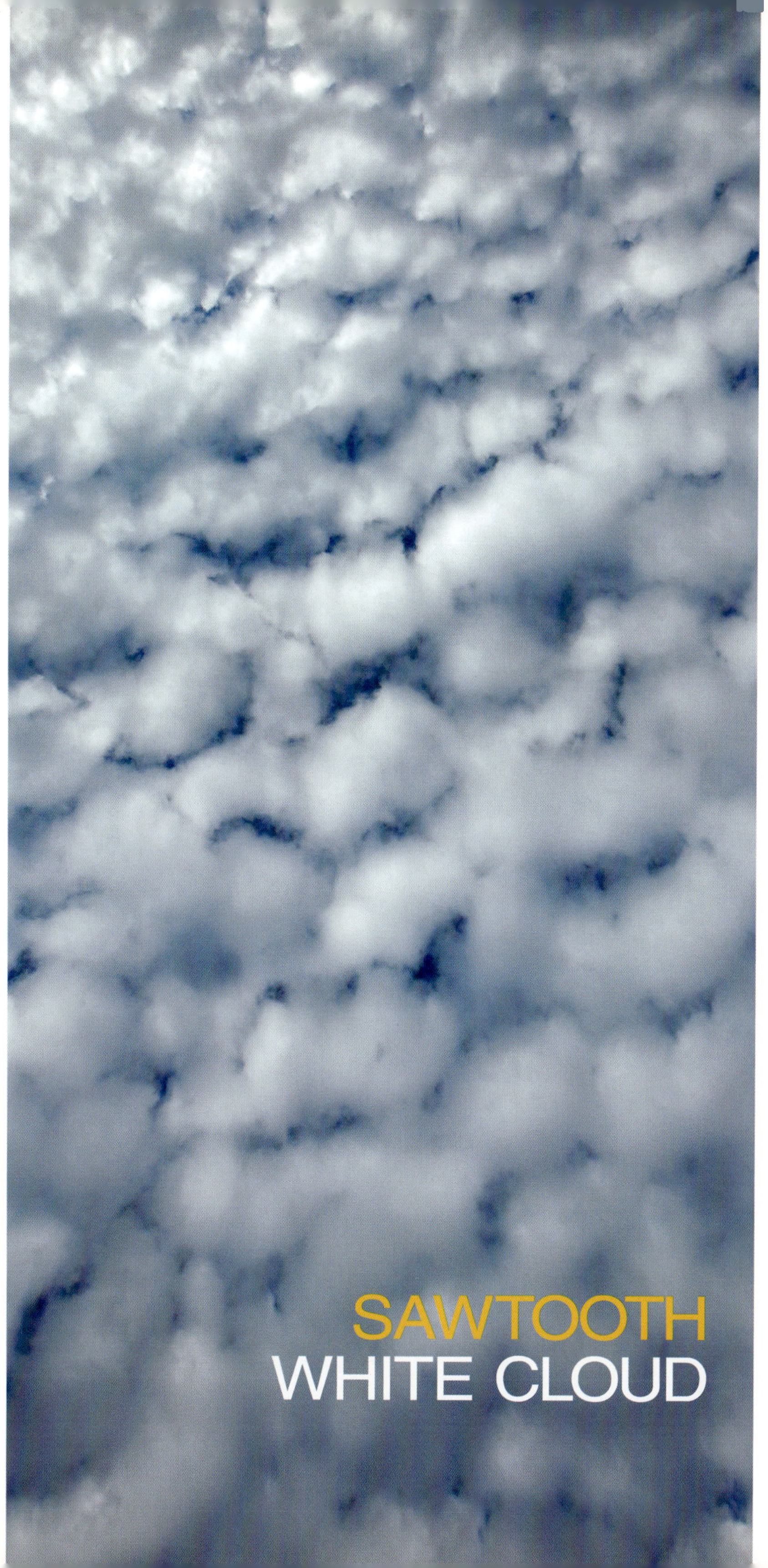

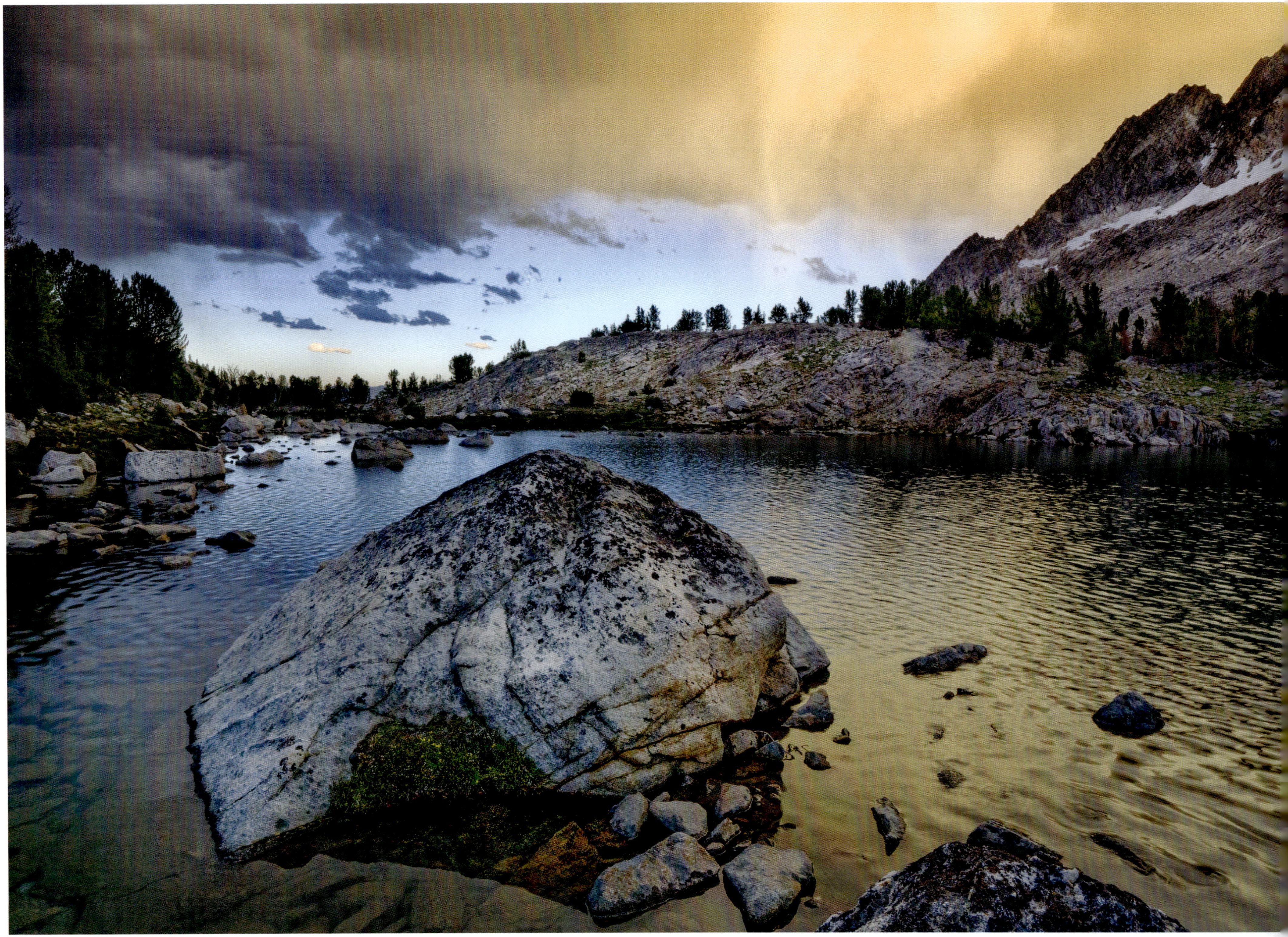

SAWTOOTH
WHITE CLOUD

Printed in Canada

Library of Congress Catalog-in-Publication Data

ISBN 978-087004-600-1

Caxton Press

Published by
Caxton Press
Caldwell, Idaho
2016

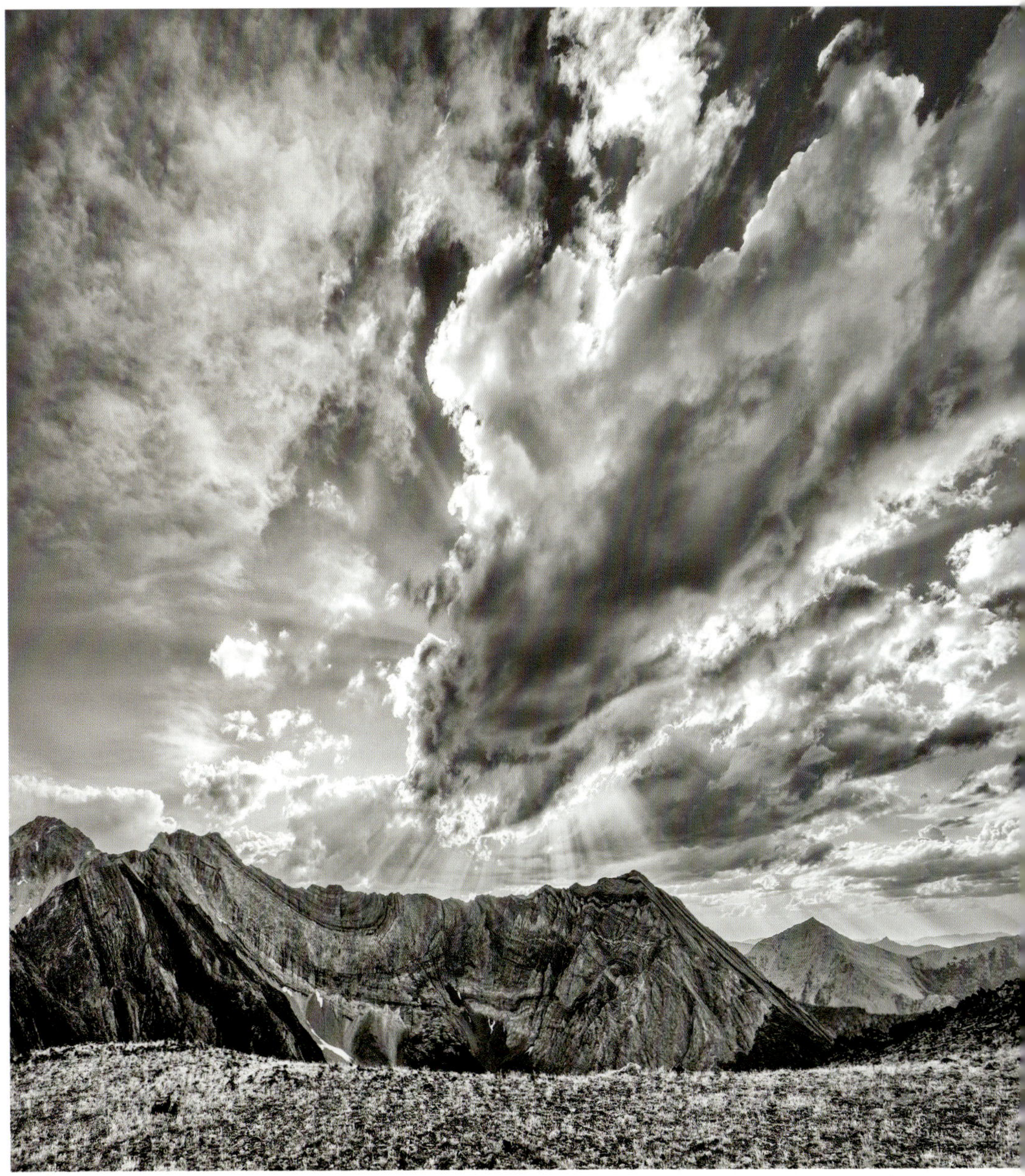

Sun rays illuminate the east face of the Chinese Wall, Railroad Ridge - White Clouds
(Opposite) Summer storm over Quartzite Lake - White Cloud Wilderness

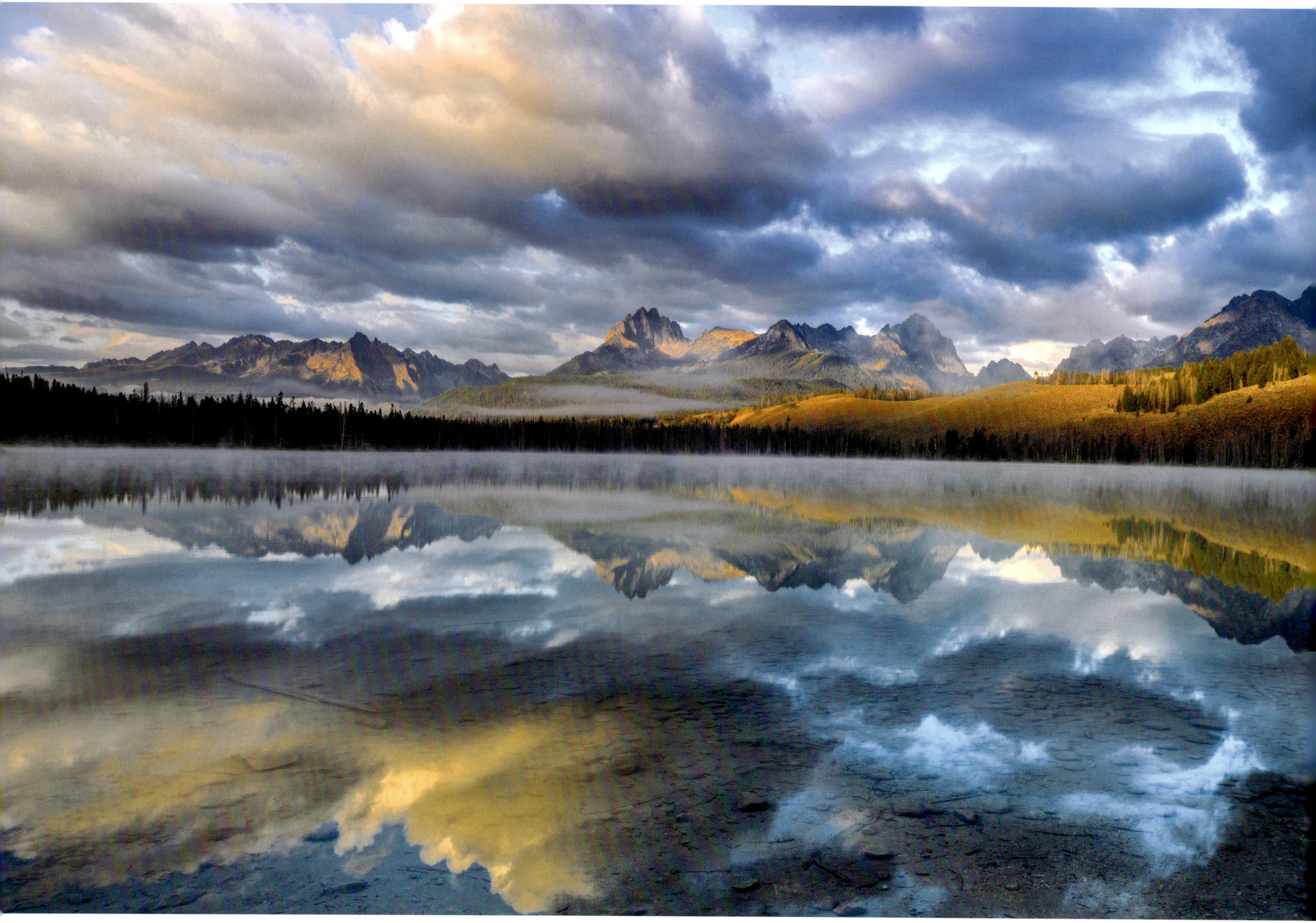

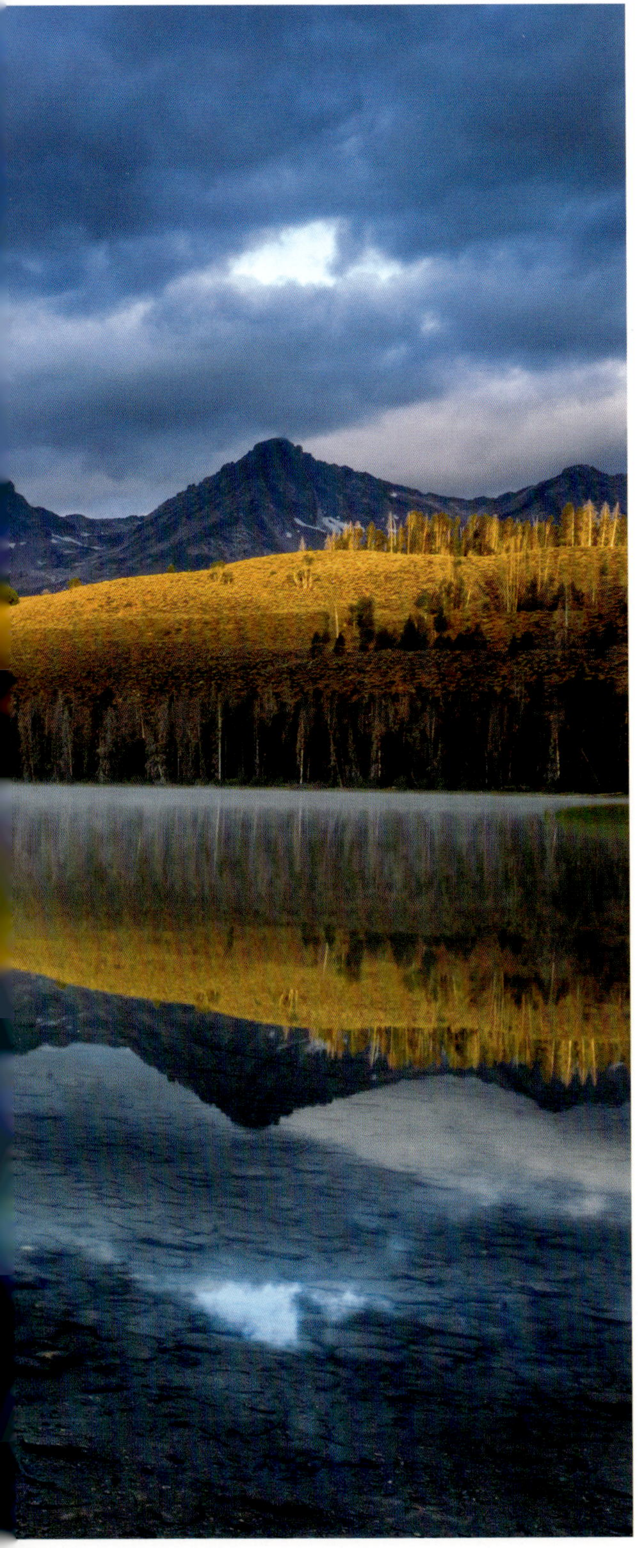

SAWTOOTH WHITE CLOUD

Photography by Mark William Lisk
Essays by Nicole LeFavour

Chinook Bay on Little Redfish Lake - Sawtooth Wilderness

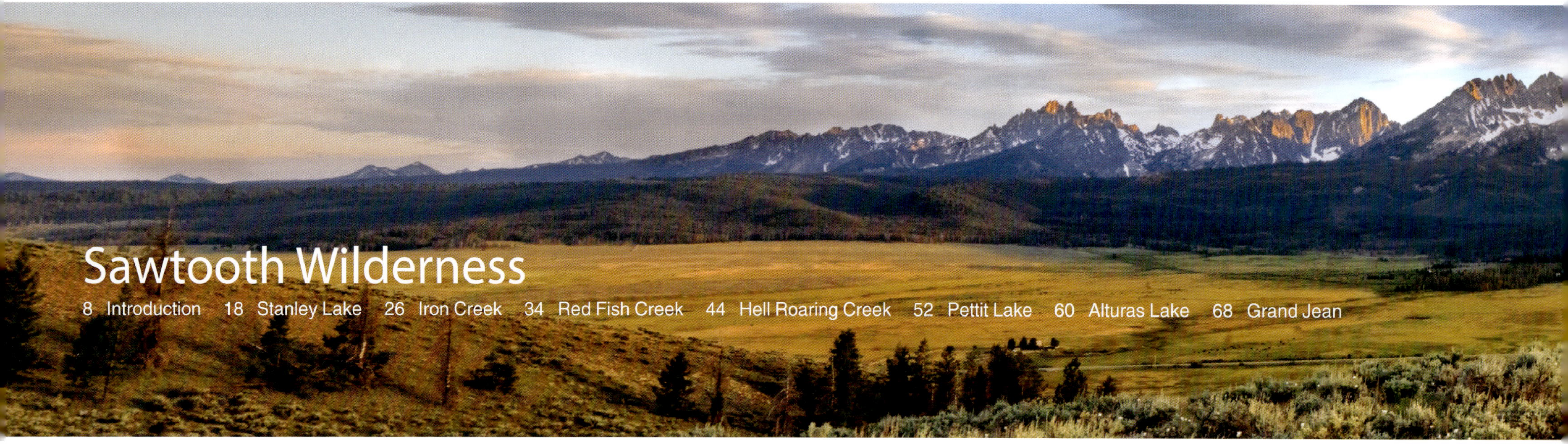

Sawtooth Wilderness

Stanley Basin - Sawtooth Range, Sawtooth Wilderness
White Cloud Peaks - Boulder Chain Lakes

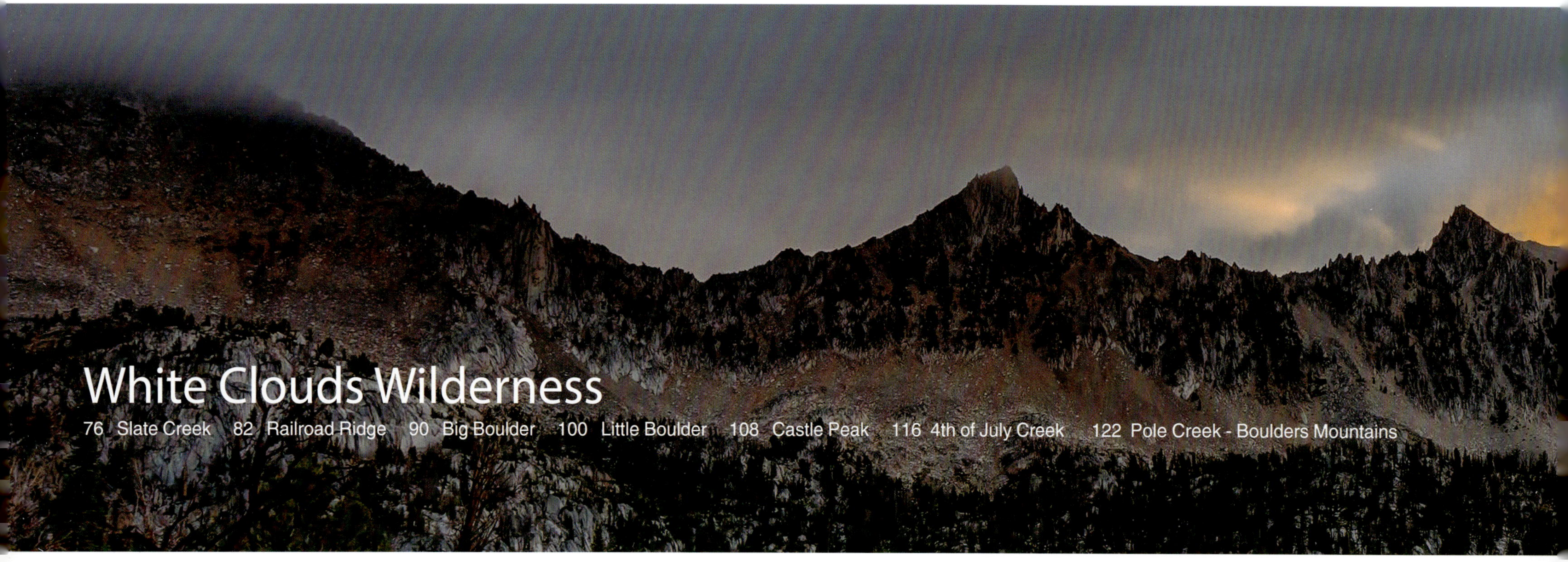

White Clouds Wilderness

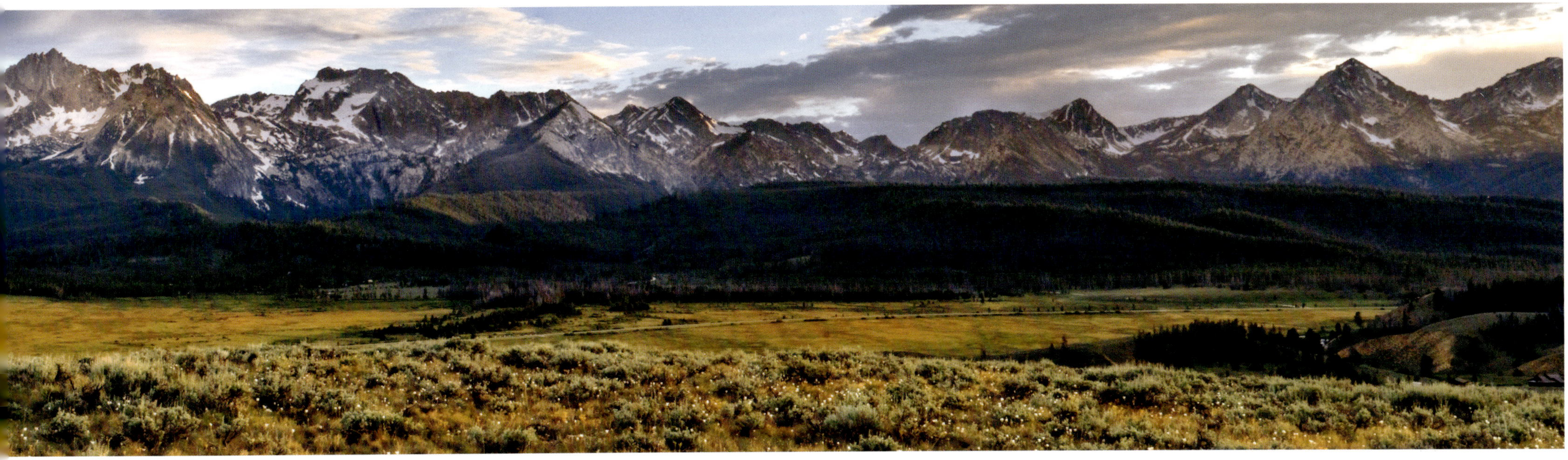

SAWTOOTH
WHITE CLOUD

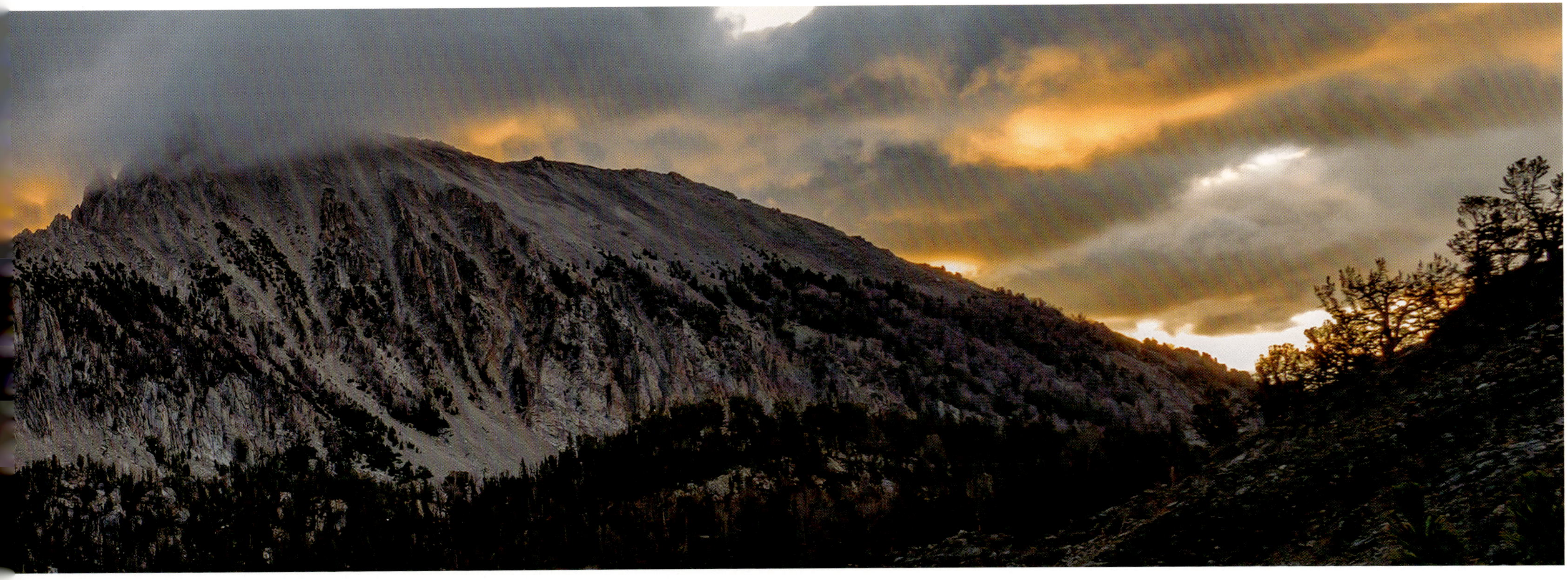

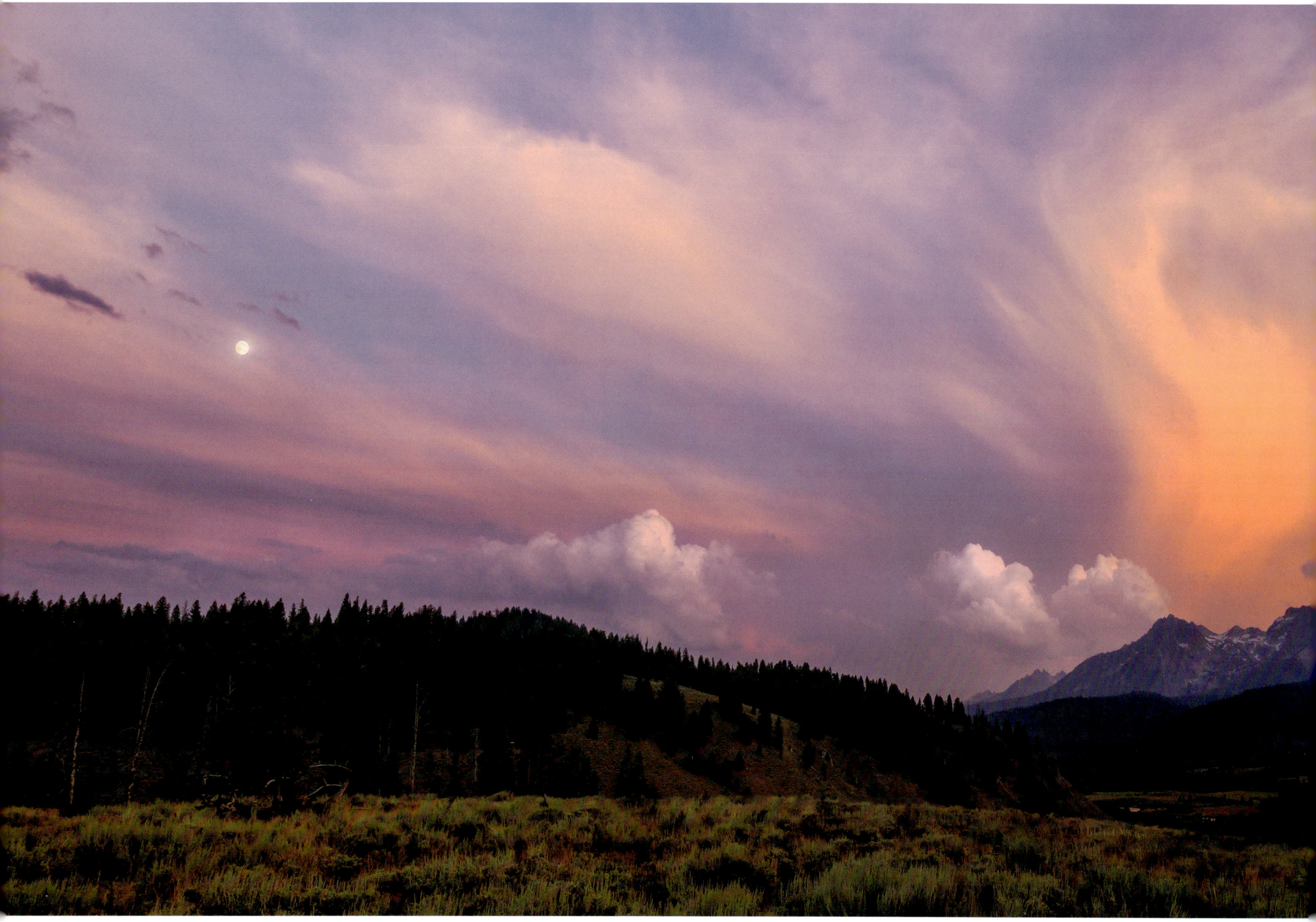

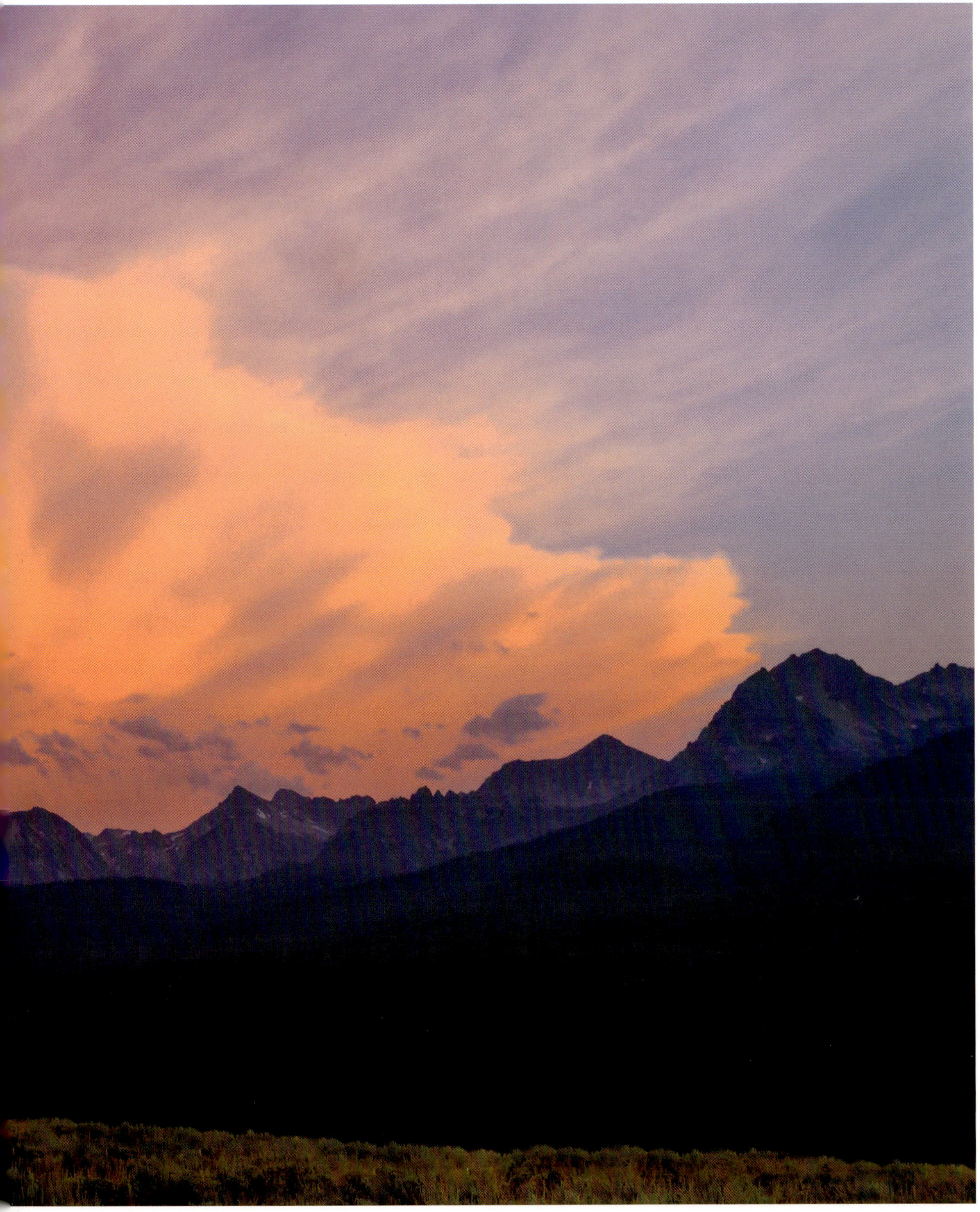

Realms above the Trees

Essay by Nicole LeFavour

THE HIGH SUN OF 10,400 FEET WARMS MY LEGS.

I lean back against a lichen-painted rock at the edge of a great curve of blue black water. Cliffs fall and the lake bottom vanishes to a depth greater than my eye can measure. I've found a hollow in the huge field of granite boulders, rounded by glaciers more than six thousand years ago. The wind howls through stone crevasses and here, at the top of the earth, water spills from a rim well above the tops of all but a few of the neighboring peaks.

This is the barren ground of the White Clouds Wilderness, where lakes meet the sky. A female hummingbird, plain brown, has just stopped to hover near me out of the wind. Small grey, rabbit-like pika call from the boulder field, making trips with mouths full of grass. This will be hay for winter, still months away. Earlier, small tan ruby crowned kinglets flew up, letting out sharp wails as we picked our way through the rocks to the lake. Backpacks light, supplies and heavy items down in base camp, I followed Mark and Jerri Lisk: Jerri carrying a tent, food and gear and Mark hefting camera equipment. We have settled in now and have broken the silence, but rest respectfully in the cathedral of goats.

Plants here are low and sparse. Lichen is often the only blanket for the earth. The few trees at this altitude are mere bushes two to five feet high: pine bonsai, ancient, twisted and perched in small pockets of soil on the mountain side.

Warm thunderhead over the Stanley Basin - Sawtooth Range

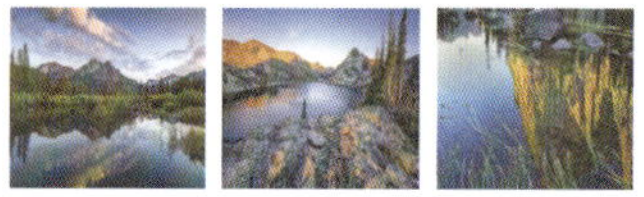

Huge cutthroat trout rise in the dusk, sipping insects from the water's surface. These are the decedents of fish carried here by pack string or aircraft half a century ago. They have stayed because the outlet is a sheer drop. The sky and the snowfield the only inlet. There is nowhere to go. The kinglets will fly South when the snow comes. The goats and pika will winter over. Lower down in the valley, the loud Stellar's jays will remain with the hawks, ravens and golden eagles which pass through from time to time.

It has taken me three days to get here; three and one-half hours from the Capitol city by car and then two days on foot. And tonight, this is where I will sleep. Like nearly every major trail which leaves a road to climb up into in the White Cloud or the Sawtooth ranges, the journey starts in sage brush; low, dry, south facing slopes, parking lots matted with cheat grass which quickly gives way to bunch grasses, tiny blueberry-like whortleberry, aspen, stands of lodgepole pine and wild flowers.

Here, up high in late July, in the shadow of a massive serrated ridge at the far end of the lake, an immense snow field still calves great hunks of ice into the water. Winter is never far here. It snows all summer long, resting as a high, white mantle on the peaks in early morning, gone by noon. The cold settles with snows which last days or even weeks in October. North slopes hang, white with frost, soon deep in layer after layer of frozen crystals. By spring, great cornices hang from the peaks and ridges. These form where snow is blown and clings to rock; snow binds to snow, forming stiff curved walls topped with overhanging faces, like frozen waves hanging above bowls and valleys of white.

I grew up in the world between the Sawtooth and White Clouds mountain ranges, along the Main Salmon River whose headwaters flow from the wide glacial valleys that formed ten thousand years ago at the feet of the Sawtooth range. In the Sawtooths, jagged granite walls rise above hundreds of stone-rimmed lakes. Huge quartz crystals hide in caverns and small glaciers still lie tucked on north faces of peaks, melting to form creeks and streams. Hundreds of pinnacles of all sizes jut into the air under that deep deep blue alpine sky.

When I was eleven, my family moved to Robinson Bar Ranch about 14 miles as the raven flies from the lake where I sit. The ranch lies on the Main Salmon River at the base of the White Clouds. It was once owned by Frank and Bethine Church, the political force behind passage of the 1964 Wilderness Act.

Earlier in the day, as Mark, Jerri and I followed goat trails up through little patches of alpine meadow toward the lake, history was being made far away in Washington D.C. Congress was debating designation of the land around us as the nearly 91,000 acre White Clouds Wilderness, a designation which passed into law and was signed by the President less than two weeks later. The White Clouds have now, after decades, joined the Sawtooths and Frank Church River of No Return Wildernesses as lands free of motors and wheels, managed to minimize the impact of people on the silence, the plants and the animals that are native here. Though local people love the land deeply, wilderness designation has often been highly controversial, especially in Custer County, the vast majority of which now lies within the boundaries of wilderness areas.

I walk away from the tent through the moonlight and it is so silent that when I stop in a boulder field above the lake, in a spot where the half moon reflects broken into shards of light off the water at the far end, all I can hear is the sound of my own pulse in my ears. Here, high above the creeks and waterfalls, above the trees, birds and animals that wander and graze the valleys below, the silence is heavy and palpable.

Wild of this kind is extremely delicate. I wander gently here, stepping on rocks rather than moss or lichen. I'm careful not to turn stones, not to leave channels or deep marks in the dirt. I want those who come after me to believe, as I sometimes do, that I am one of the first humans to pass here.

Most people in America live along paved streets, in cities or in suburbs which lace the earth with concrete and grass lawns, far from the mountains. They live in places where wooly mountain goats and pika exist almost as mythical creatures. People all over the world may live their entire lives without experiencing a place where the sound of human beings can be completely absent or where a person can walk for hours or even days without seeing another soul. Very few people will ever hear a silence like this. A tiny percentage will see stars in darkness deep enough that they can clearly see the great curve of the Milky Way

As a child who never anticipated that I would spend eight years in elected office and become a State Senator in the Idaho legislature myself, I met Frank Church in the late 1970s when his helicopter landed in a field near our big creaking lodge. He was a U.S. Senator and I learned later had sold our ranch to eliminate any possibility of conflict of interest as he began work for the preservation of 2.3 million acres, not in the White Clouds out our back door, but in the dry canyons and wooded acres of roadless land north of us, along the remote Middle Fork of the Salmon. This was the land I later walked for four years as a wilderness ranger, having spent three years on a fire lookout and two fall seasons off-trail gathering bottles

(Opposite) Camping on Railroad Ridge, the northern edge of White Cloud Wilderness

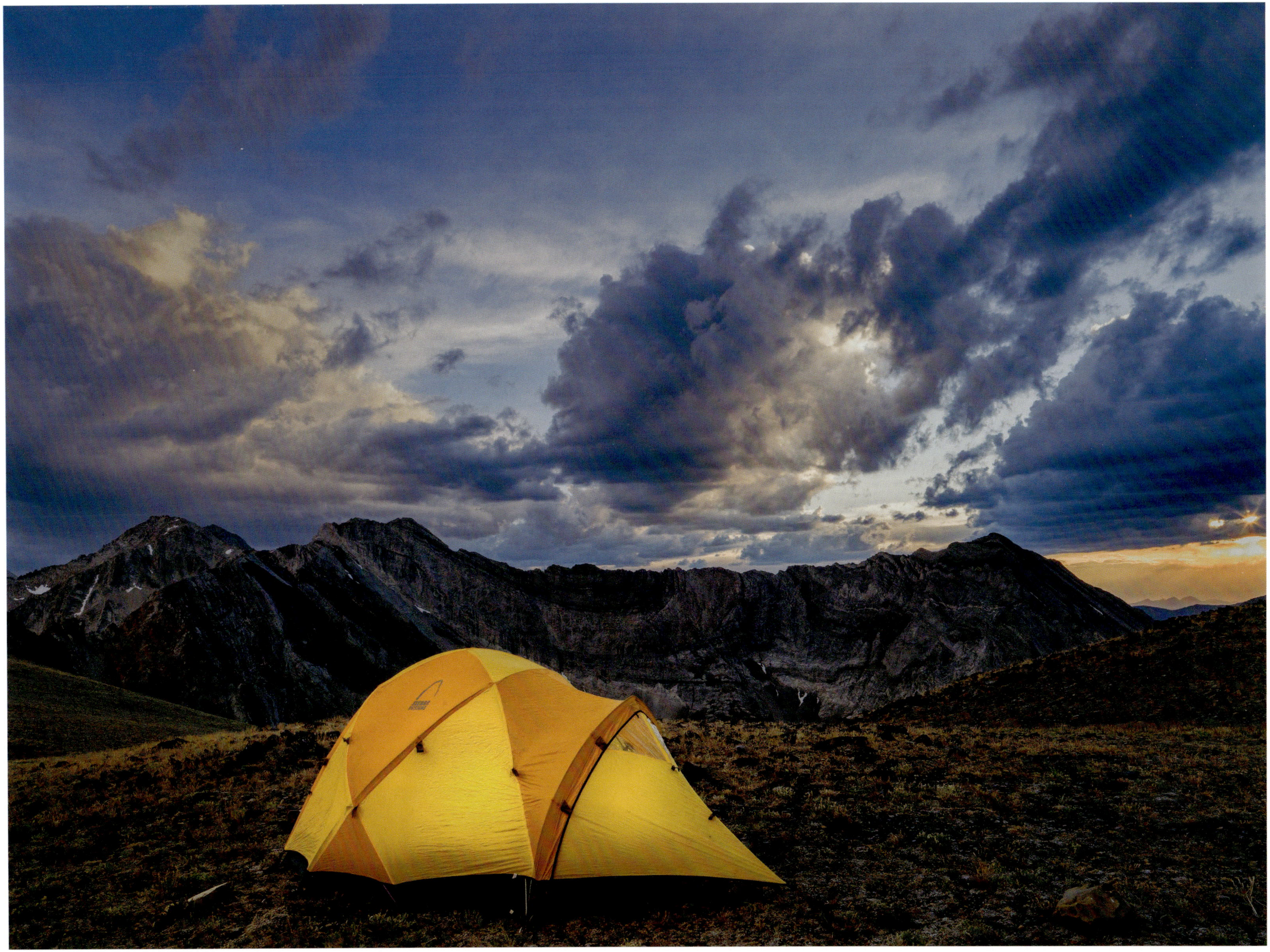

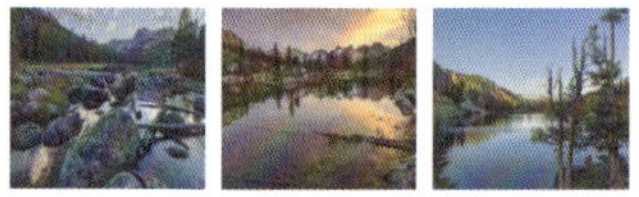

of water from high lakes above 8,000 ft.

But the White Clouds and Sawtooth Wildernesses at only one eighth the size combined, hold well more than twice as many high lakes. In the White Clouds forty lakes lie above 9,000 feet. In the Sawtooths more than twenty do. The two ranges, and especially the White Clouds account for the reason that Idaho has 111 peaks over 11,000 feet of elevation. In the White Clouds many of the lakes are higher than the tallest peaks in the Sawtooths. And while the Sawtooths hang huge and visible from the Stanley Basin and beyond, the White Clouds are all but invisible to those passing on roads traveling to and from Stanley and Challis or Sun Valley to the South.

Up high, looking down from the lake rim, the valley is lined with the silhouettes of limber pine, often just skeletons on rocky slopes or knolls. Roots deep and twined in crevices of bedrock, these towering grey and brown trunks with their bare arms have drawn strikes of lightning year after year.

Clouds pass over. They rise out of the valleys to the West beyond Grand Jean and the Wood River, the moisture coalescing white and then towering grey as it billows warm and wet, thousands of feet above the peaks. When the sky is clear on the desert plains of Southwestern Idaho, it can still rain in the Sawtooths and the White Clouds, soaking afternoon and evening rains which keep the high valleys green. And the clouds blow off of Castle or O'Calkins Peaks and fade, often evaporating completely into the sky in the desert air of the East Fork of the Salmon, Copper Basin or over the sage filled valleys to the East.

Evening falls. Mark, Jerri and I wander the lake edge as the wind settles. We walk the lichen fields to the outlet. A wide span of slow water gurgles under boulders, through massive hollow spaces, and down where it slides off the face of the mountain, toward the next lake 900 feet almost directly below.

We have made the climb on a whim, extending our time away from base camp below, making do with whatever food we had, wanting to sleep this high and near the stars. In truth we do not have enough food for three of us for two days and so our stomachs growl and we make a soup from wild sorrel, Mark's spice mix, Jerri's beef jerky and the last of a little tube of pesto I carried. We settle in to sleep, having tucked our tents amongst the rocks. My tent is ancient, borrowed from my mother who, working as a hunting and fishing outfitter out of our ranch, slept many nights under its yellow rip stop and curved "covered wagon" tent poles.

The sky is a darker blue above 10,000 feet. The dry air and thin atmosphere refracts less light, so the dark of space is a clear backdrop to the thin few thousand feet of sky above us.

Mark rises in the night to shoot the stars. I hear the zipper on his and Jerri's tent several times as the moon swings across the cirque basin from the South East to the West. Earth spins against the great depth of sky in the darkness and the silence presses, broken only by rockfall, evidence of goats high on the cliff faces we will see at morning: a nanny and tiny kid, white and desperate to scale an impossible wall to where they feel safe, out of our reach, as we walk out to leave the place in silence.

But tonight, we curl in the rocks. Stars smear circular lines between the ridges. Mark's camera clicks. He stands alone in the dark, freezing still in time the stark land he loves, these high barren places where the work of water, ice and wind on stone and soil is like a story told, like a reality hidden everywhere but in the land of deserts; and here, high in these silent bits of fragile wild, these delicate realms above the trees.

Sawtooth Wilderness
217,088 acres
1937 Sawtooth Primitive Area created
1972 Sawtooths are designated as wilderness
Highest peak: Thompson Peak 10,751 ft.
More than 550 lakes, most unnamed
Largest lake in wilderness: Sawtooth Lake 8,430 ft. of elevation
Highest lake: 9,750 ft.

White Clouds Wilderness
90,769 acres
1972 included in the Sawtooth National Recreation Area
2015 White Clouds Wilderness created
Highest peak: Castle Peak 11,815 ft.
More than 100 lakes, most unnamed
Largest lake in wilderness: Quiet Lake 9250 ft. of elevation
Highest lake: 10,449 ft.

(Opposite) Limber pine skeleton on Goat Lake Ridge - White Cloud Range

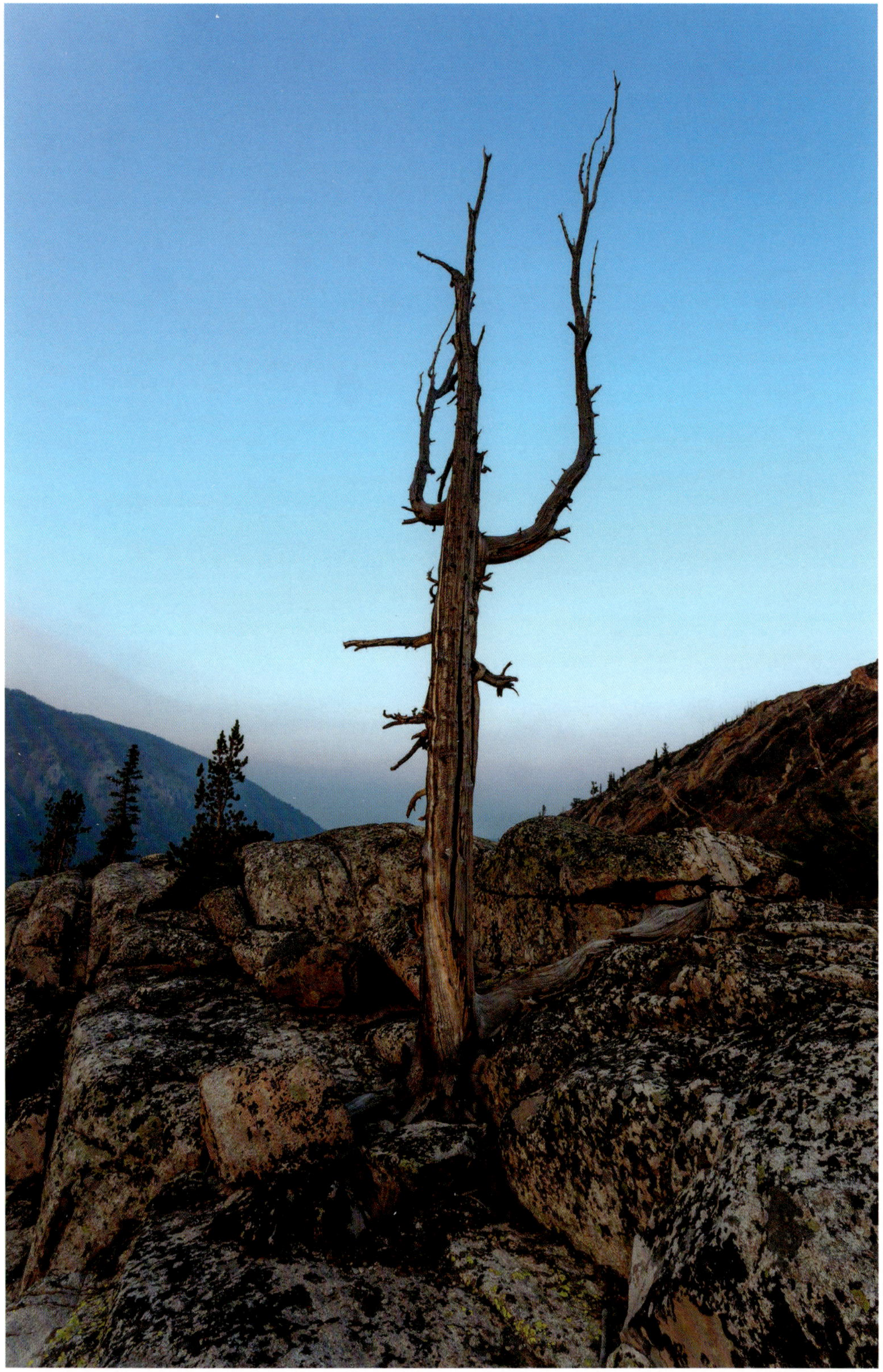
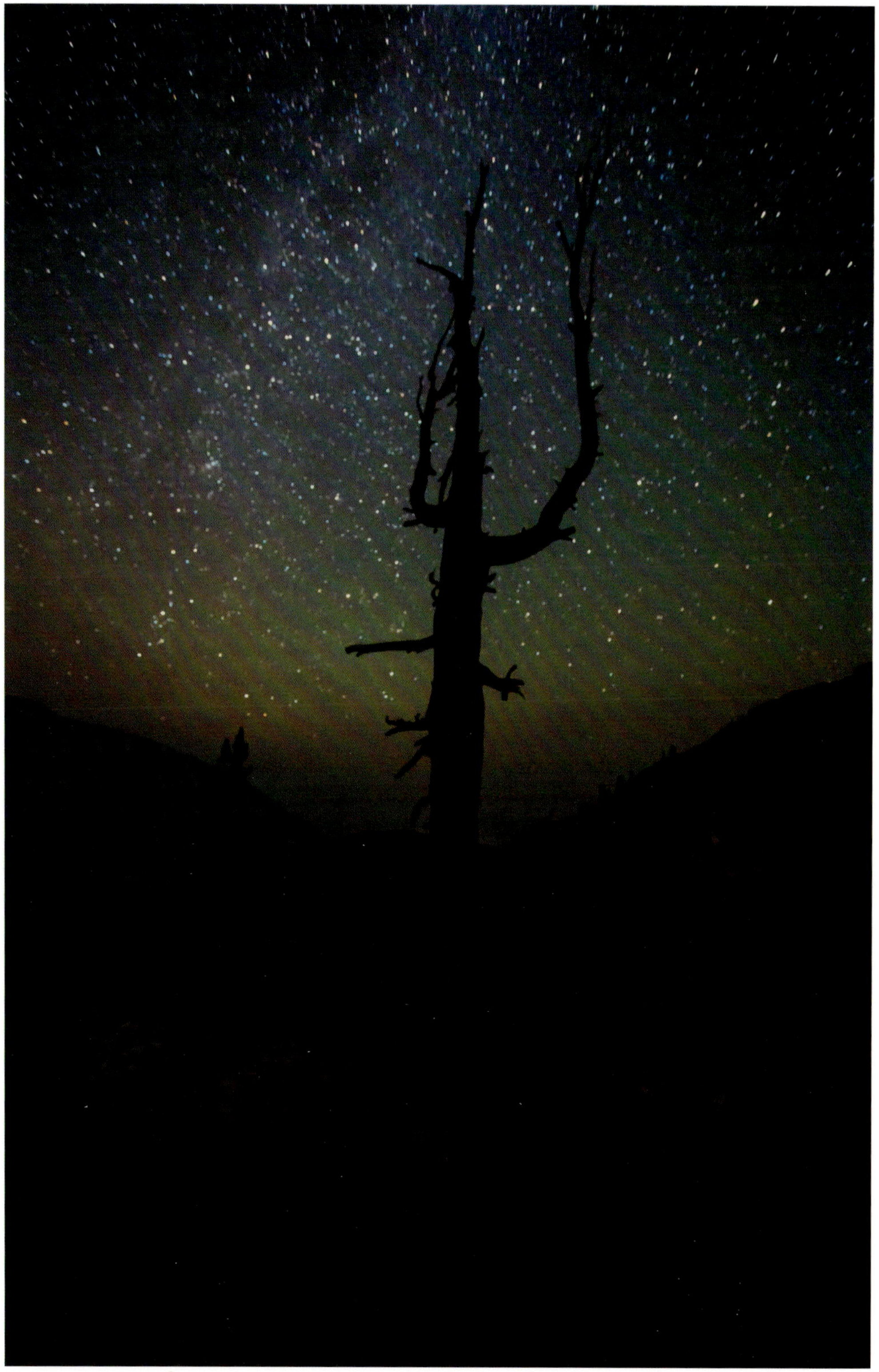

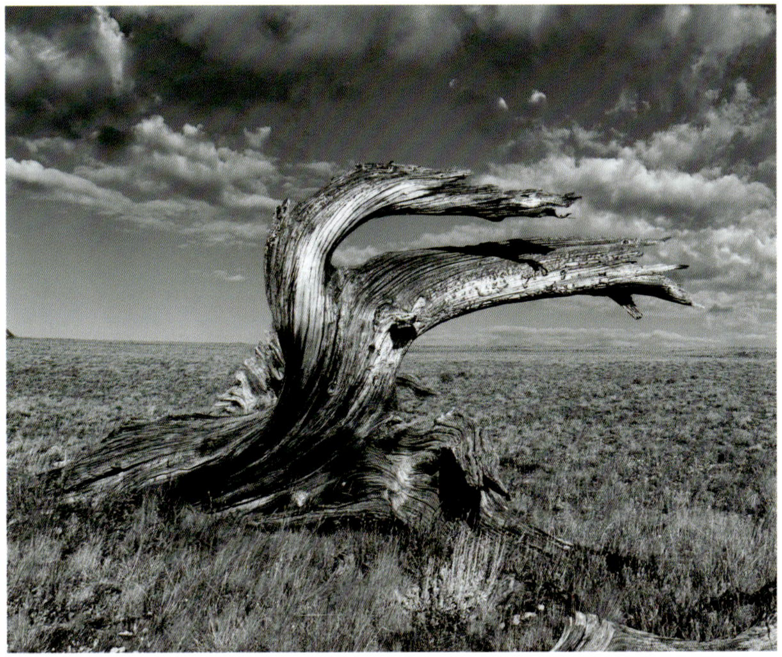

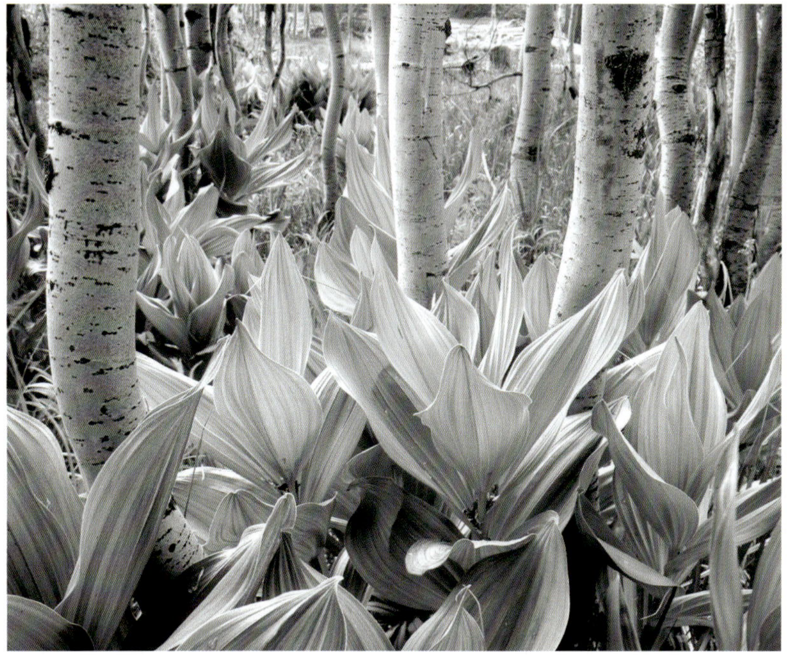

Old pine snag along Railroad Ridge, White Clouds

Skunk cabbage, Boulder Mountains

(Opposite) Elephants head blooms along Meadow Creek, Sawtooth Range

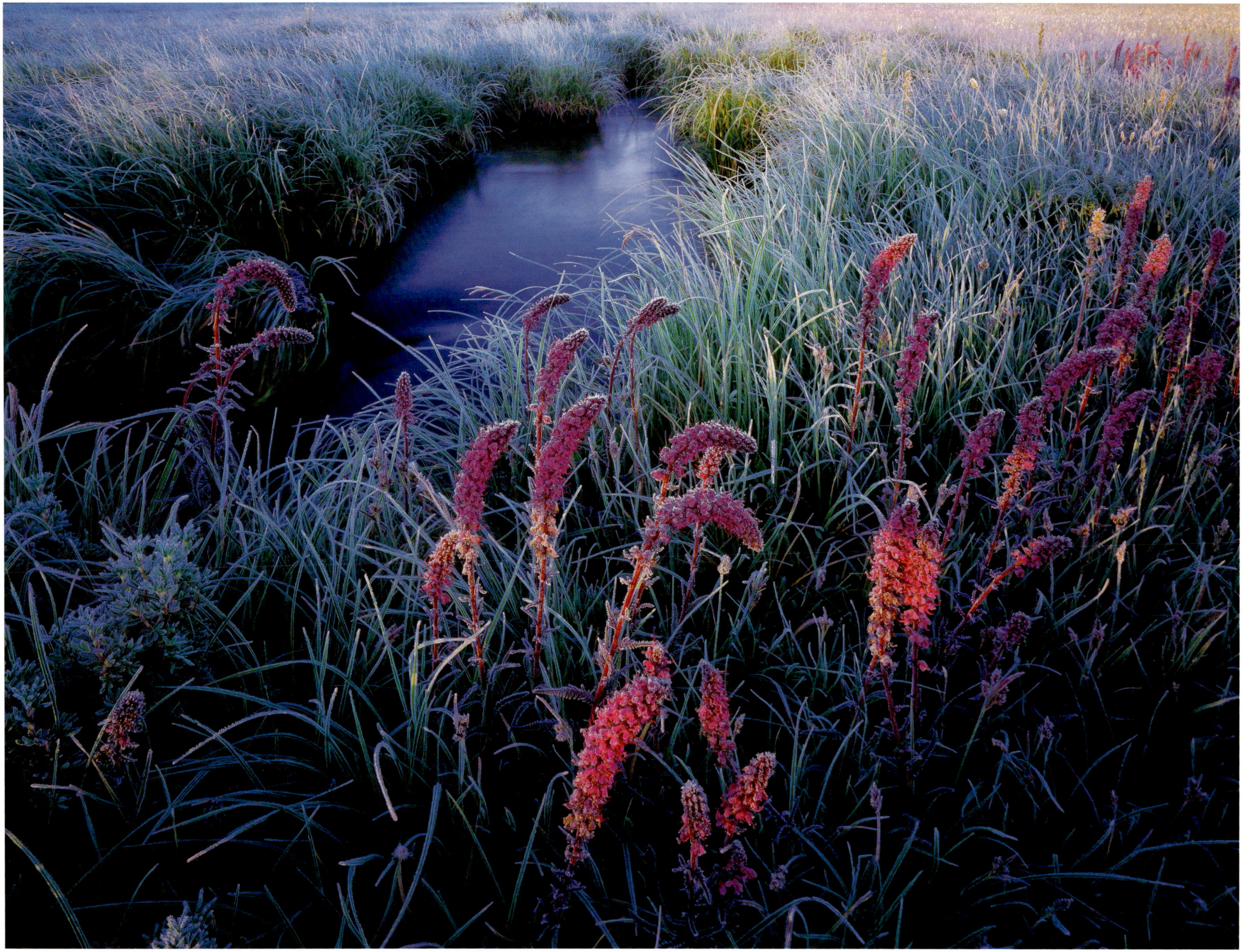

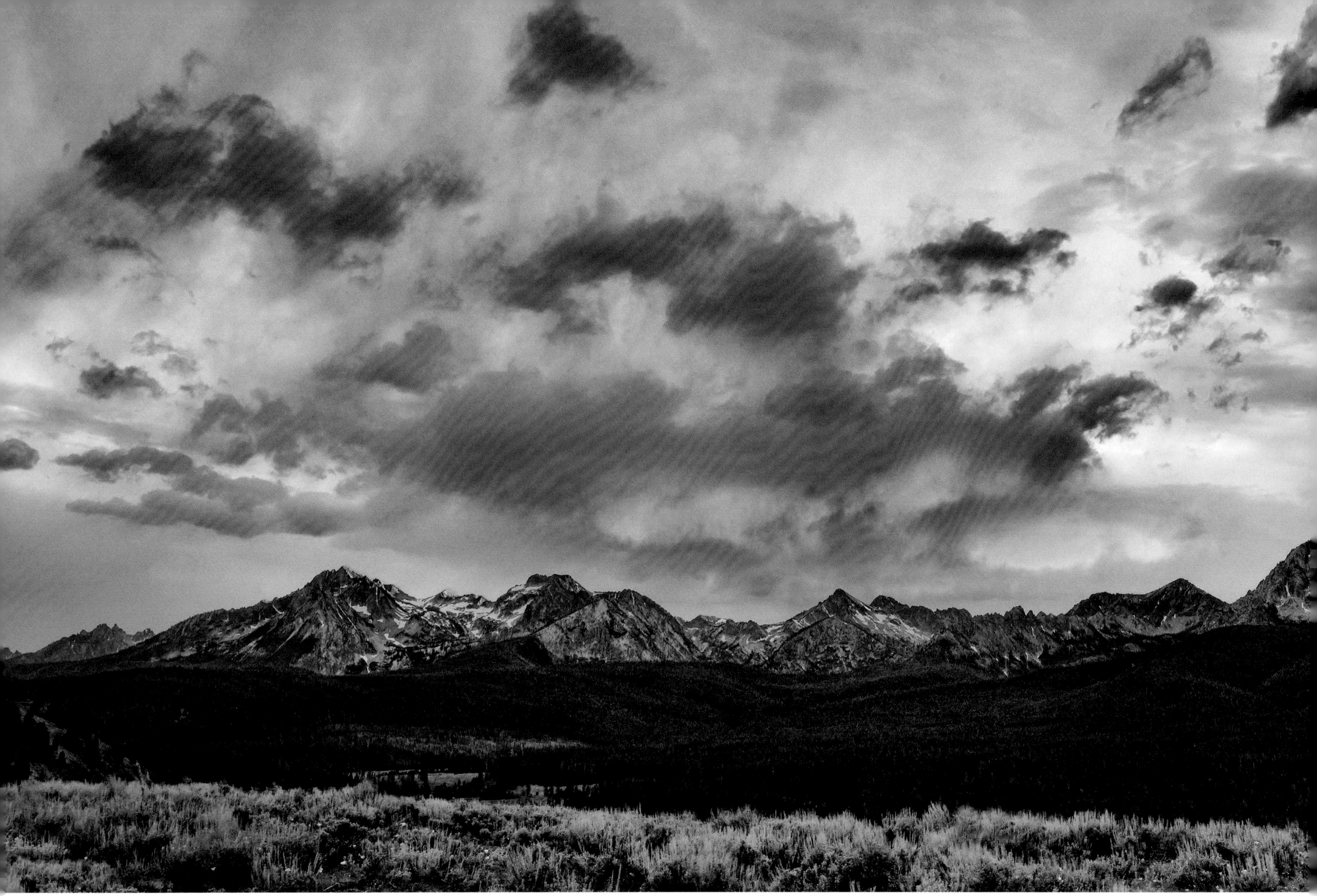

Stanley Lake | Iron Creek | Redfish Lake | Hell Roaring | Pettit Lake | Alturas Lake | Grand Jean

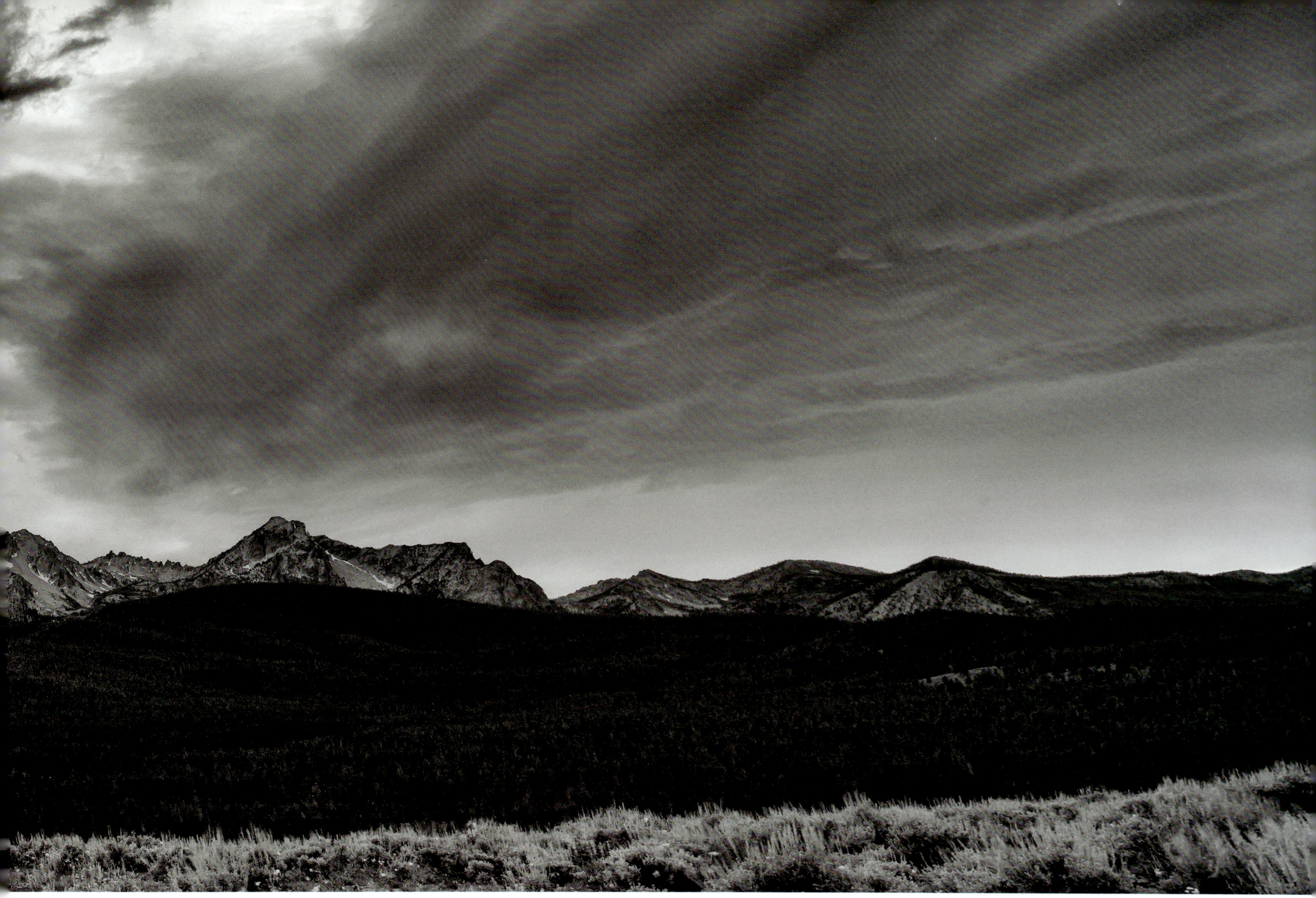

Sawtooth Wilderness

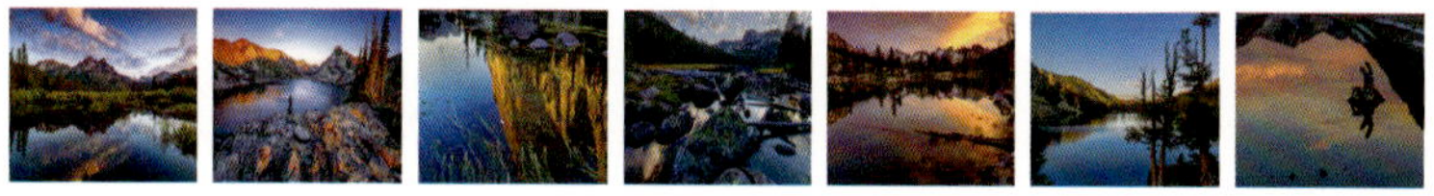

Stanley Lake

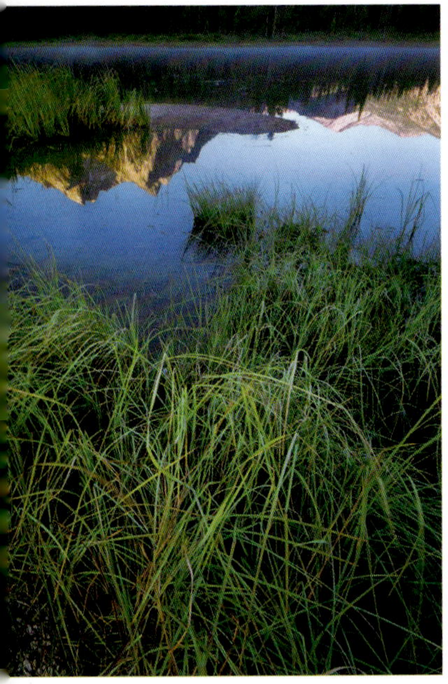

Stanley Lake
Stanley Lake Creek
Valley Creek
McGown Lake

McGOWN TOWERS WITH ITS DOUBLE HULK.

Peaks flush. Stanley Lake lies glassy. Its surface pulls sky and cloud to earth as if water were a funnel for memory and what pours into us in this light is all we know. But through the trees the trail climbs slowly, in and out of meadows and lodgepole pine, deep grass, sedge and reed tangles wet as the sun warms. Feet make a hollow rhythm on the black winding line of ground. Visiting tanningers flit, yellow and orange. Beaver swim an arrow's head through the water into the willows. They nibble bark and mound twigs into a dome. But day fades until the light again stains the tips of the peaks, leaves pockets of water, cracks in the peaks stuffed with yellow stonecrop glowing sulfur yellow in the falling of day into night. Staring up, we are swallowed by the stars. In this oblivion we become humble. Small. Imperfect. Never singular. We rise and dissolve like dunes of sand or waves, ripples on the lake, swirls in sediment deep in the dark.

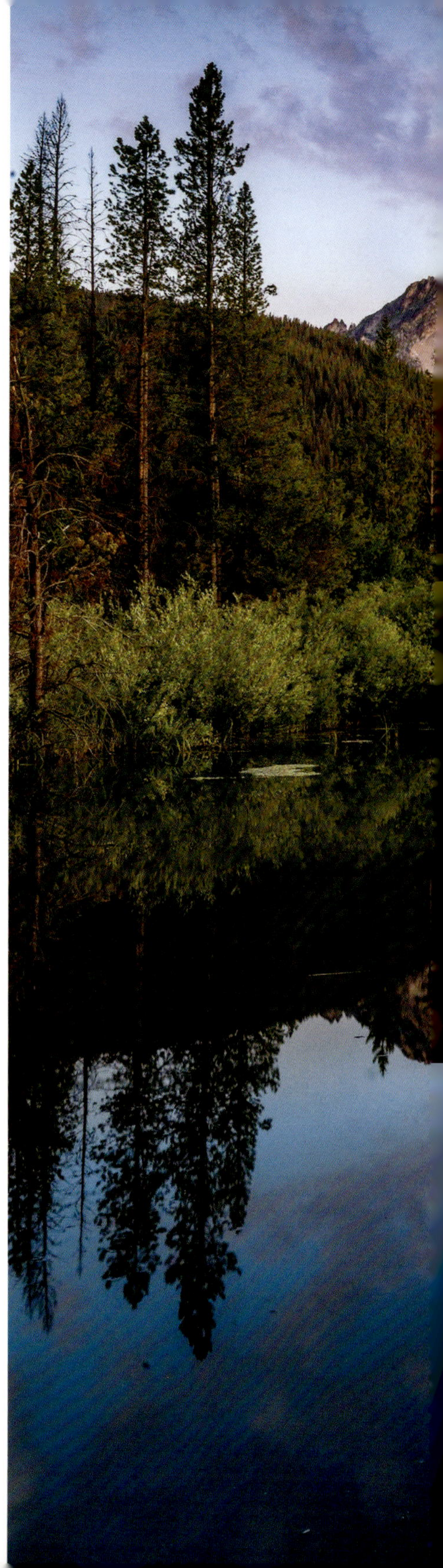

(Detail) Long grasses line the shoreline of Stanley Lake
Mc Gown Peak reflects into the backwaters of Stanley Lake

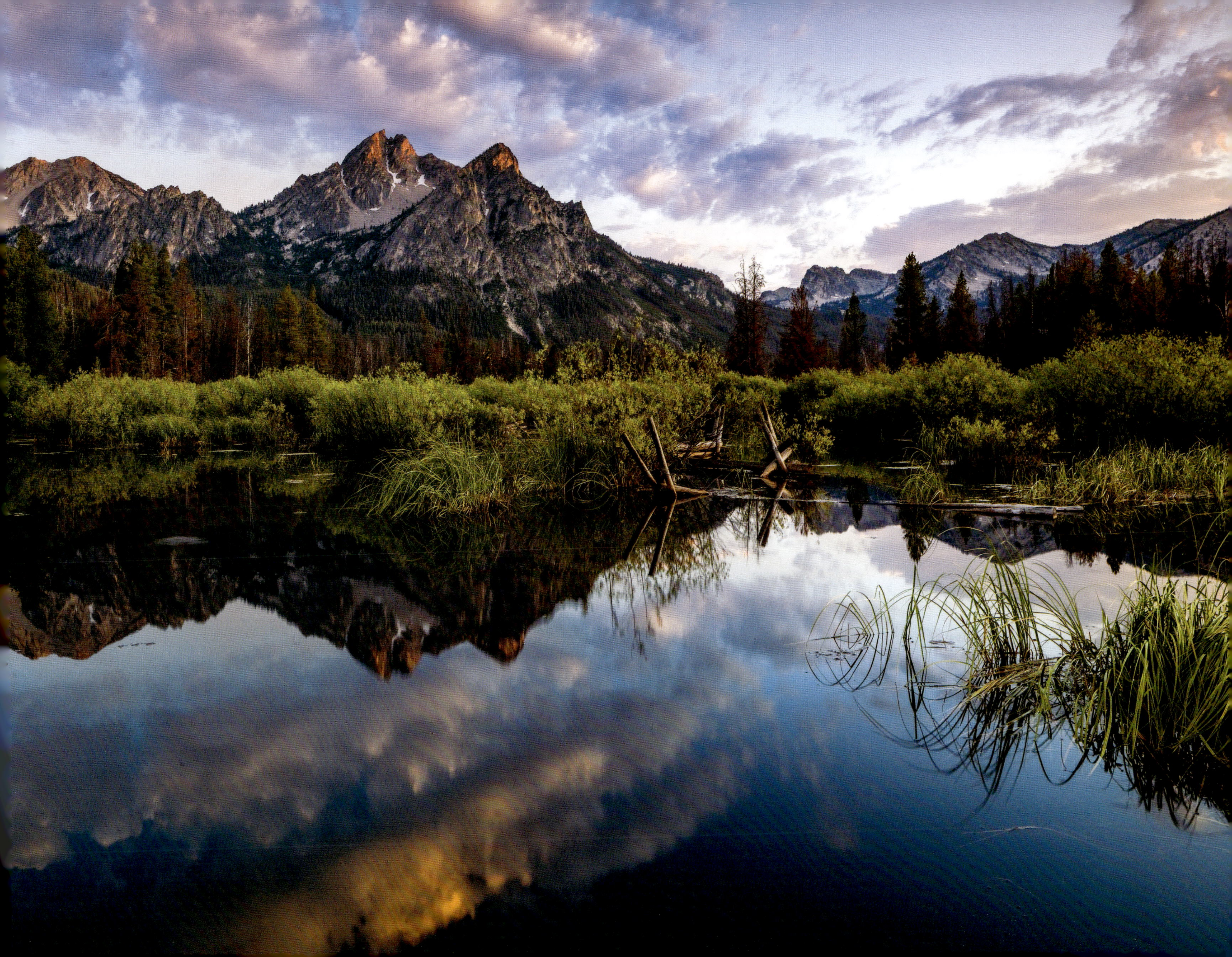

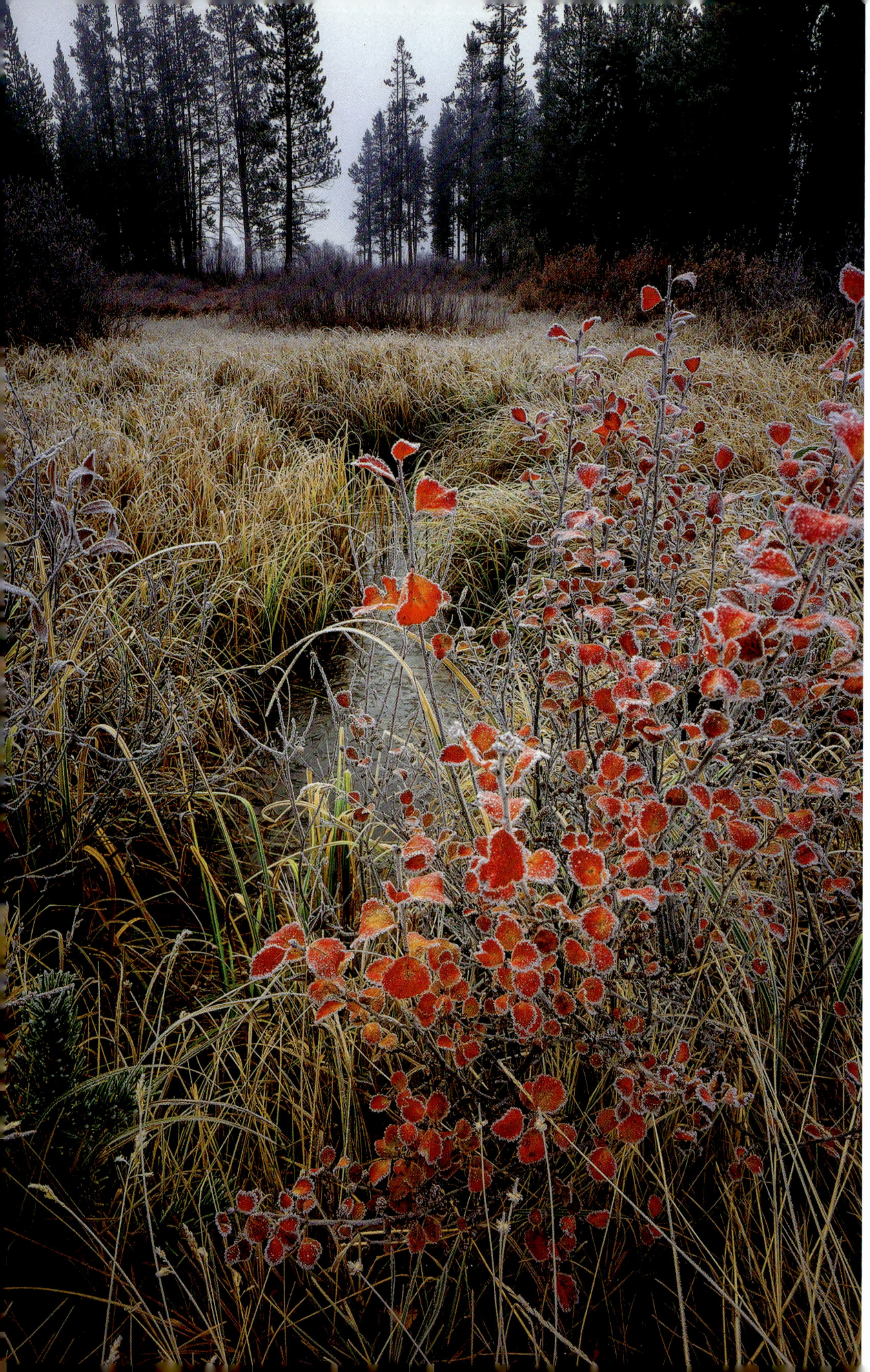

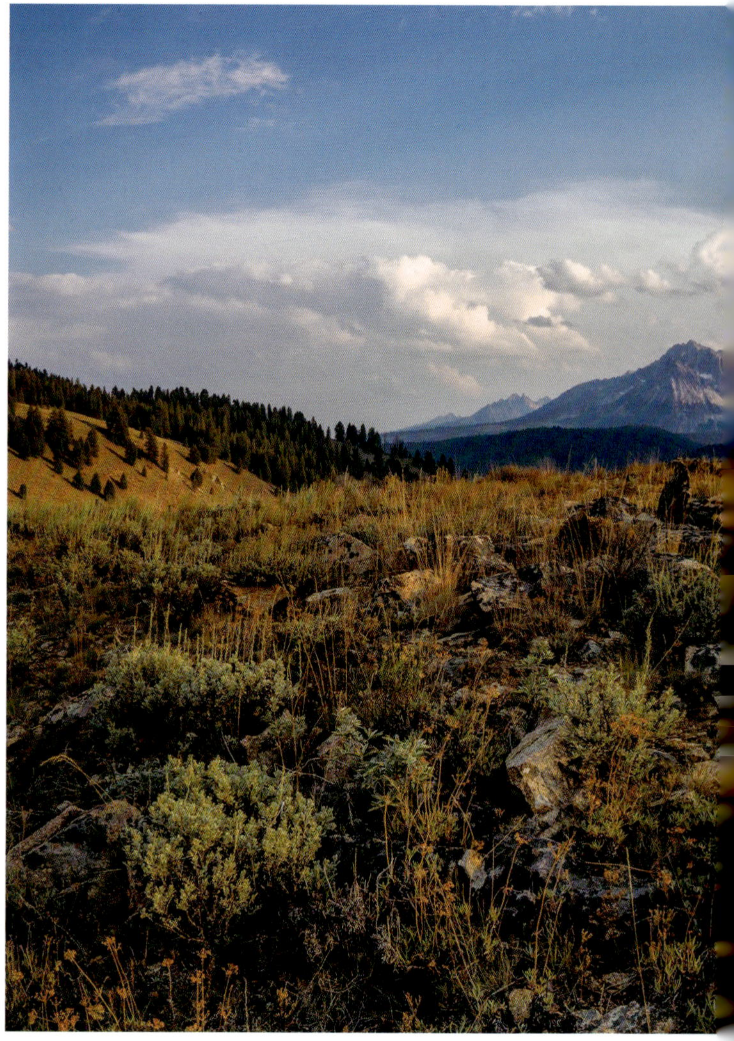

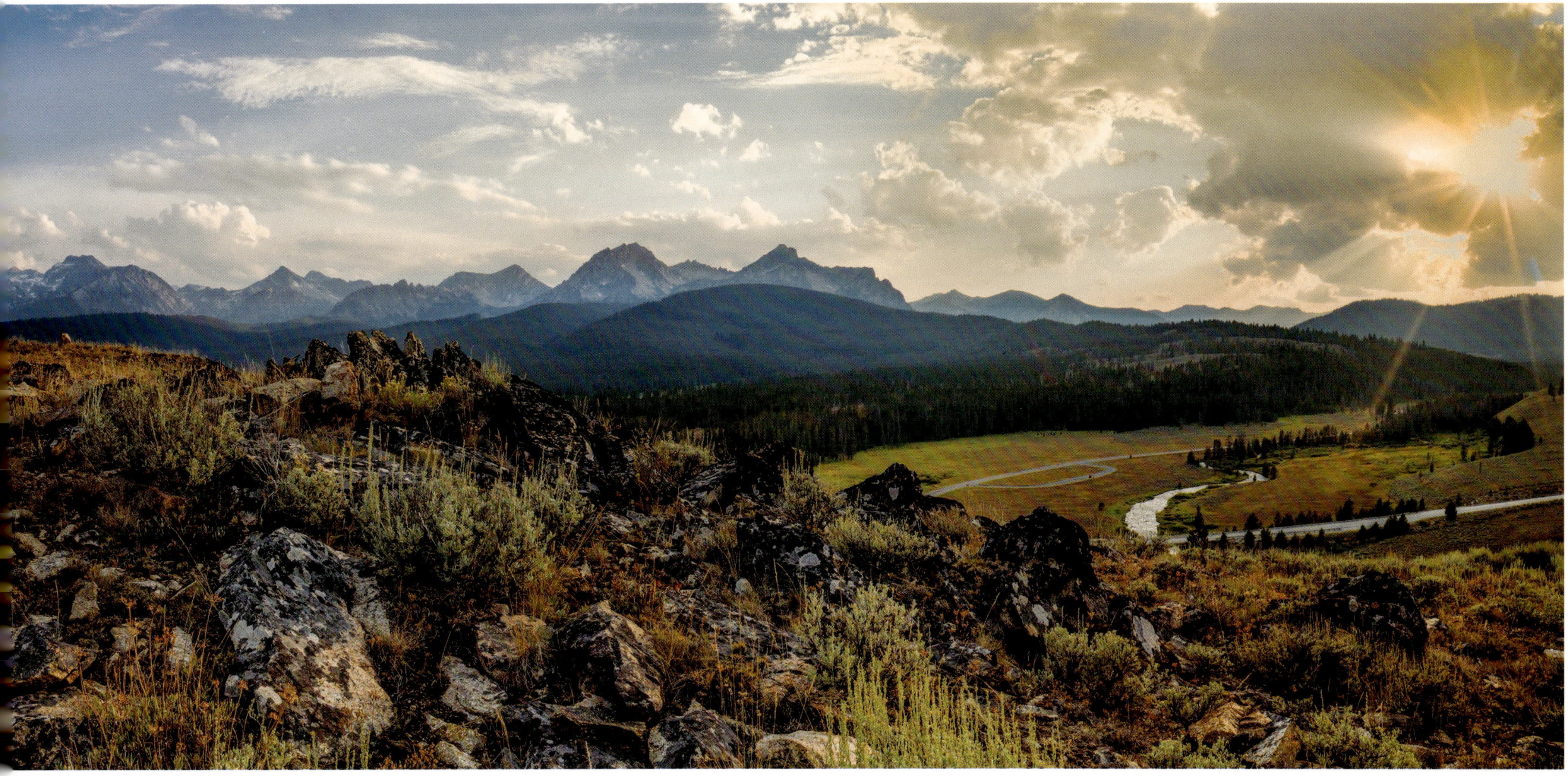

(Opposite) *An early frost turns leaves red in the back waters* - Stanley Lake
Sunset over Stanley Lake Creek - Stanley Basin

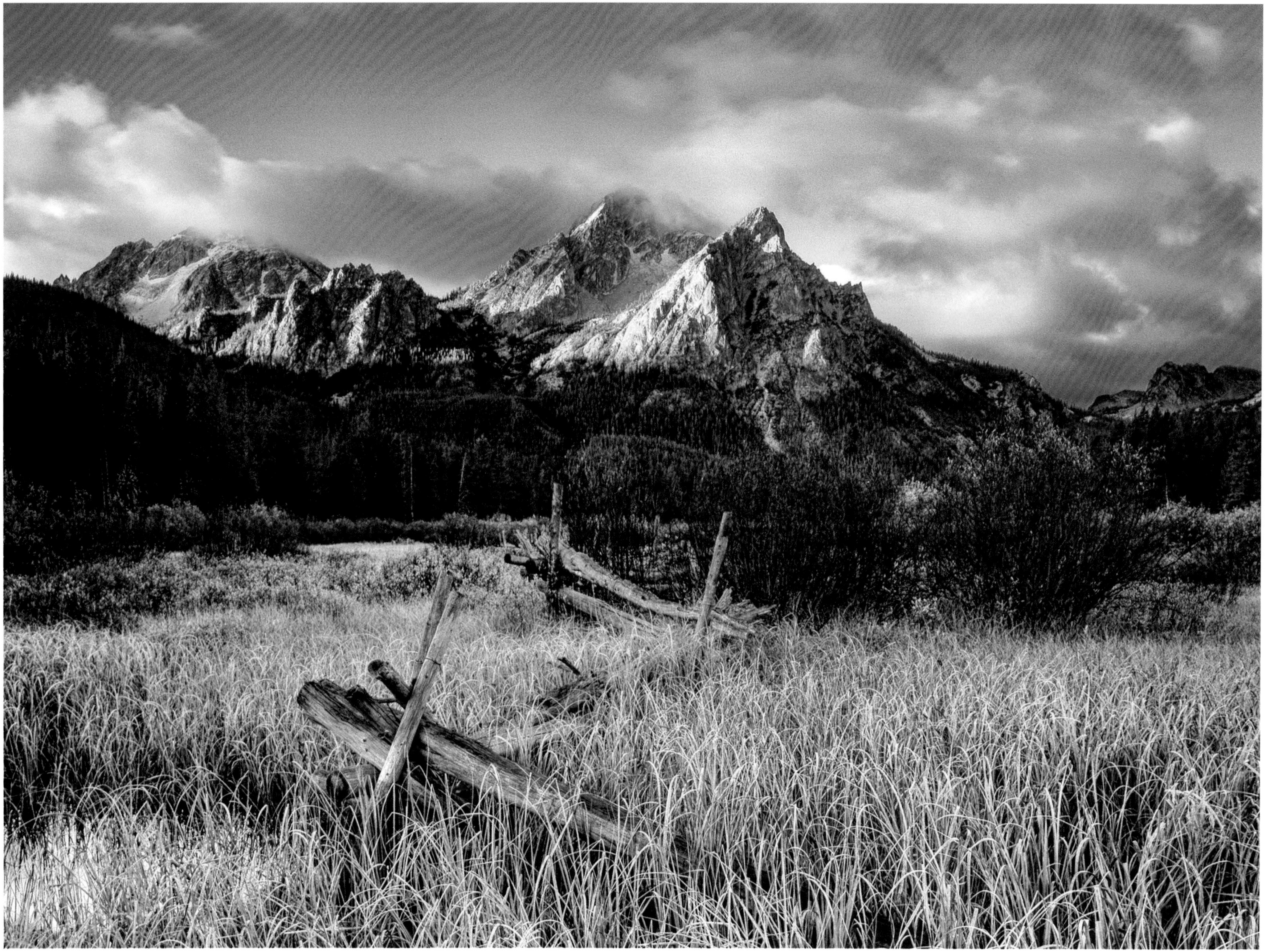

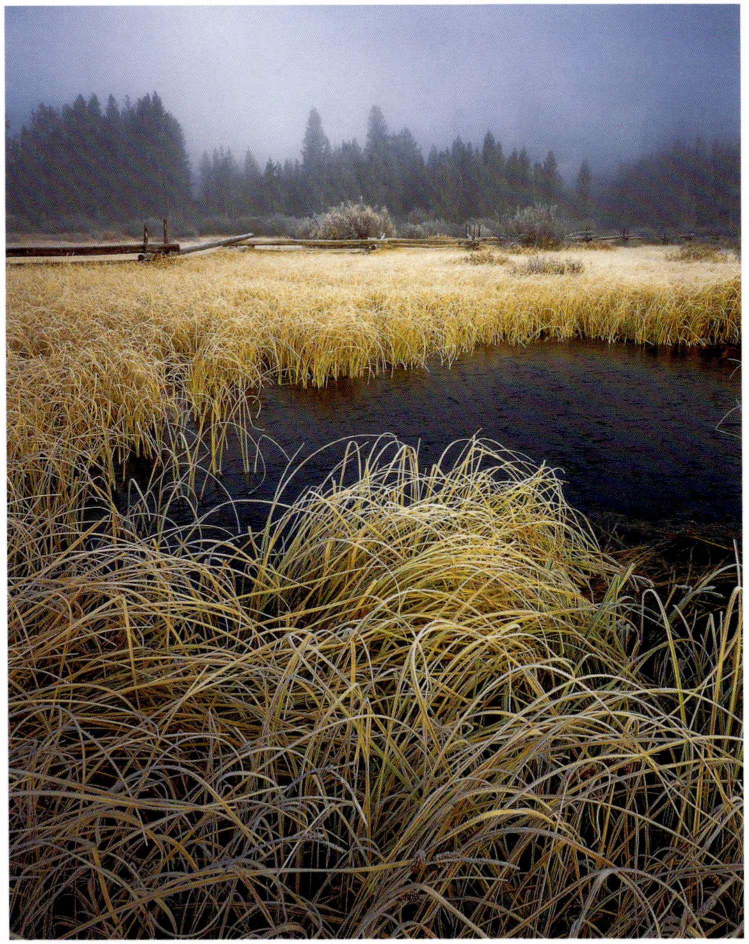

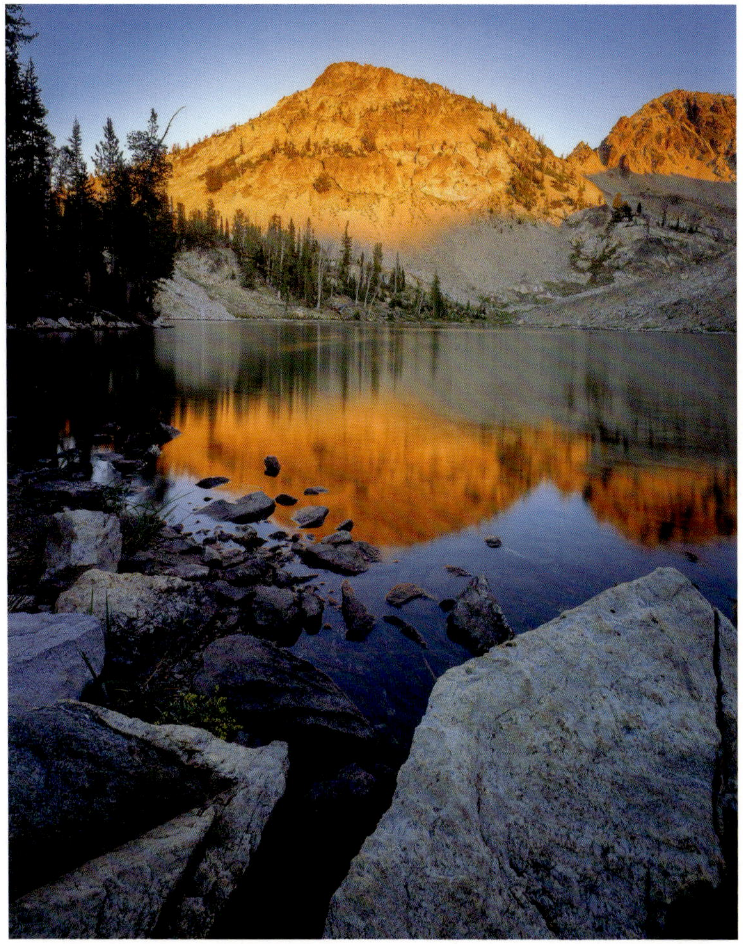

Back waters near Elk Meadows - Stanley Lake

(Opposite) The classic Sawtooth fence and McGown peak - Stanley Basin

McGown Lake - Sawtooth Wilderness

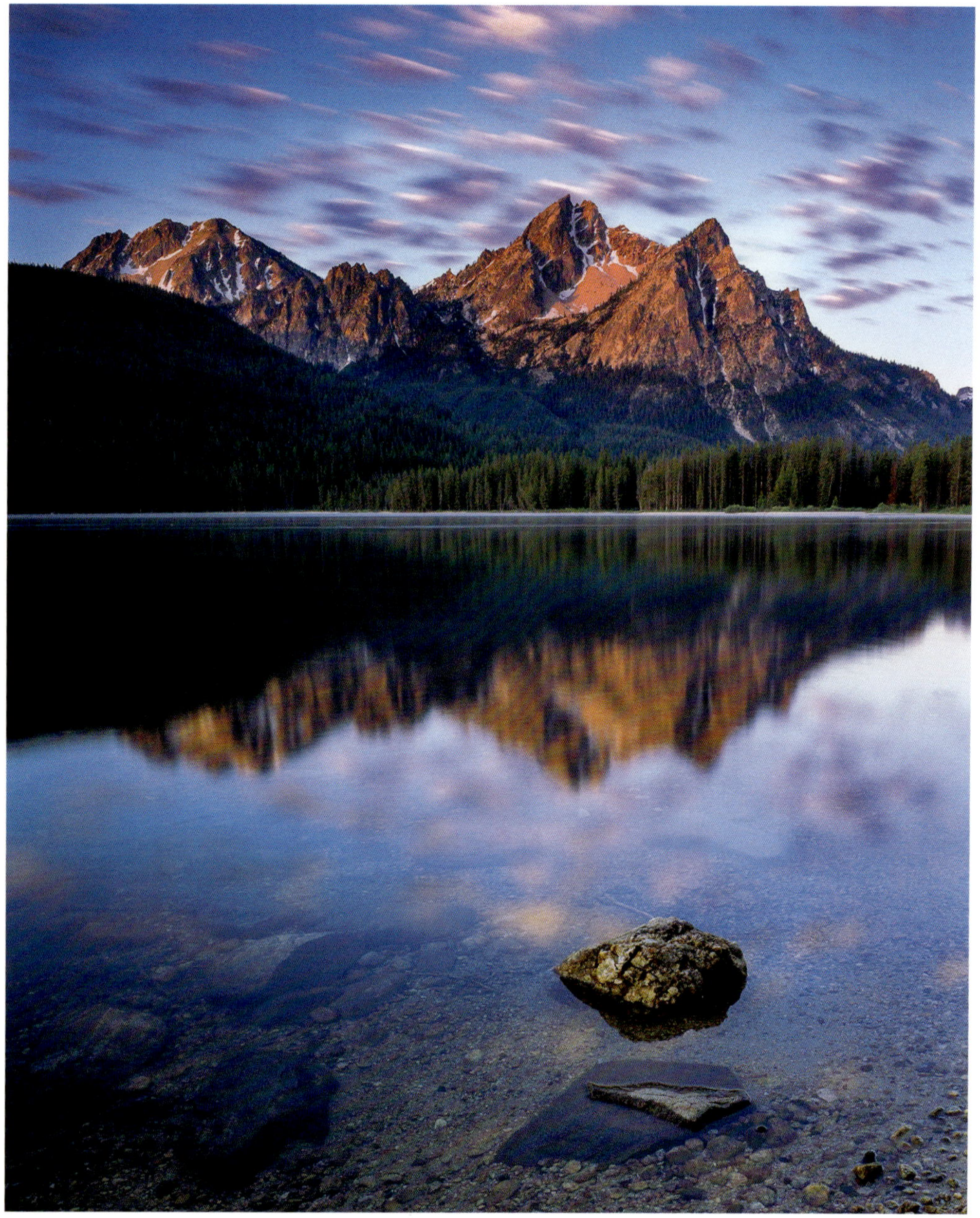

McGown Peak Stanley Lake

(Opposite) Valley Creek flows into the Stanley Basin near its confluence with Stanley Lake Creek

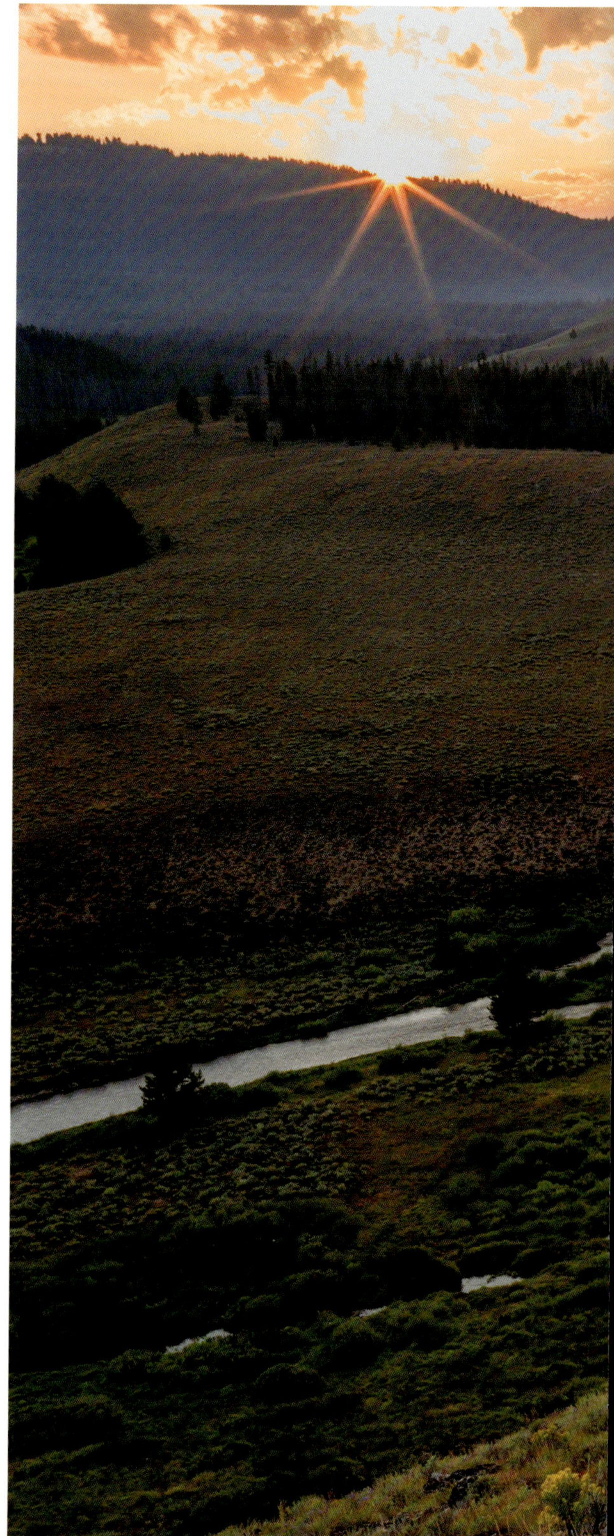

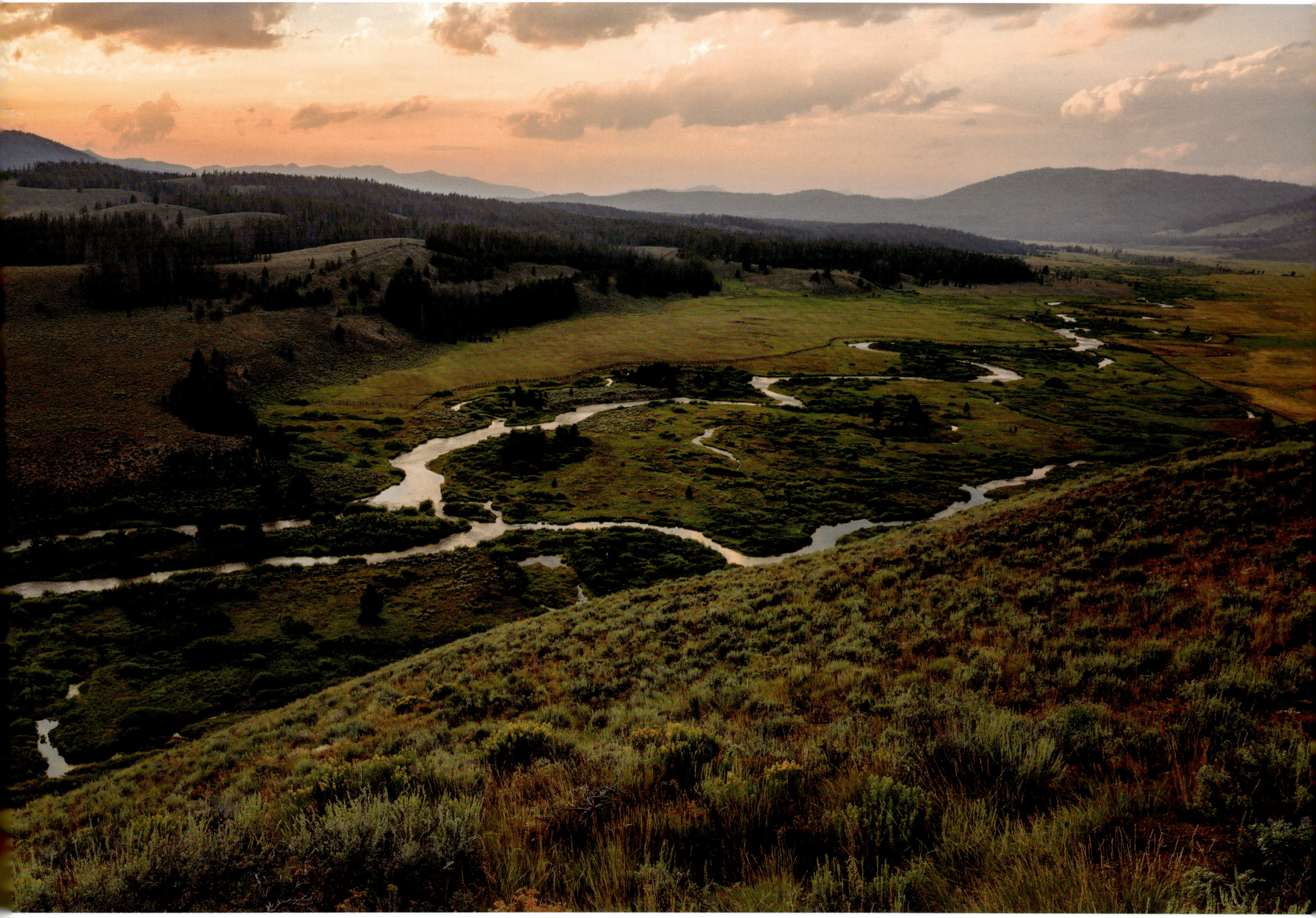

Iron Creek

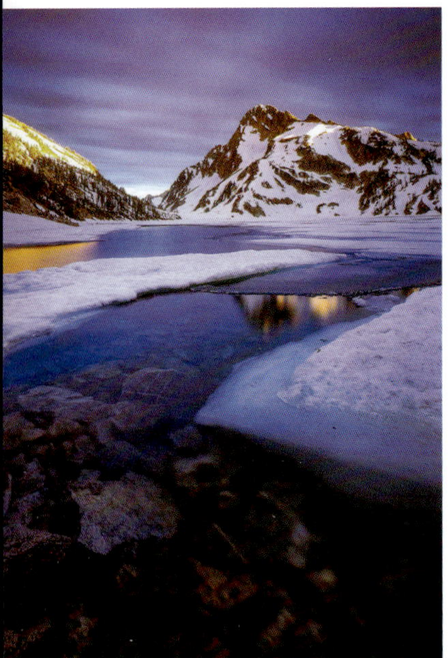

Alpine Lake
Sawtooth Lake
Goat Lakes
North Fork of Baron Creek

WATER TURNS FROM MIST TO LIQUID, a film of ice on stone in the wind. Peaks push for space against all that draws them: gravity, time, the law of all that rises and how it must fall. But where the crown of the earth sits, thorns of stone encircle an oval of water. The sky holds delicate every scrap of light and air that passes. Between the worlds of different lakes, bits of land host grass, moss and lichen. Between the boulders anything that can, grows. These are tiny things, pulling light from the sky while summer lasts, braced for snow higher than the clouds. Water once stood turquoise, taller than the mountains, walls of glassy cold melted, left footprints which became lakes, gifts from the ice age, like the peaks themselves.

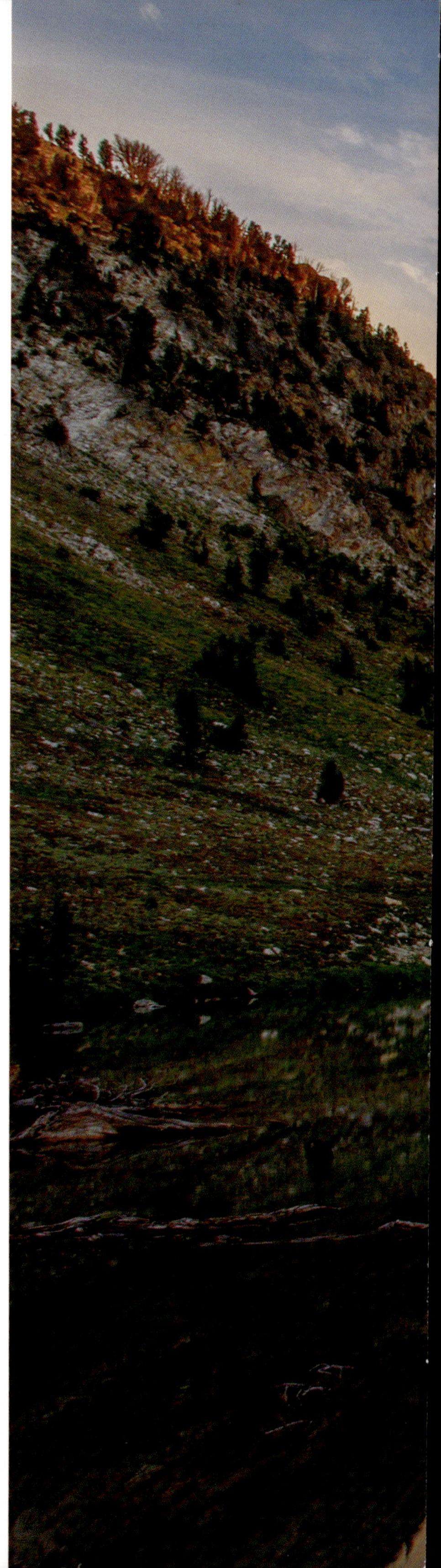

(Detail) Ice covered Sawtooth Lake, early July
A small tarn between Sawtooth Lake and North Fork of Baron Creek Divide

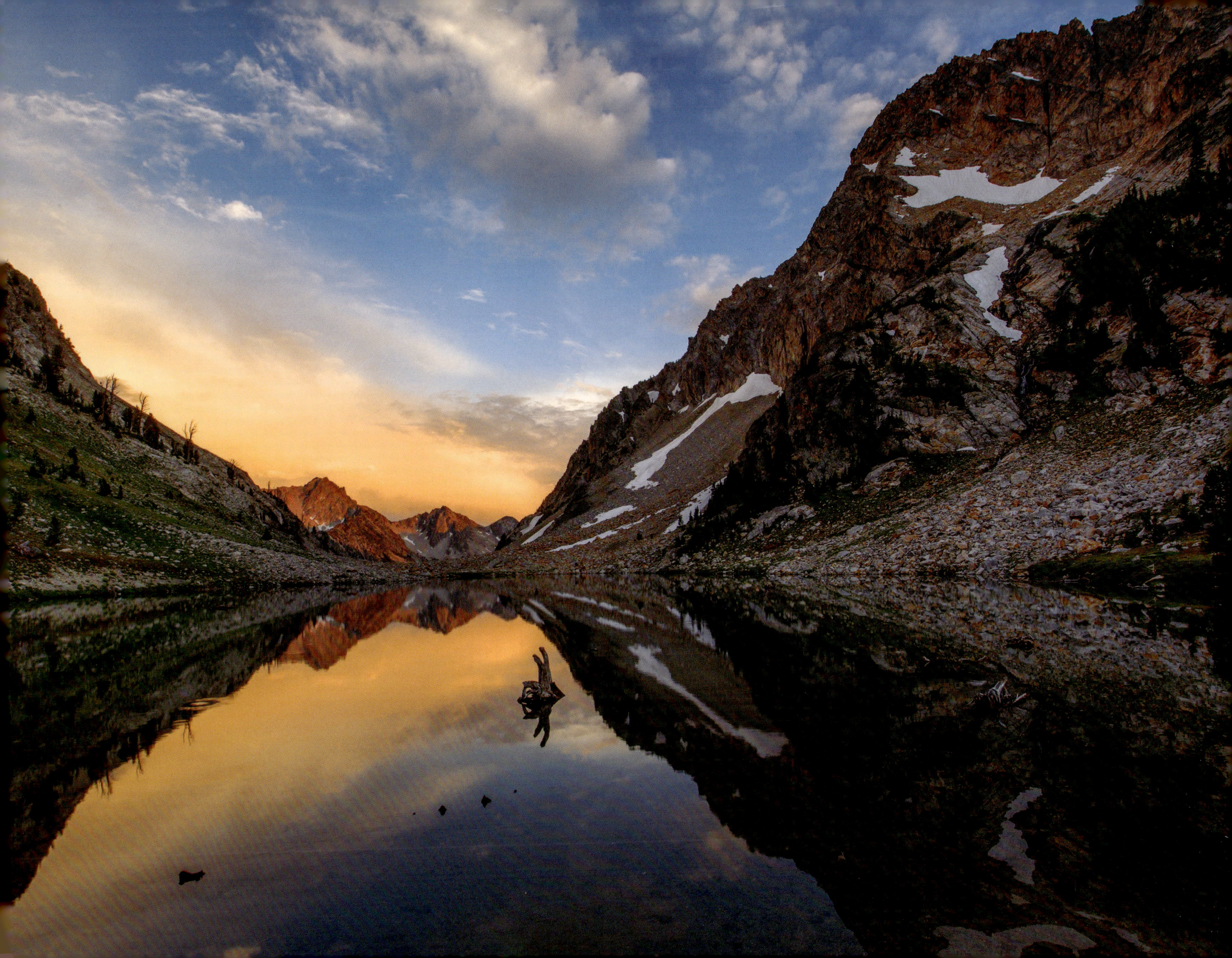

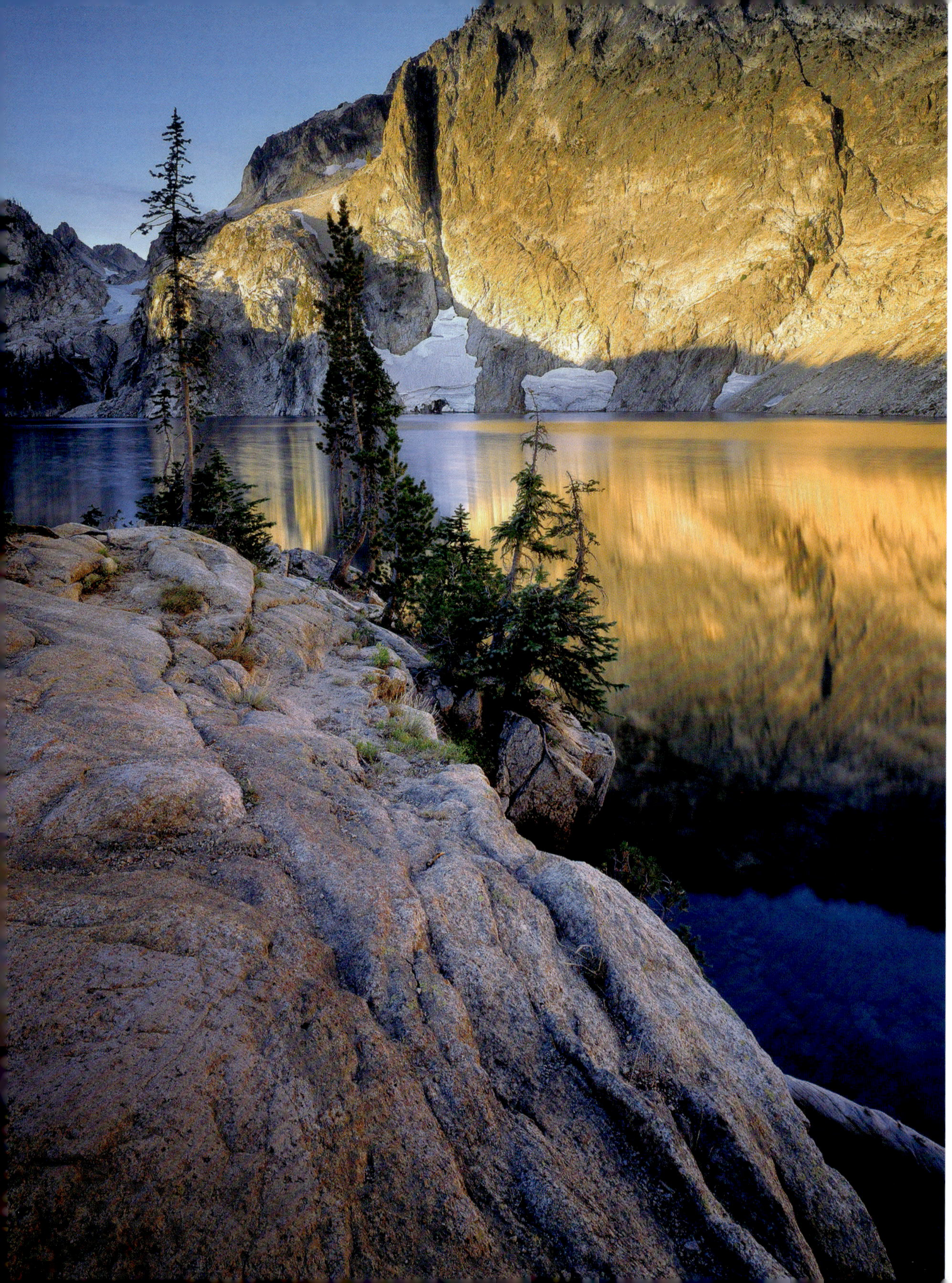

Snow fields feed Goat Lake - Sawtooth Wilderness
The largest high mountain lake in the Sawtooth Range - Sawtooth Lake

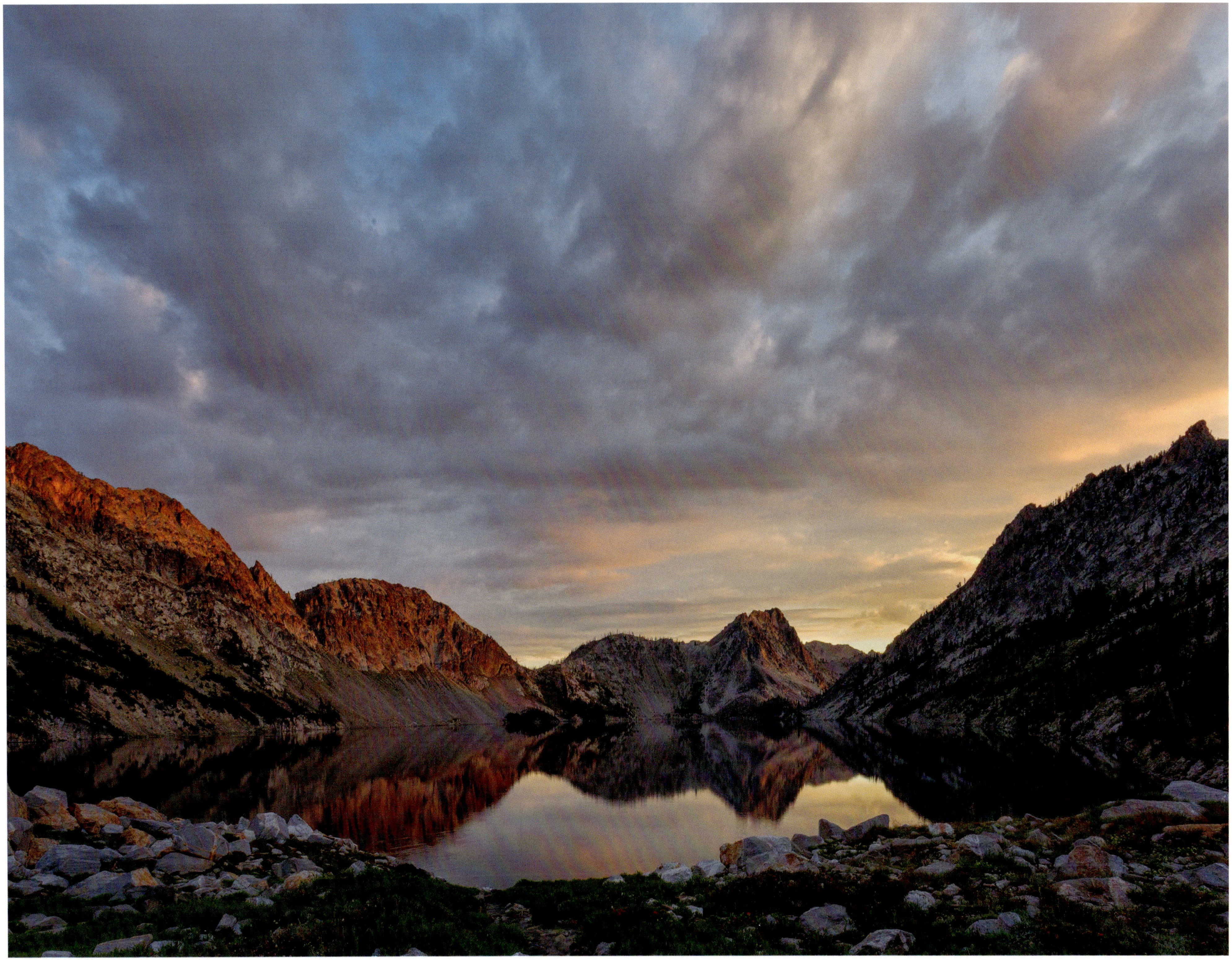

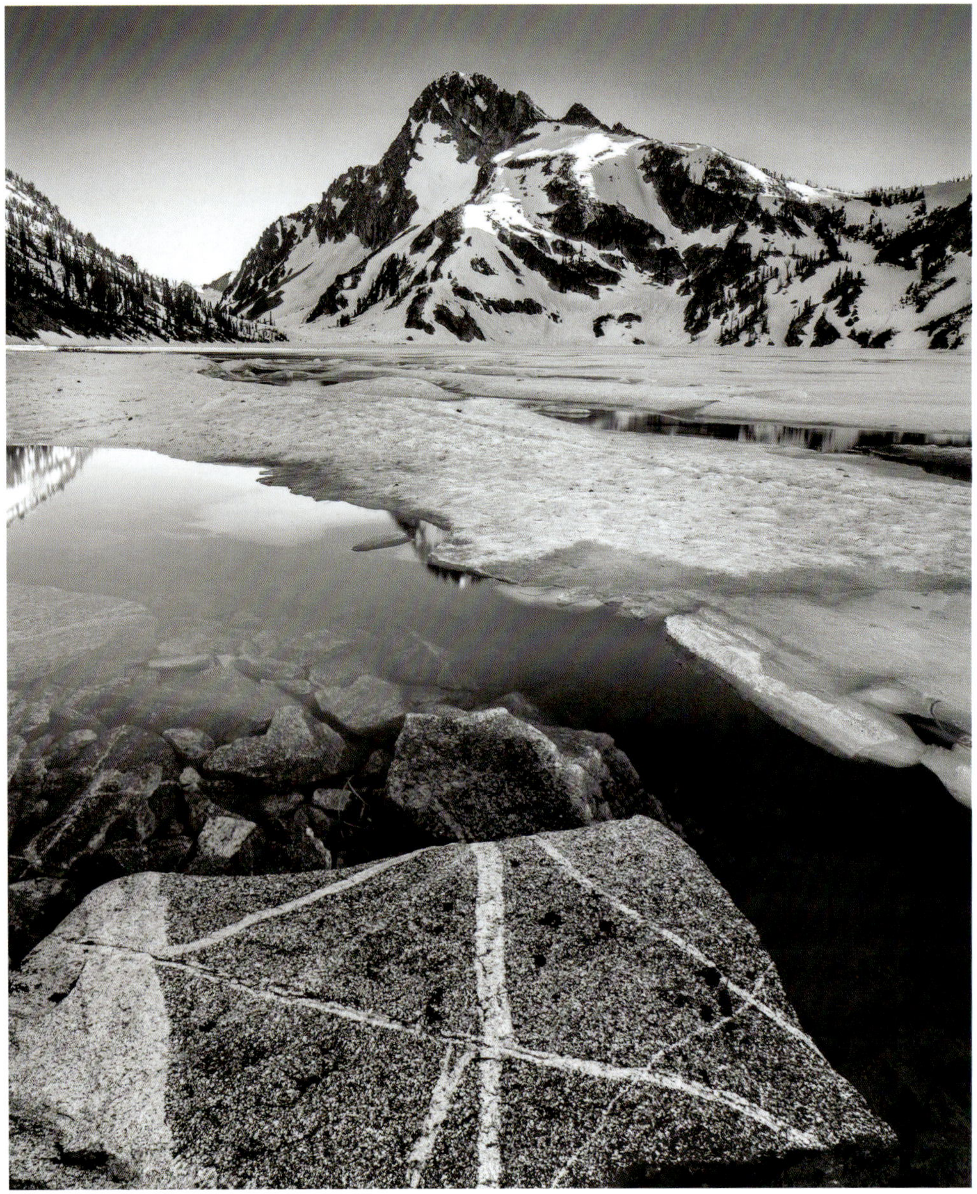

Snow-clad Regan Peak
(Opposite) Sawtooth Lake from McGown Divide

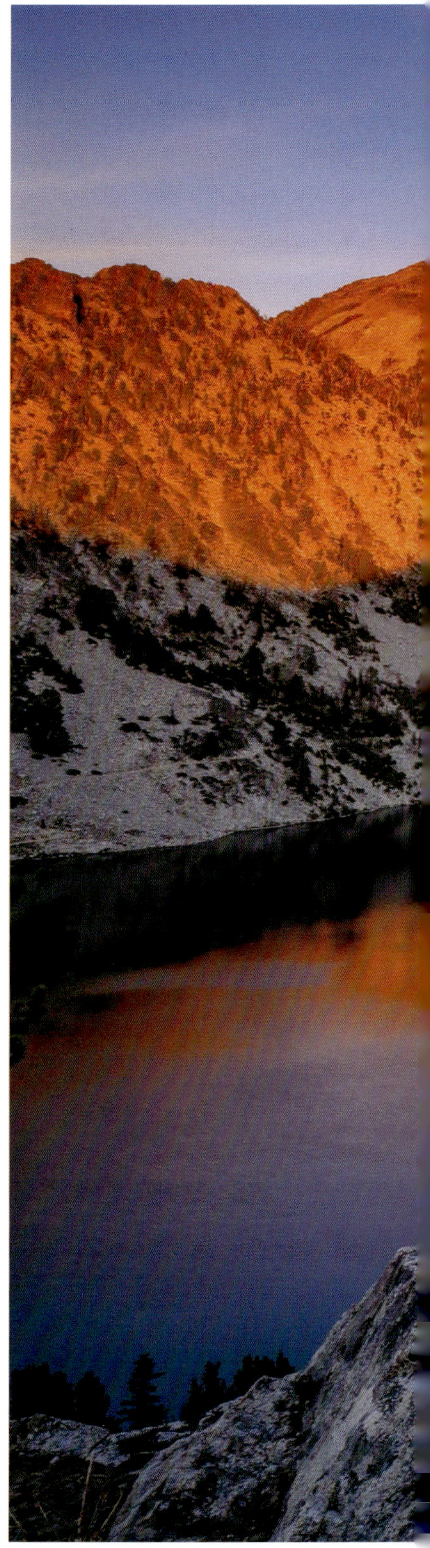

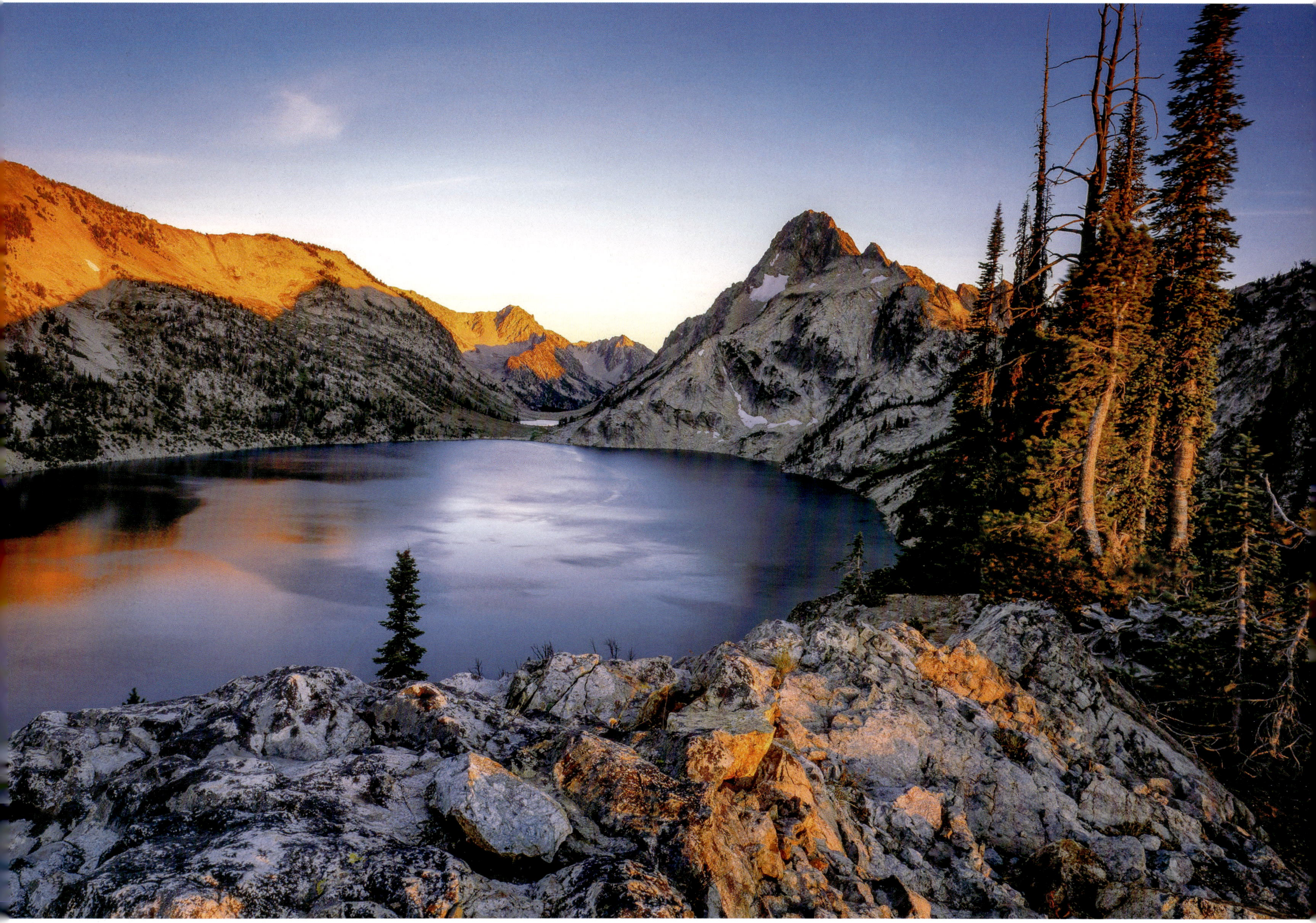

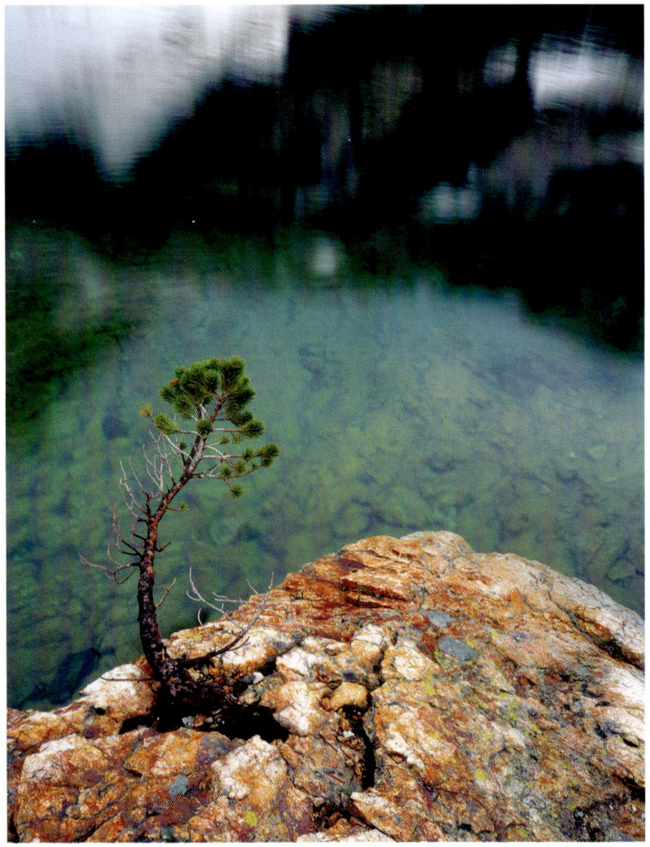

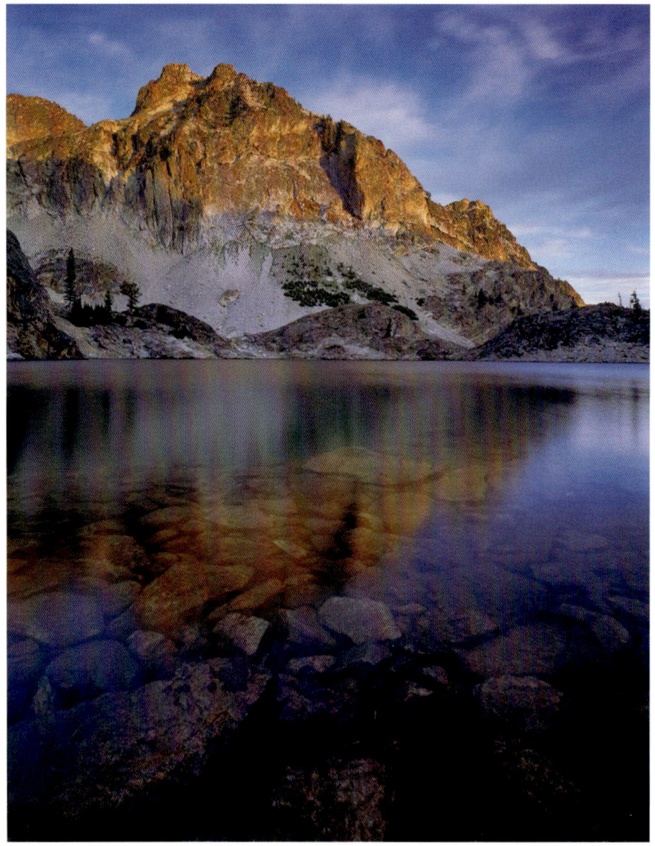

A delicate pine rests on the rocky shore of Alpine Lake

Upper Goat Lake sits just at the tree line

(Opposite) North Fork of Baron Creek Divide - Mt. Regan

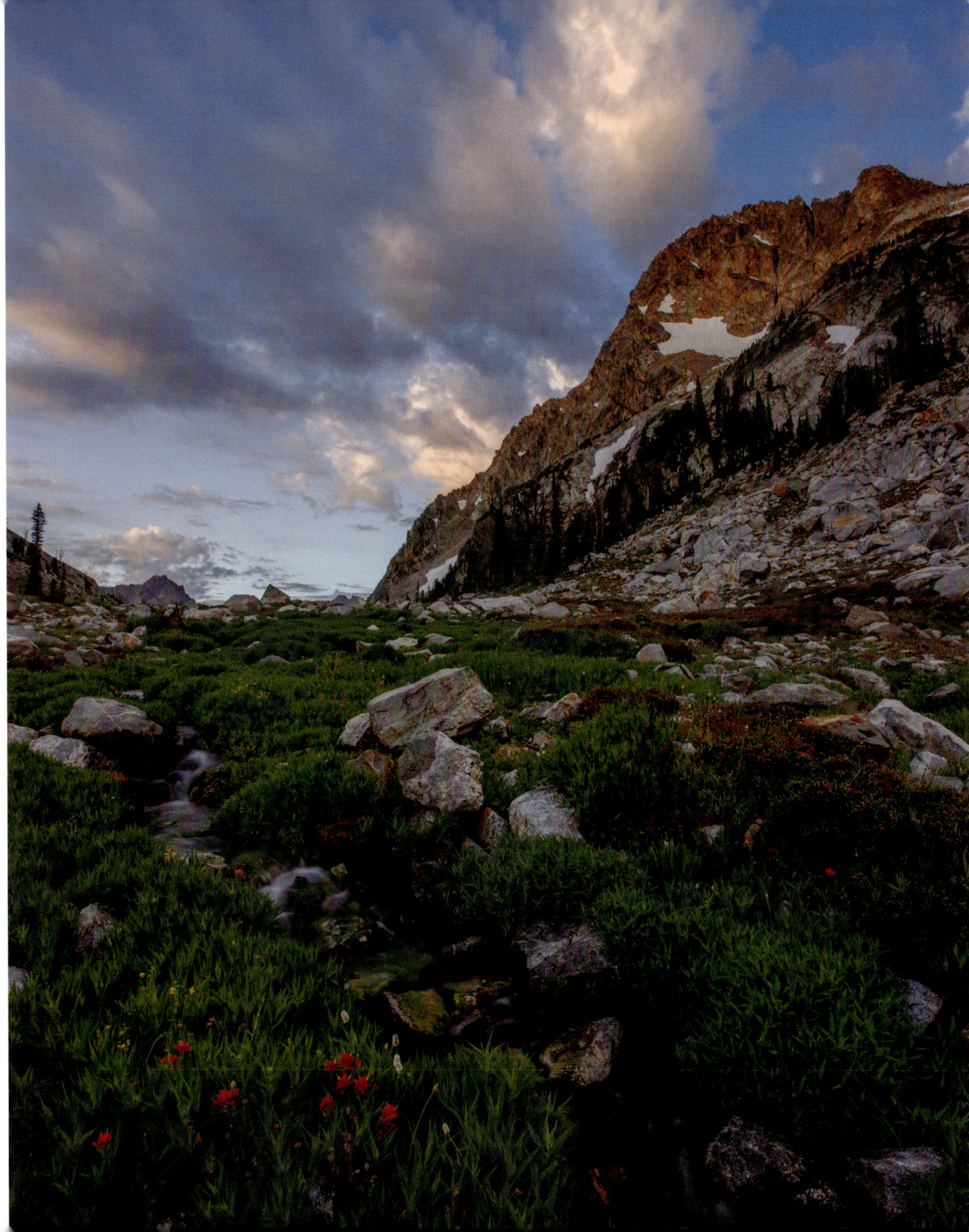

Red Fish Lake

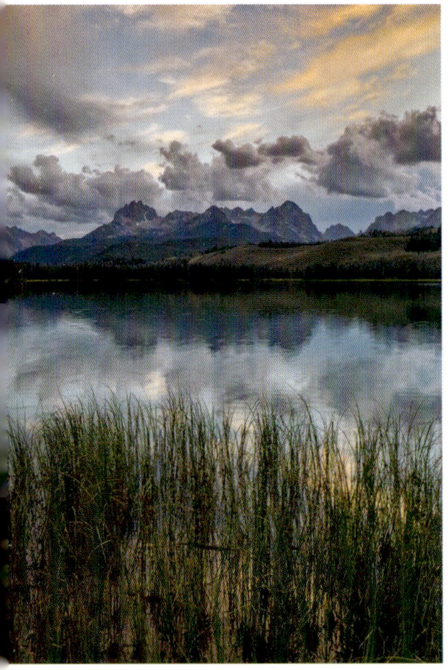

Bench Lakes
Saddleback Lakes
Alpine Lake
Kathyrn Lake
Cramer Lakes

ONCE FISH RAN THE SALMON RED, sockeye thick from the ocean, bound for Redfish Lake. In the shadow of the Sawtooths, great mounds of moraine hem the curve of deep water where the ghost fish circle in darkness. Aspens climb, turning yellow to orange, giving way to broken granite high up where only the stocked fish swim. And the peaks rise out of the Cramer Lakes, faces hanging 10,000 feet above the sea. And we climb like ants in vast stone mazes, awed by the reflection of clouds on a lake's surface, by the play of light and water in the sky.

(Detail) Sunset over Little Redfish Lake, the jewel of the Sawtooths
Fog rises from Redfish Lake

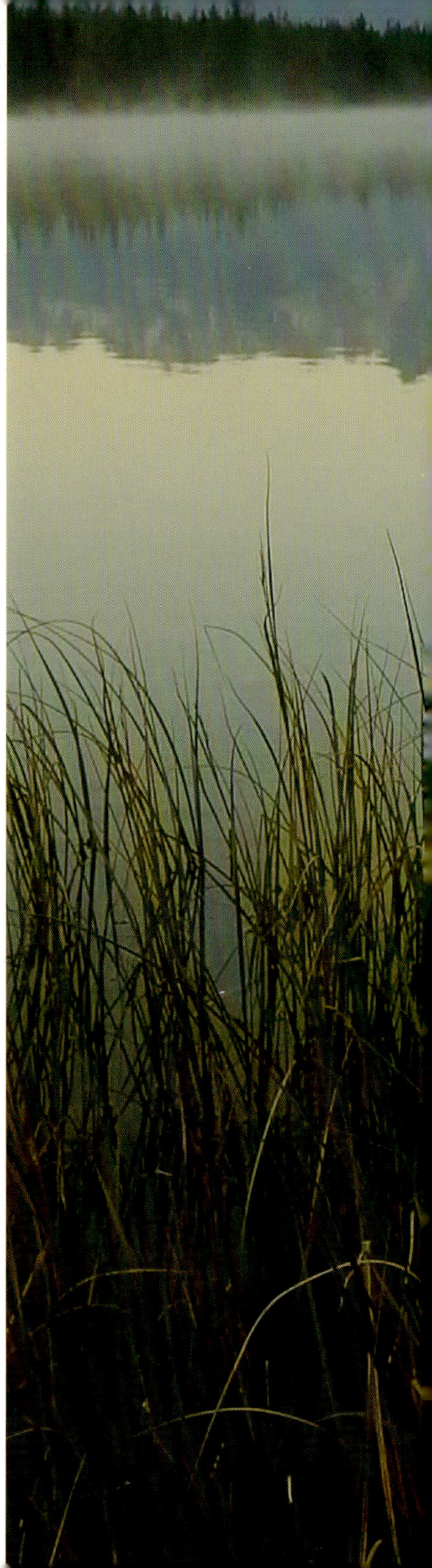

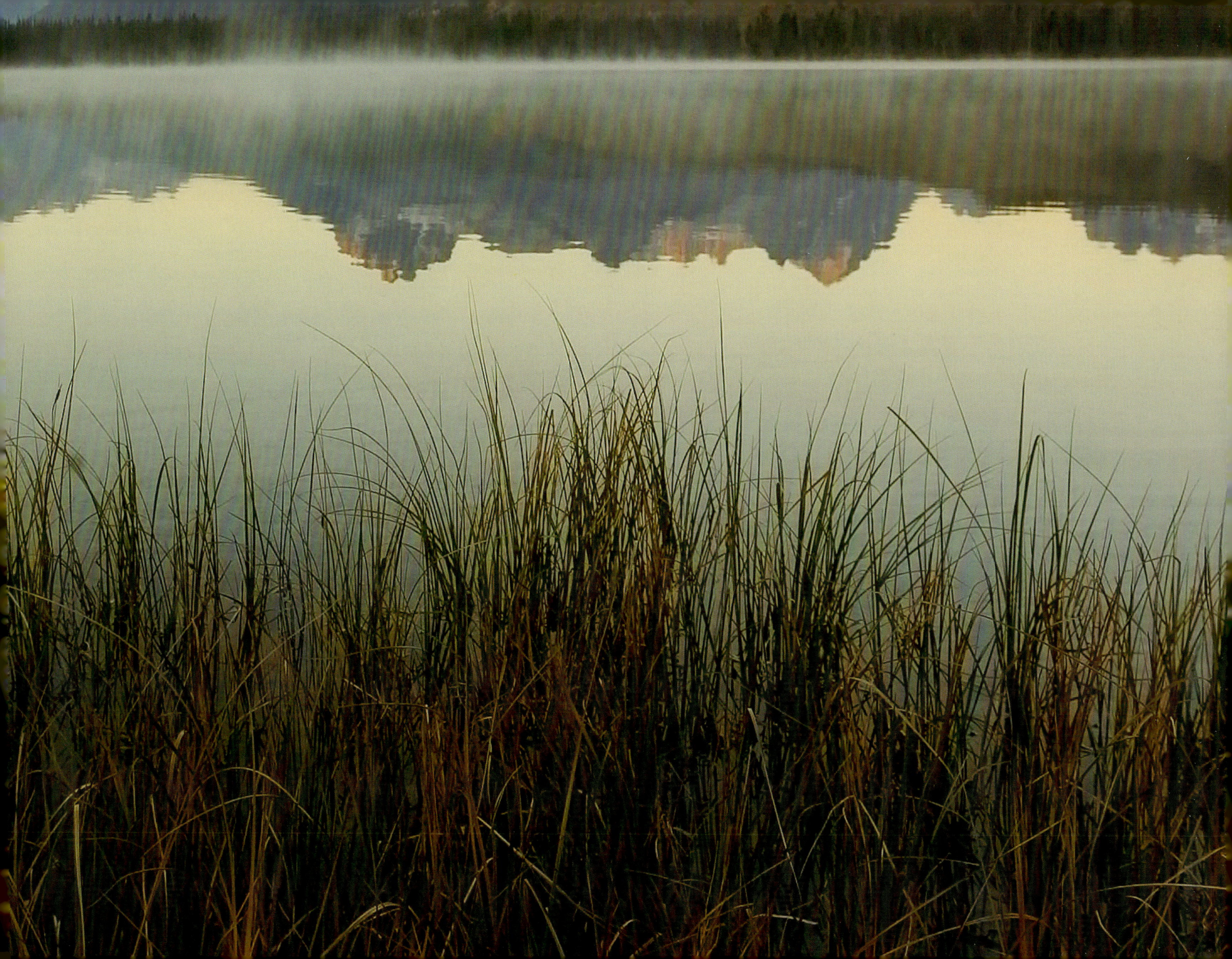

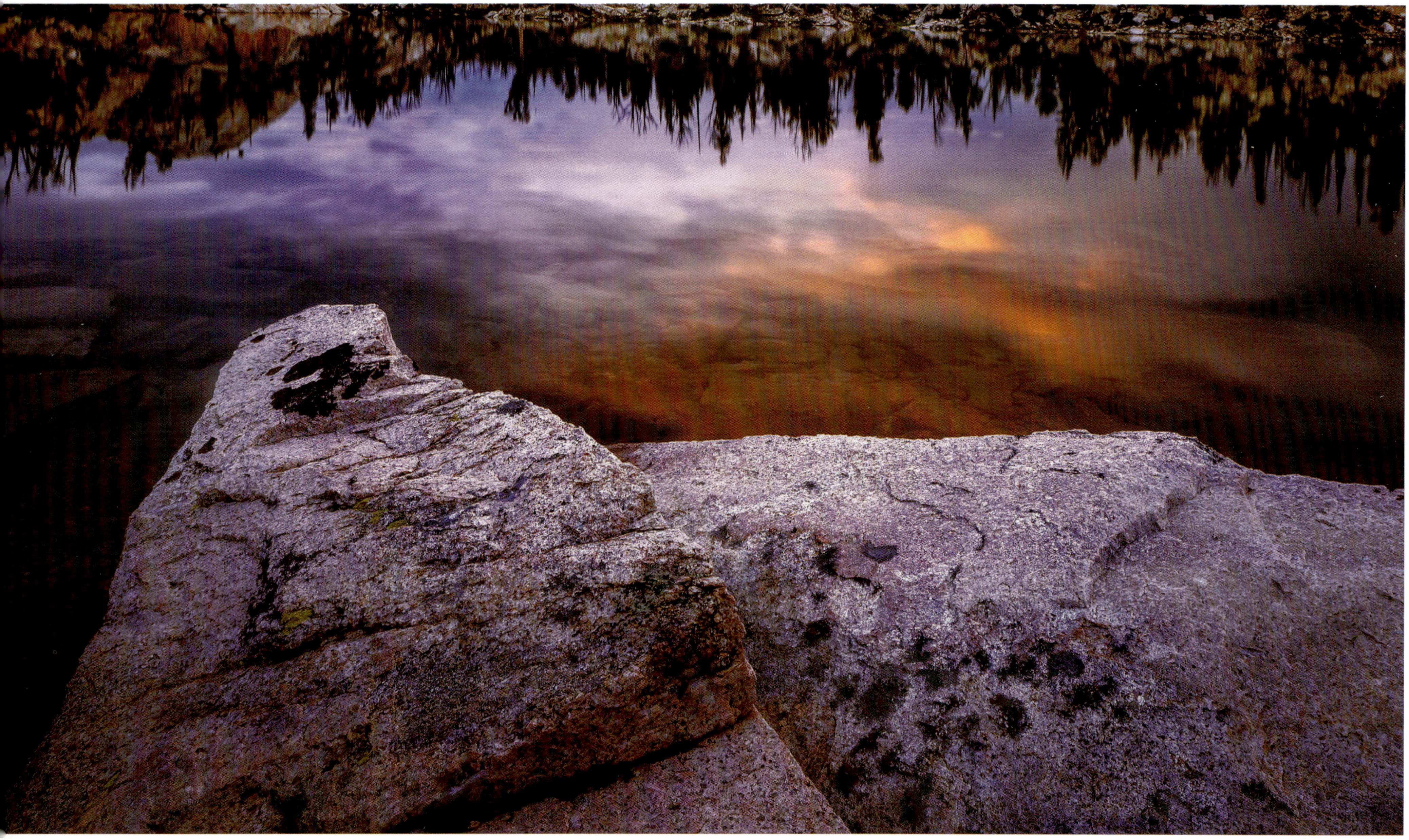

Eerie sky in the reflection of Kathyrn Lake

Heyburn Peaks - upper Bench Lakes

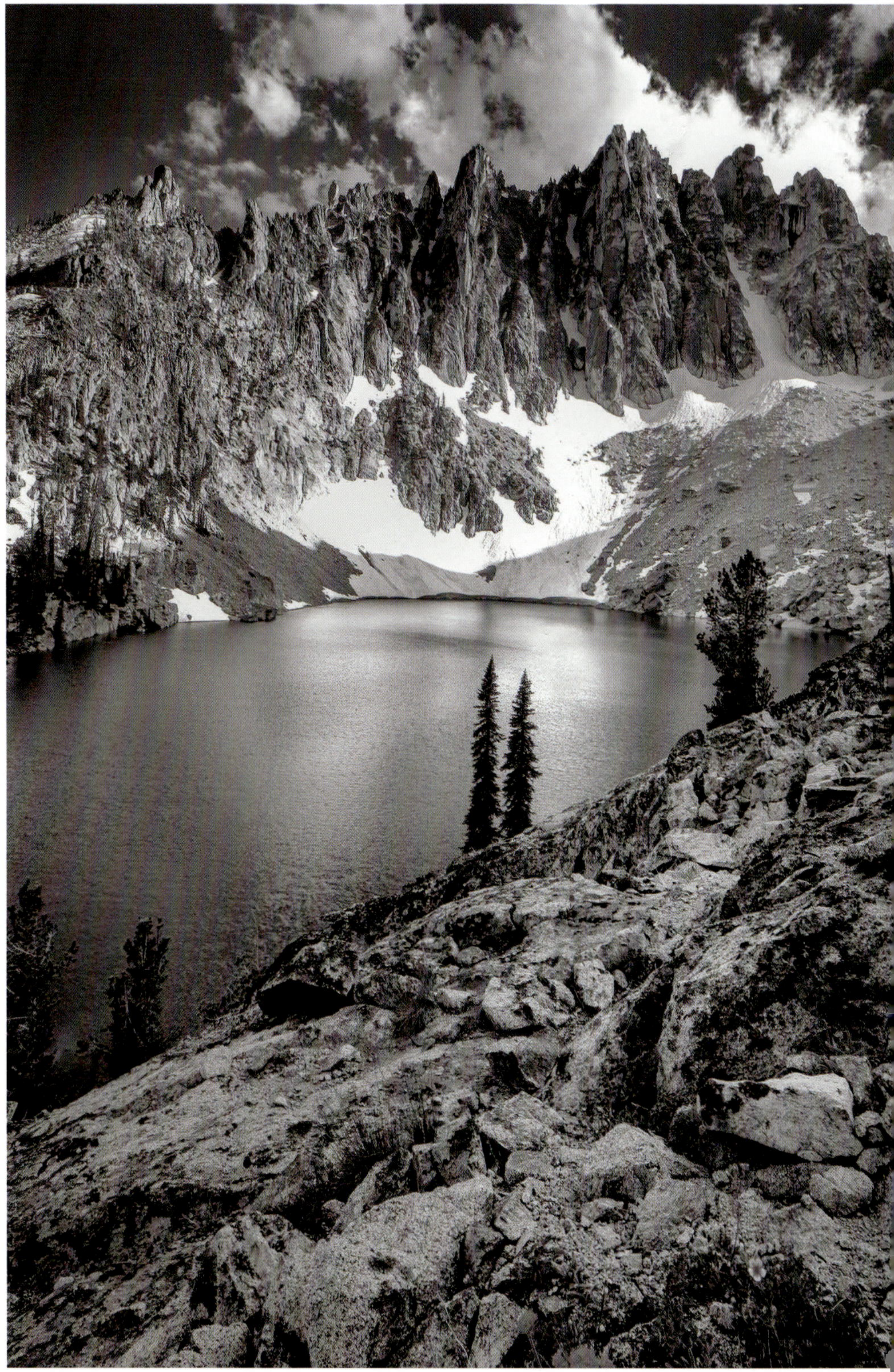

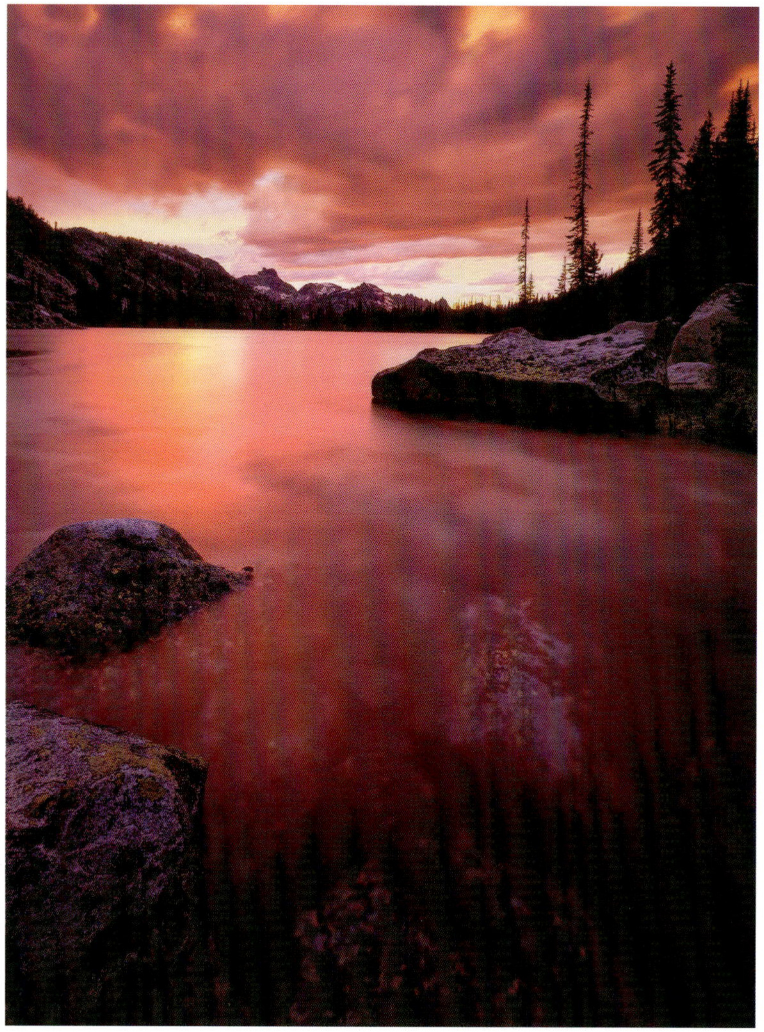

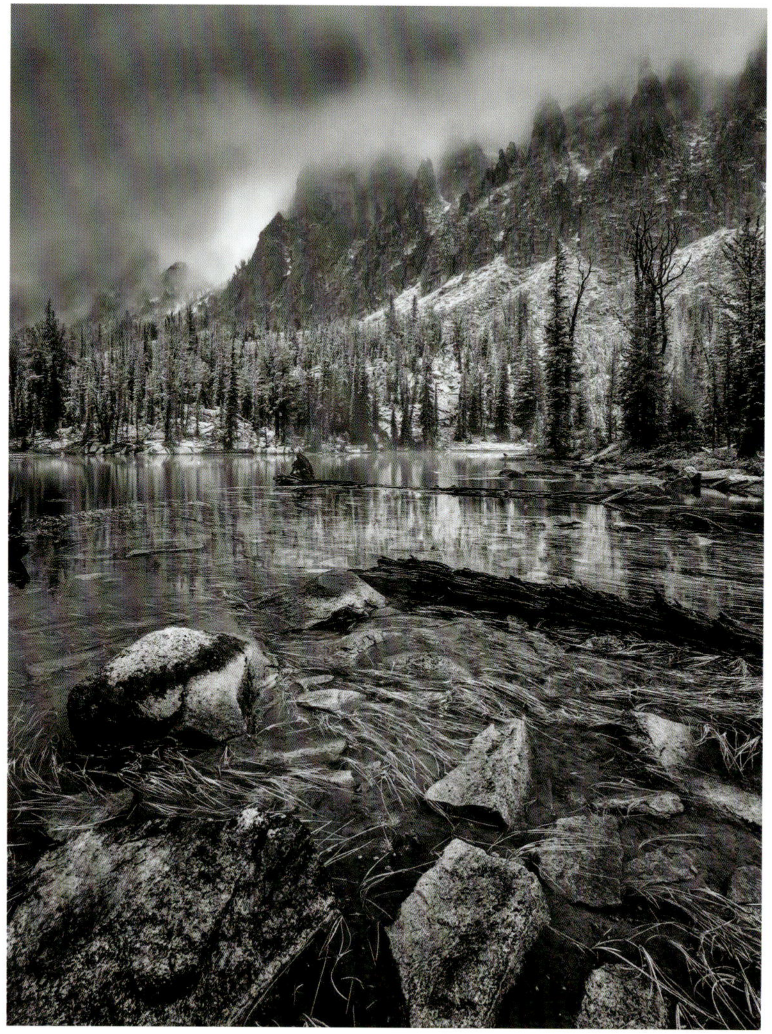

Sunset - Upper Creamer Lake
Fog from a late summer snow - Warbonnet Lake

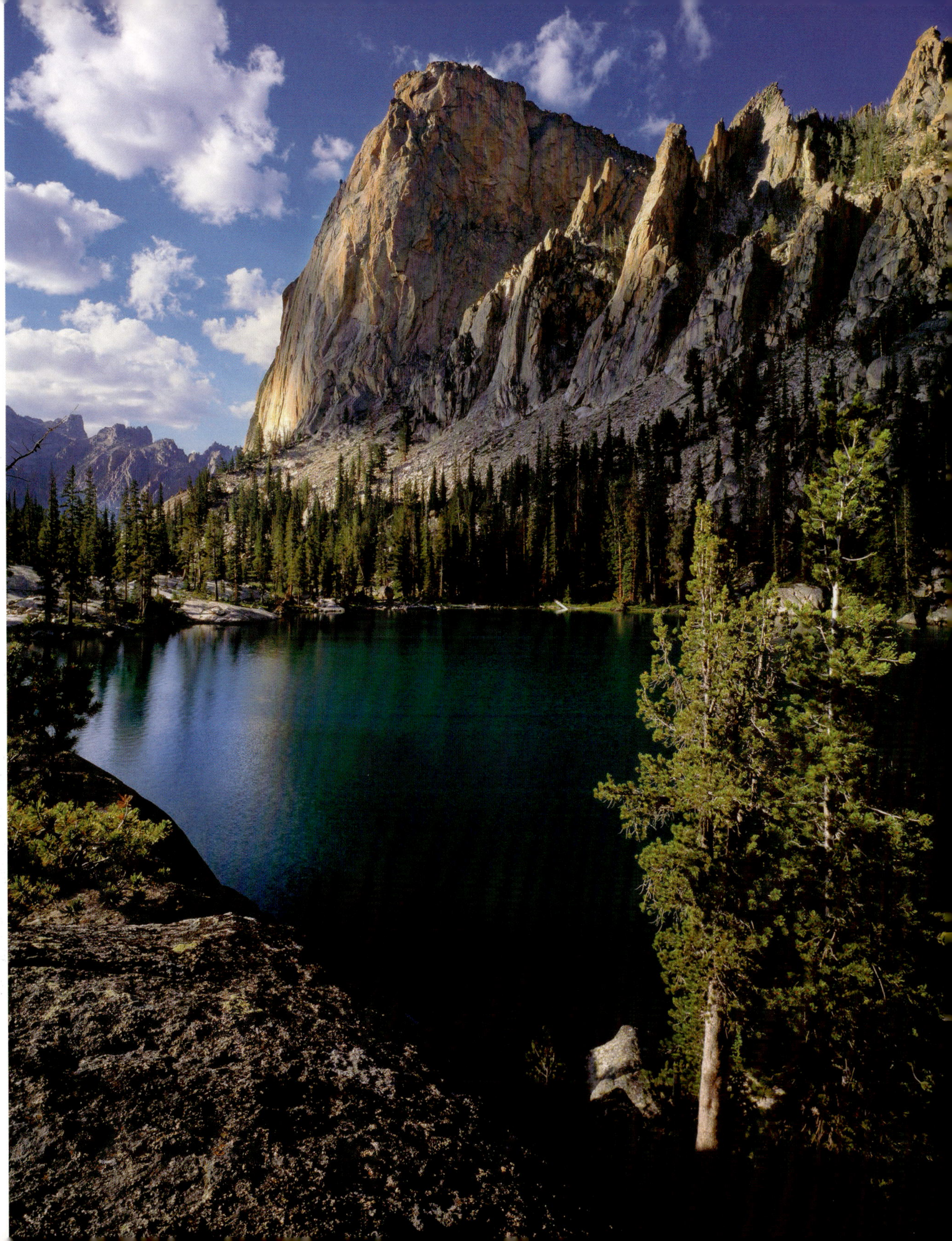

Saddleback Lake and the Elephant's Perch

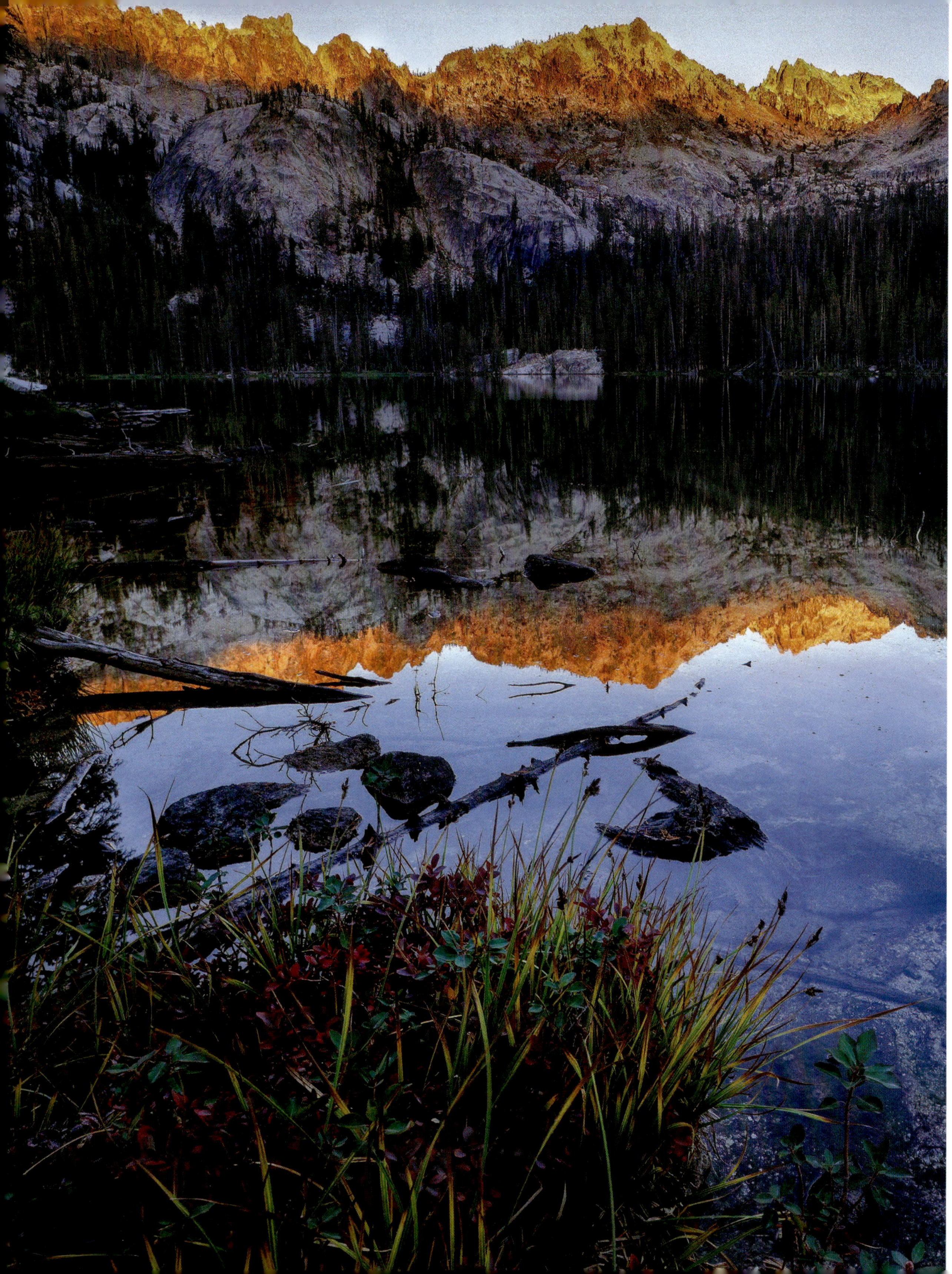

Early morning light strikes the peaks above Alpine Lake
Long grasses break the reflection of the Elephant's Perch - Saddleback Lake

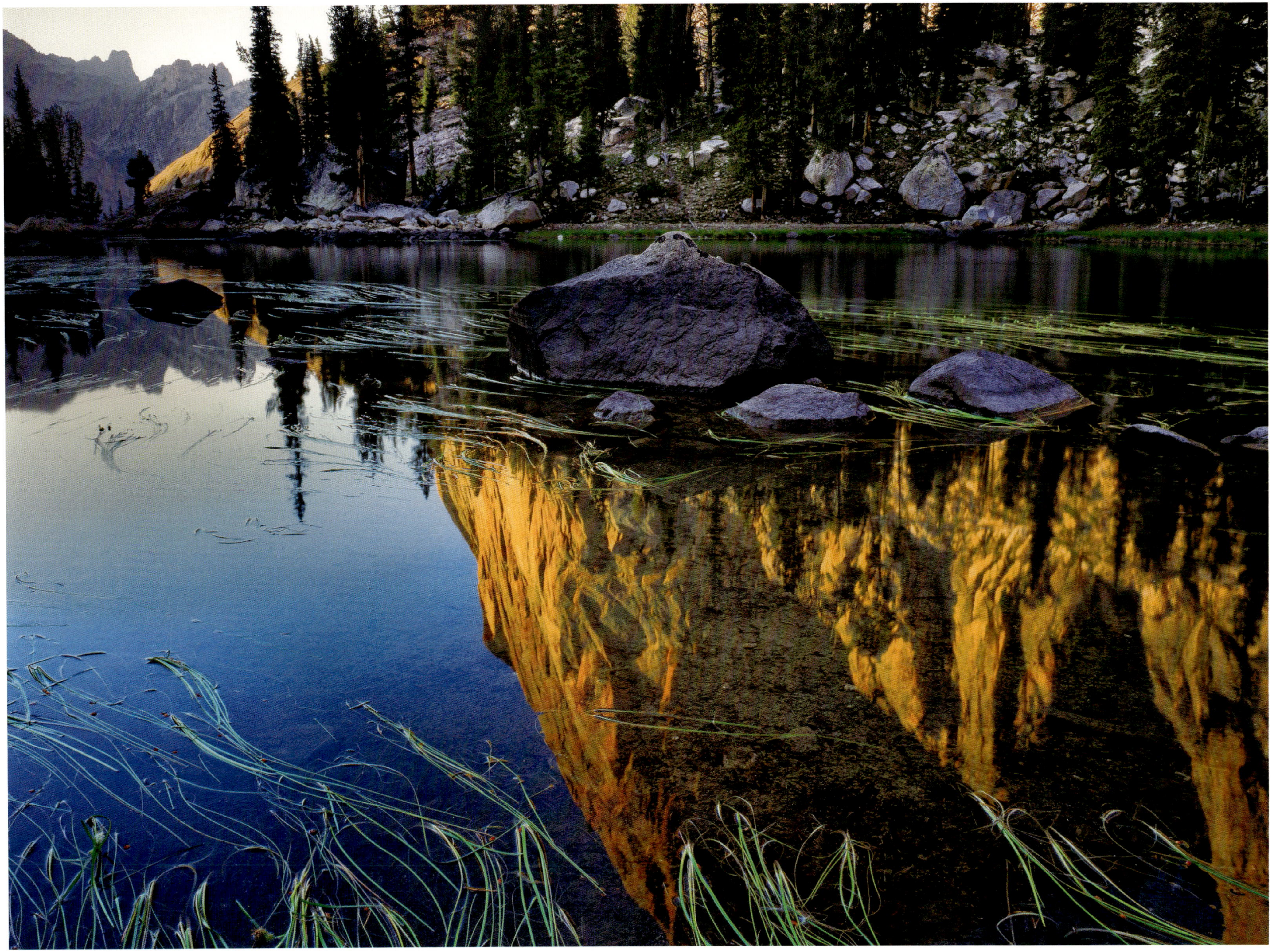

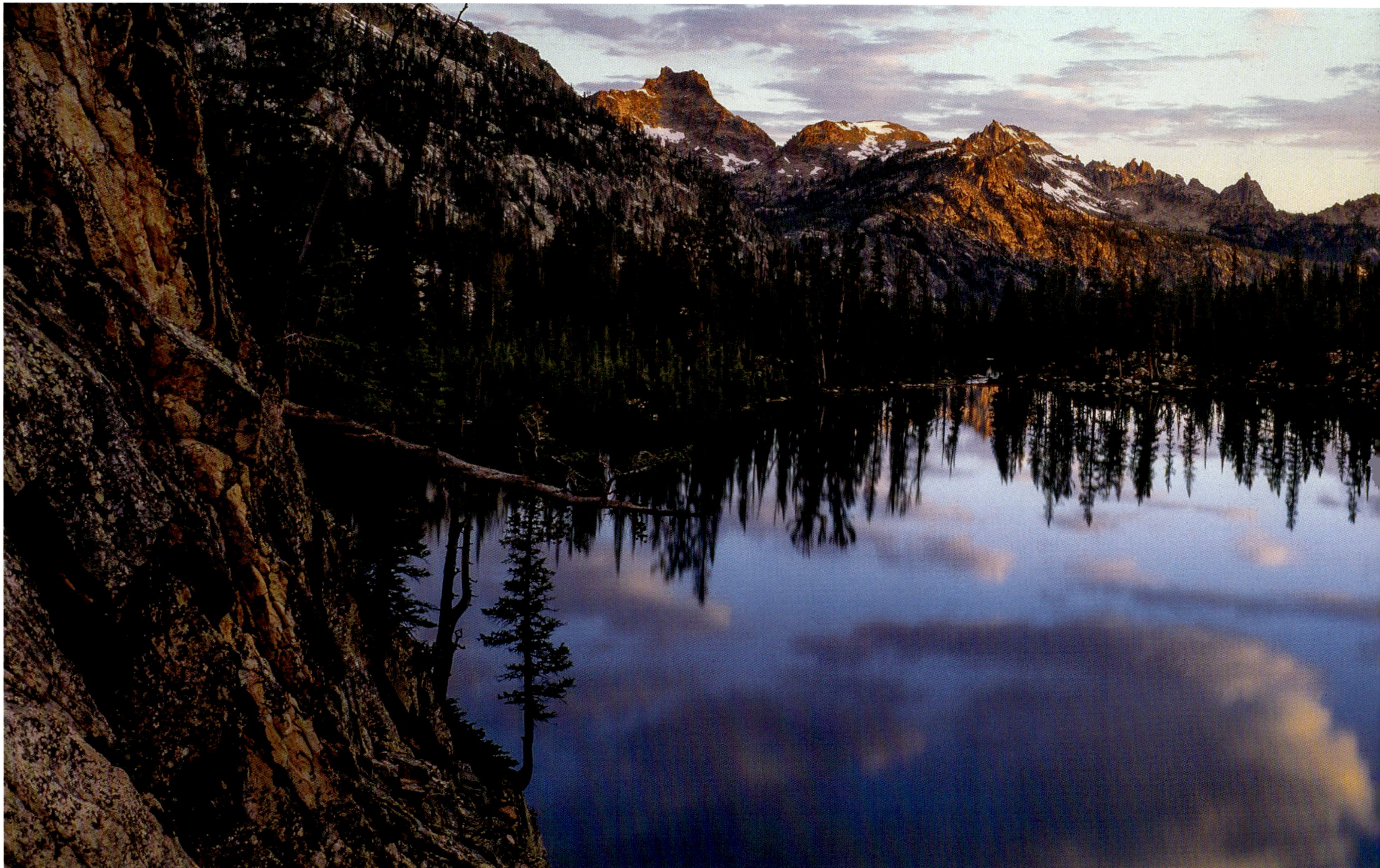

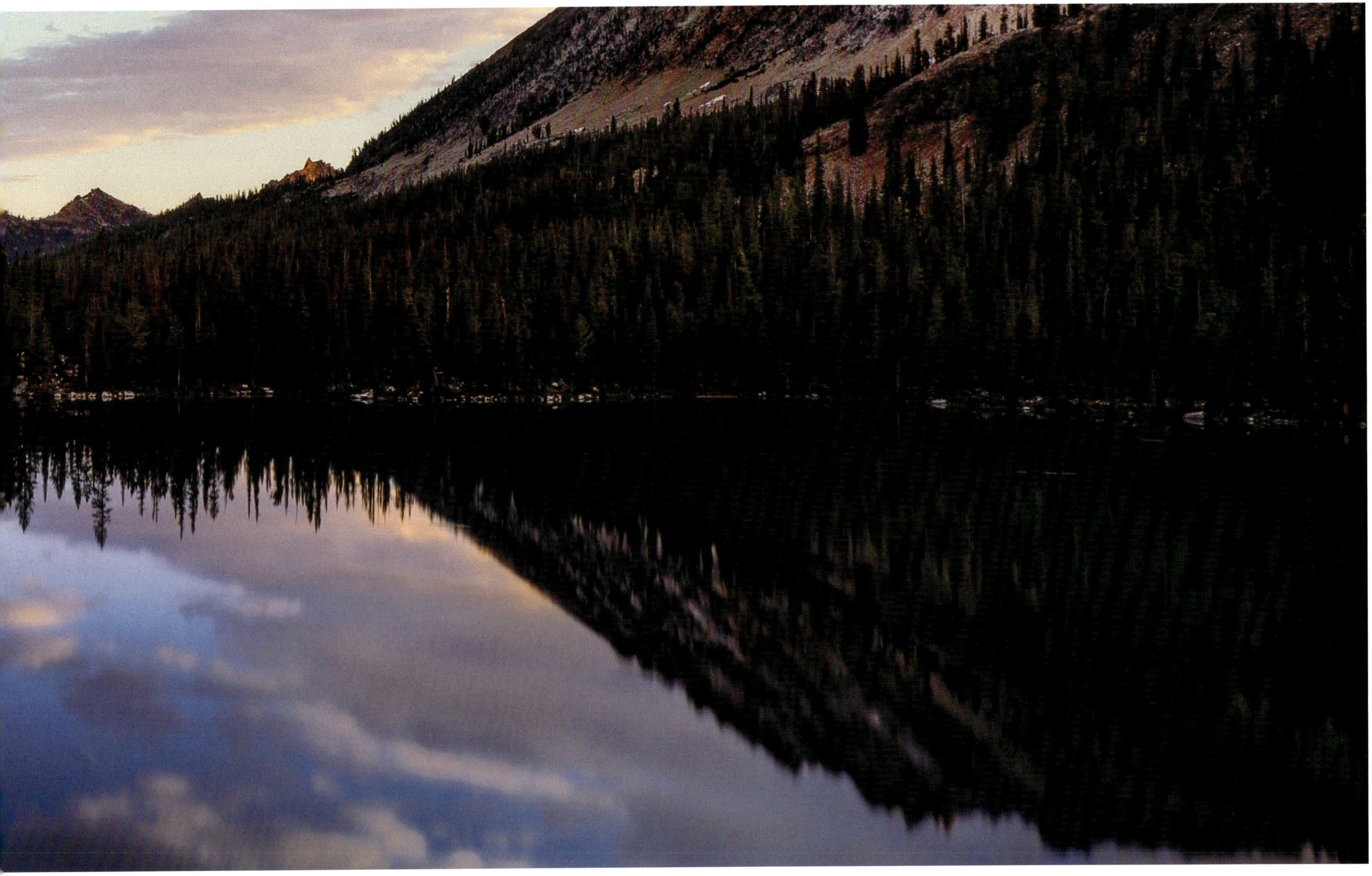

Sunrise Creamer Lake

Hell Roaring

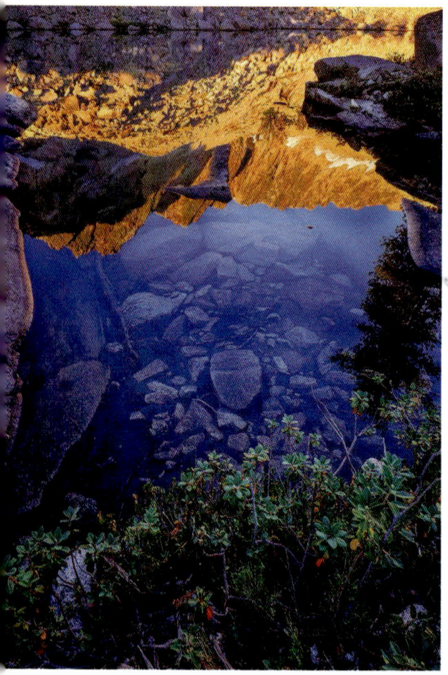

Hell Roaring Lake
Finger of Fate Lakes
Lucille Lake
Profile Lake
Imogene Lake

HELL ROARING CREEK TUMBLES, channel a jumble of cracked granite and boulders strewn by creeping towers of ice. But water settles like plates of glass in the level places. The Finger of Fate rises, part of a circle of rock faces and spires, fractured walls where climbers cling in summer. Peaks across the Sawtooths grow dotted with forms, muscled and sweaty, there where the wind touches down from the sky and the world curves perceptibly, lakes spread out in all directions, valleys falling away to the Stanley Basin or the Payette on its run to the desert far to the West. Hooves strike rock. Tack jangles, the sweat of flanks, rich, steeps the air. Mules stumble in hobbles, horses shy on the line beyond the tents. And Imogene Lake lies like a garden of islands, stone ships captained by pine and fir. Bodies lean back on the shores. They spoon bites of food from pouches, sip water carefully cleansed by filters or boiled. They creep into puffy bags to read by headlamp, then lie with the stars, with the quiet, until dawn.

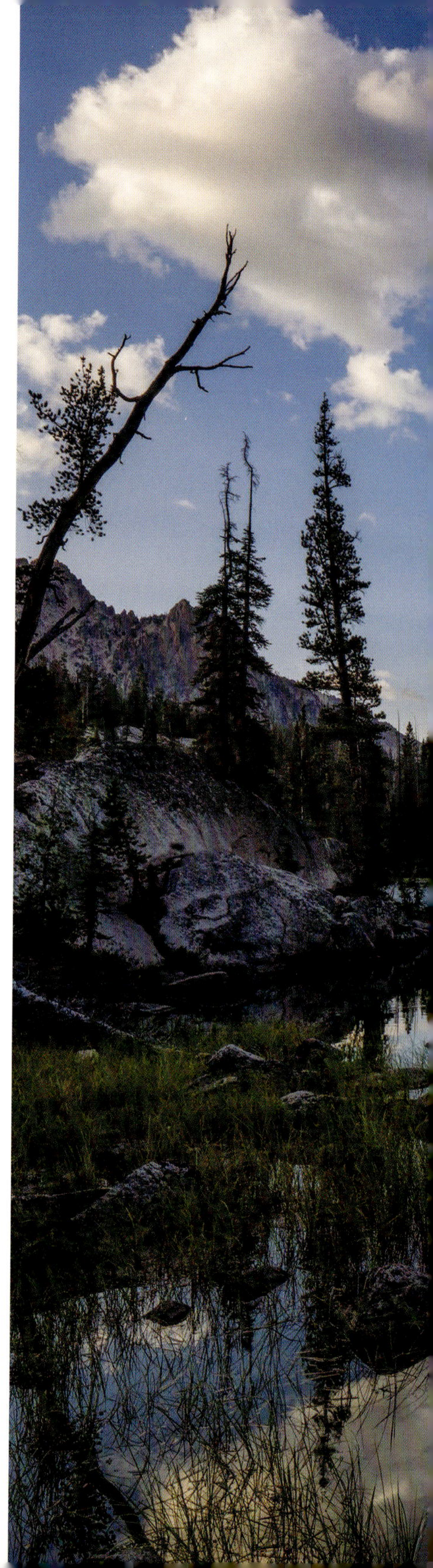

(Detail) Lucille Lake
One of many classic bench lakes - Imogene Lake

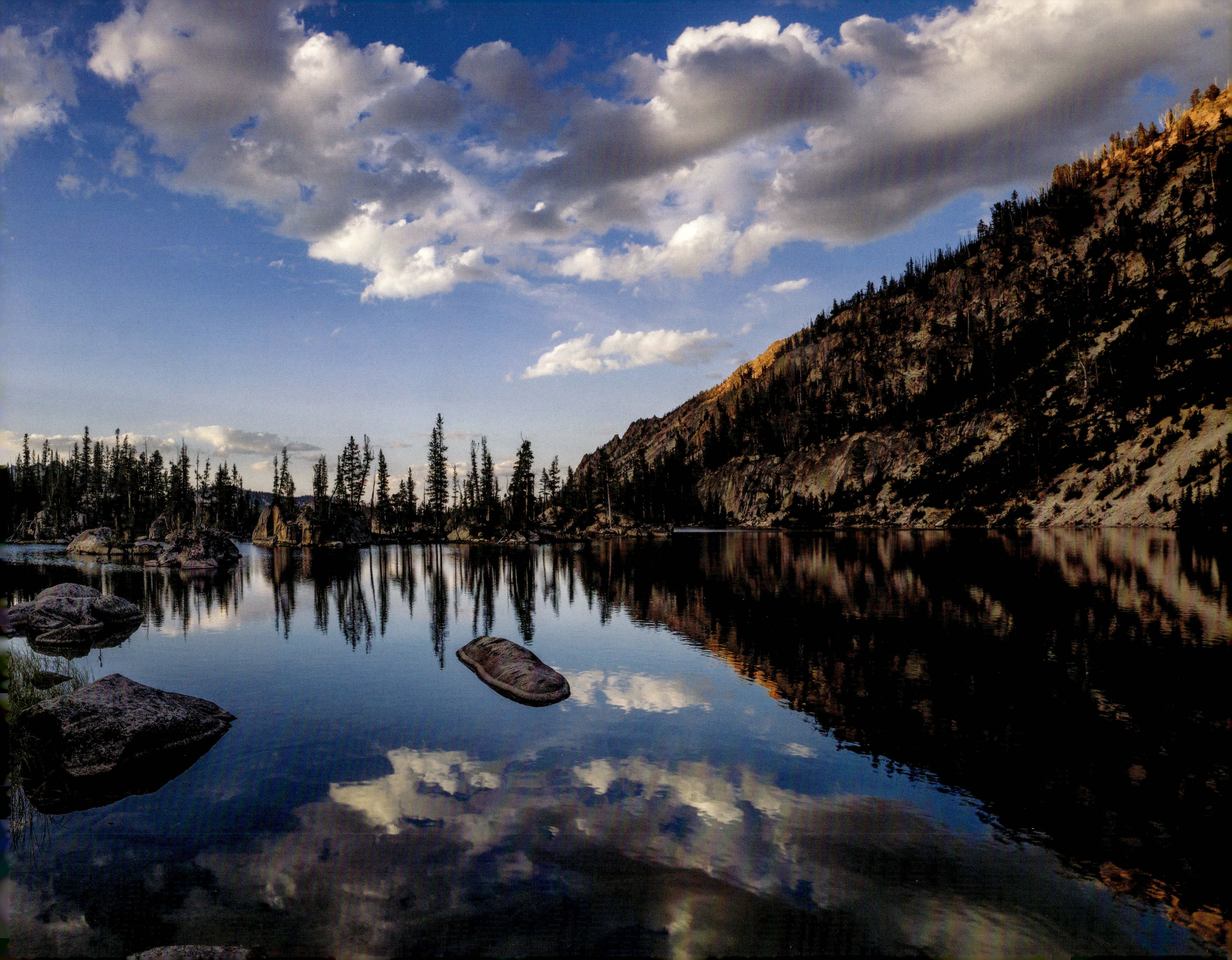

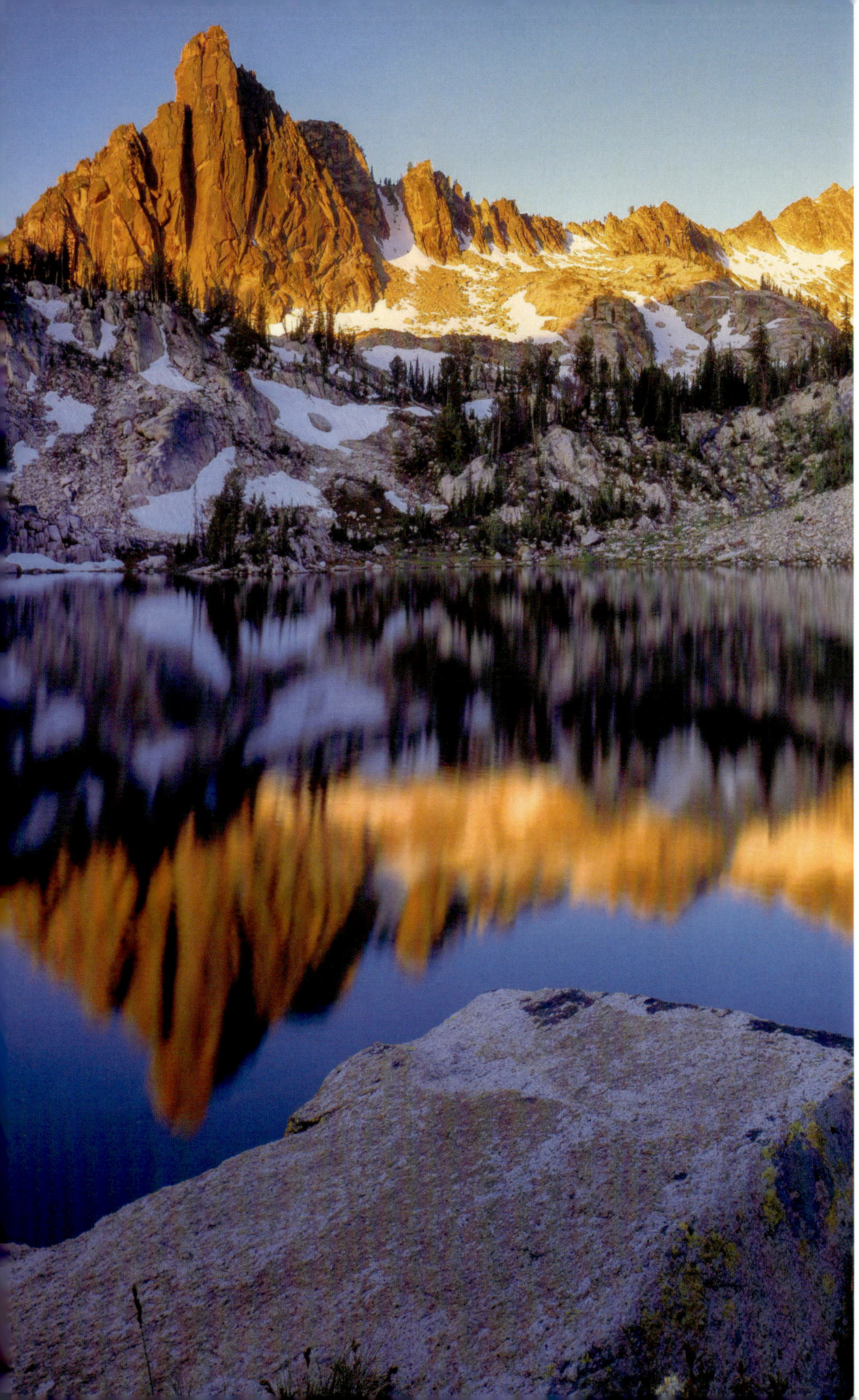

Finger of Fate Lake named for the distinctly shaped peak high above
(Opposite) Timber and boulders pile up in the outlet of Hell Roaring Lake

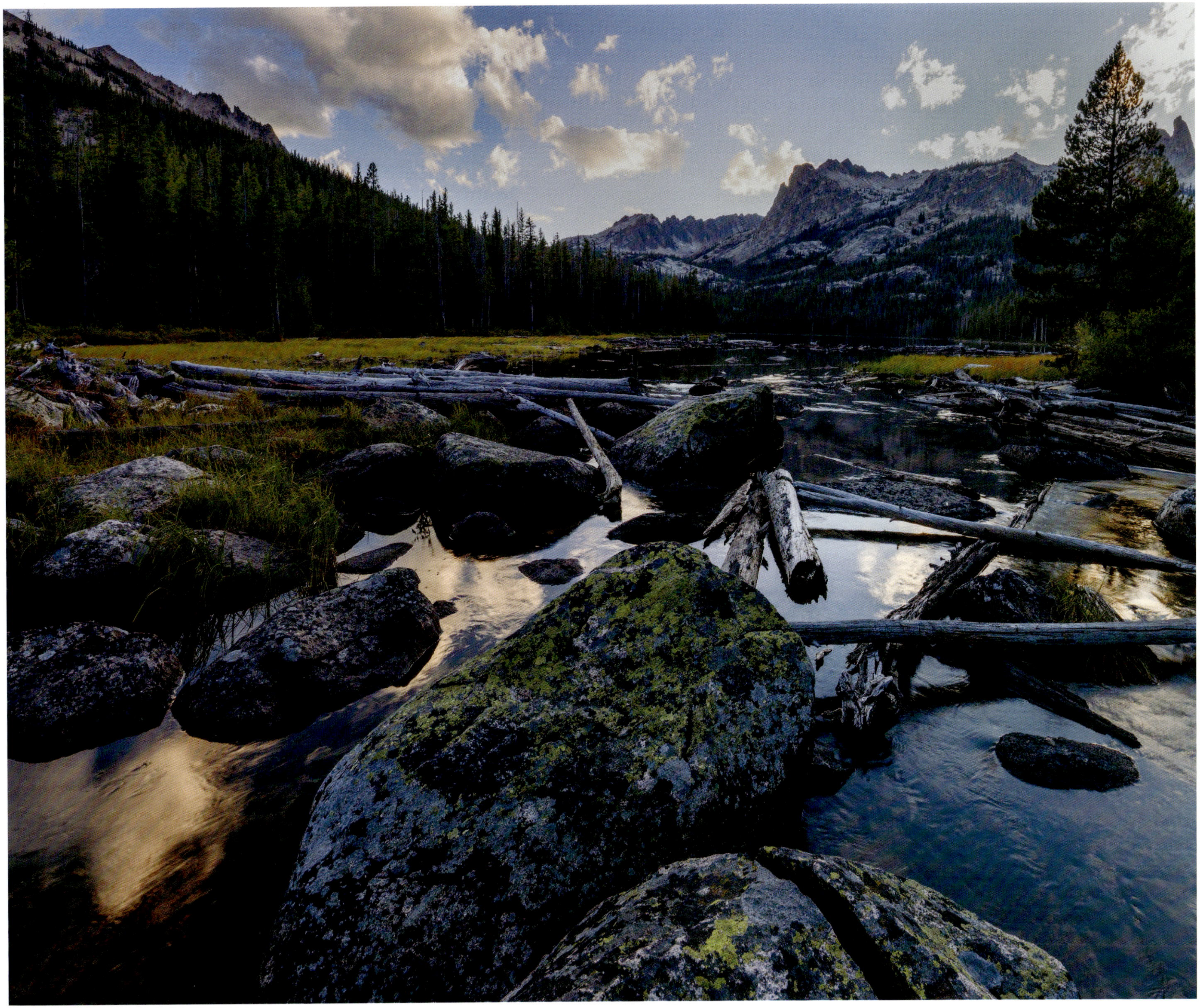

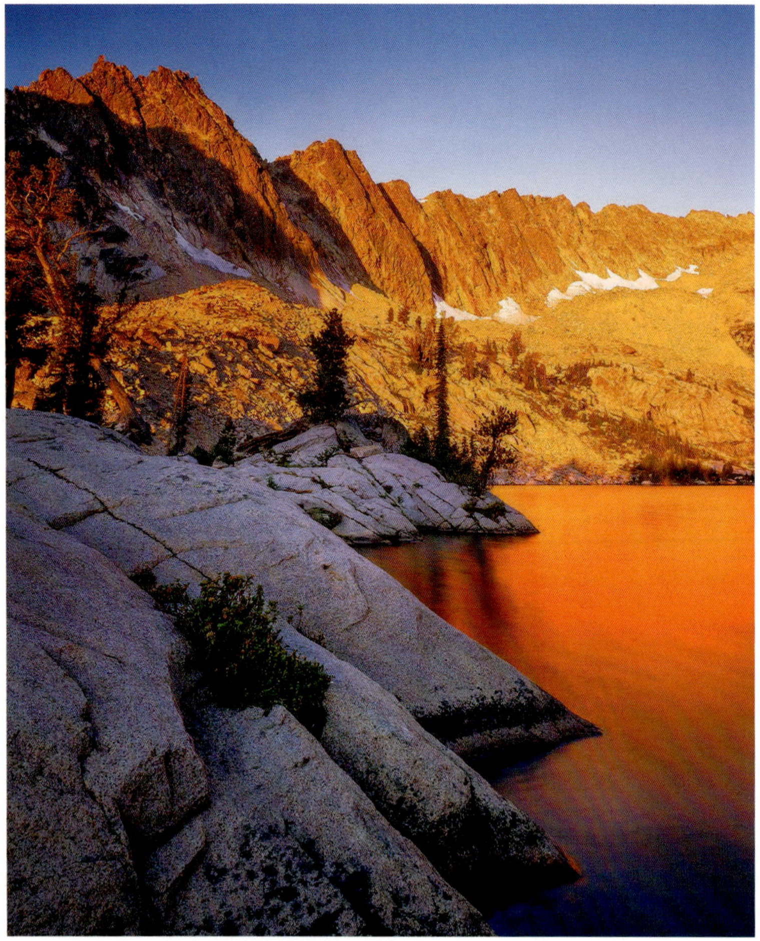

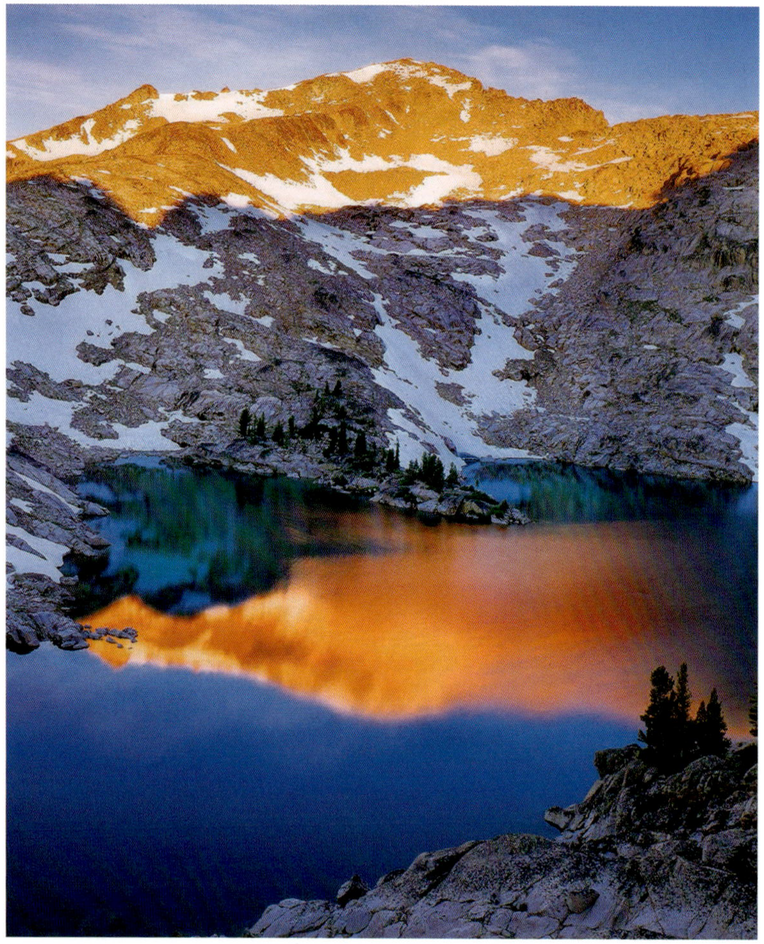

Granite shoreline - Lake Lucille

Mount Creamer reflects into the clear blue water of Profile Lake

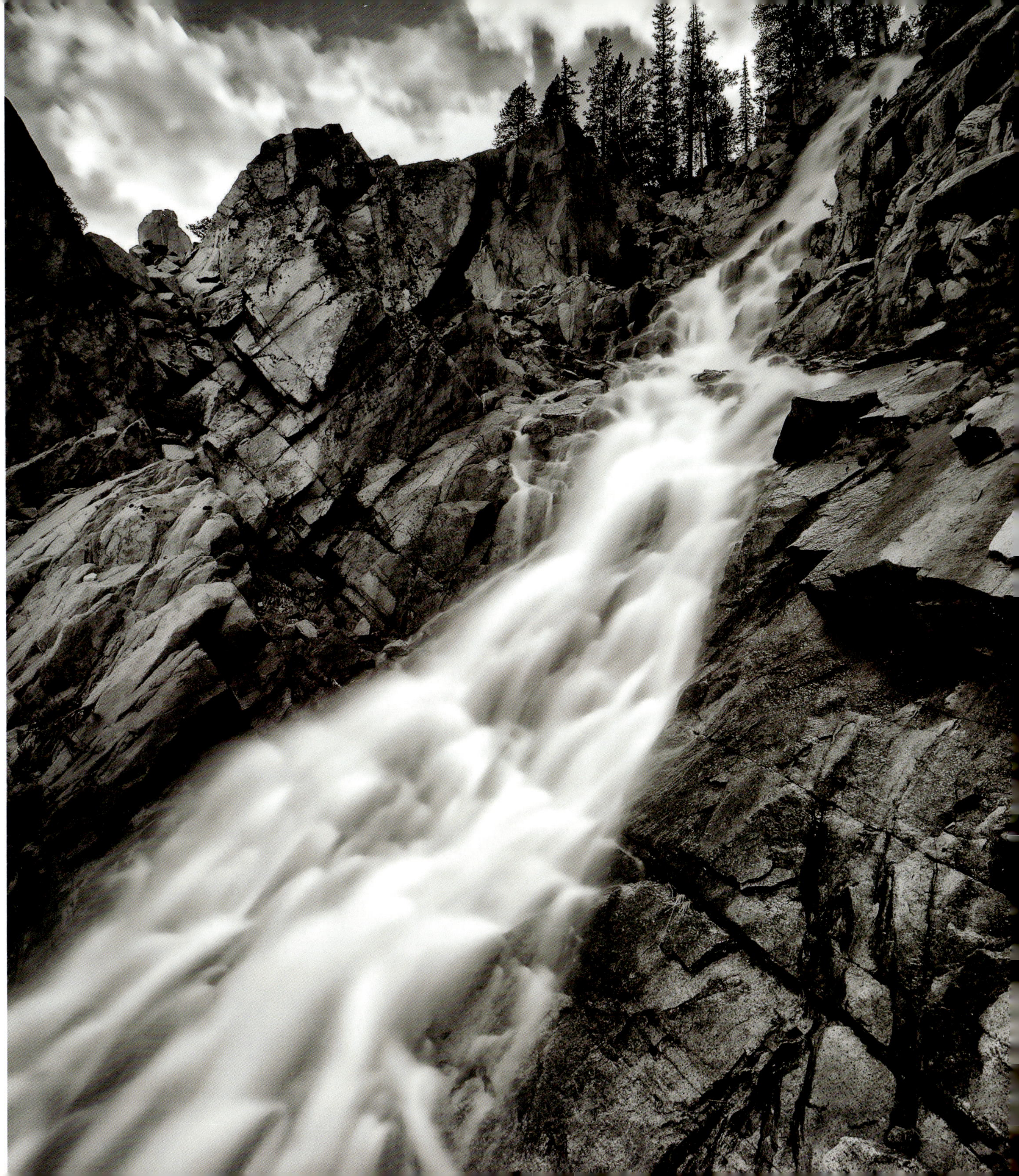

Waterfall on Hell Roaring Creek

Pettit Lake

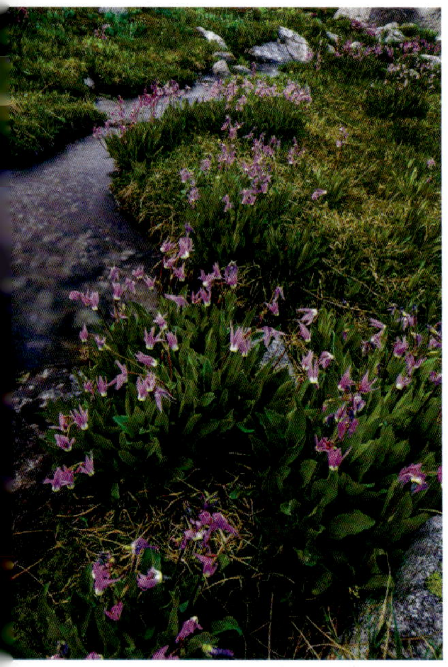

Pettit lake
Alice Lake
Twin Lakes
Toxaway Lake

EARTH TURNS. LIGHT BENDS, FILTERED.

Peaks rise, tips dipped in yellow or pink. Dull granite glows. Rafts of cloud sail in flame, captured by one lake's surface. Water magnifies sky, layering its light over rock and pale fish slipping from surface to darkness. At night, even the quarter moon makes shadows of the peaks above Toxaway, sunlight reflected from the dust of the moon, settles on the peaks until the earth spins away and the peaks stand in darkness. Stars, infinite in number, are the only light. But the depth of the sky is not static; satellites roll over planets, which pass before stars, against our own galaxy: a wide glowing stripe across the dome, wild arms flailing. And beyond that, constellations of galaxies and stars, distant and ancient, are reflected in water, still, now fading, sky cast again in color, pink, then orange, waiting for one spot on the ground below El Capitan to spin back toward the light, warmth and sun.

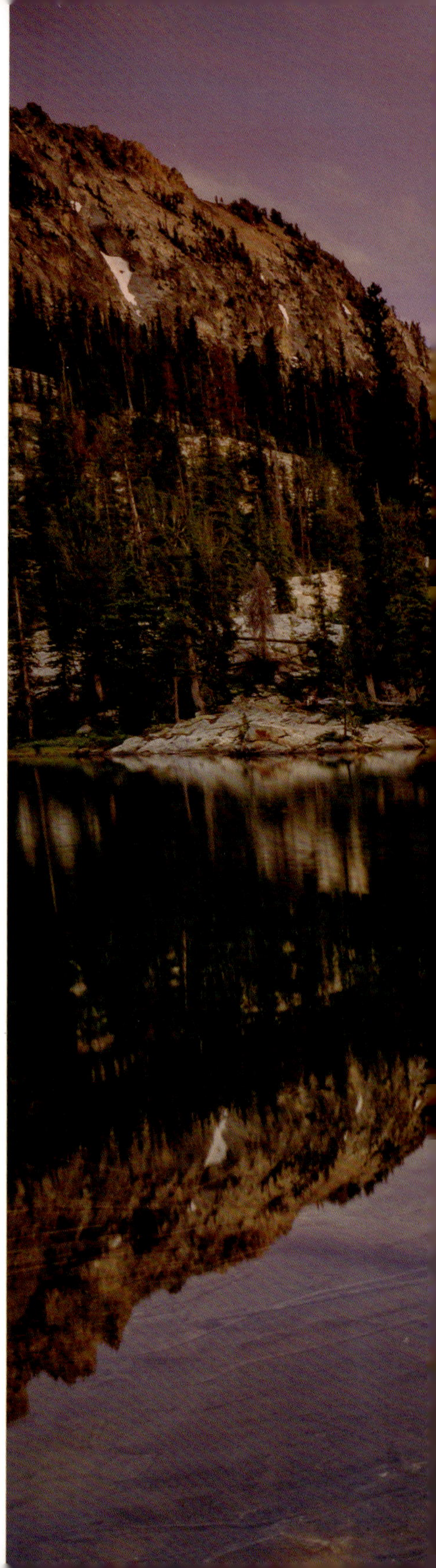

(Detail) Shooting Stars bloom near Twin Lakes
Sunset reflects from the rugged peaks above Alice Lake

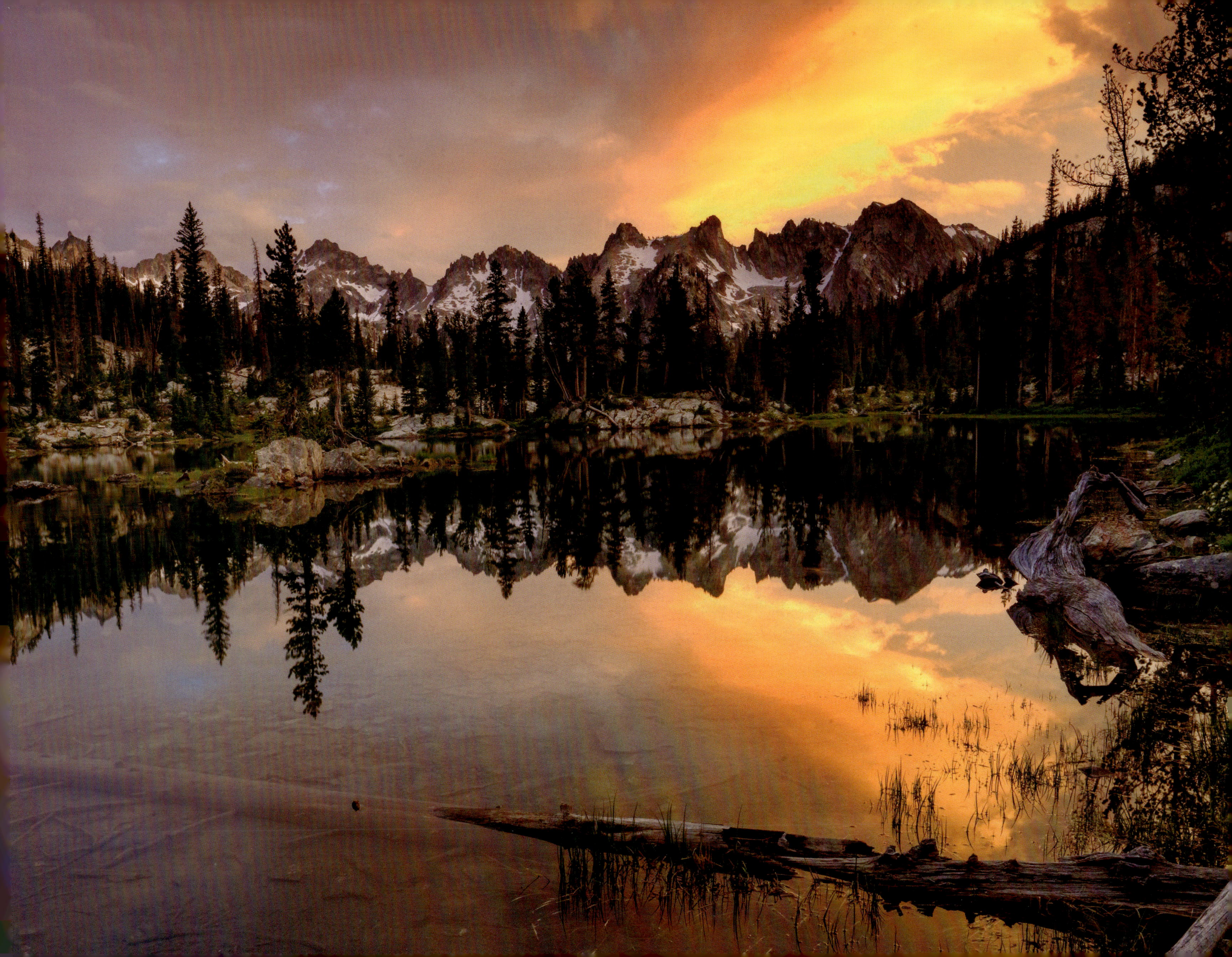

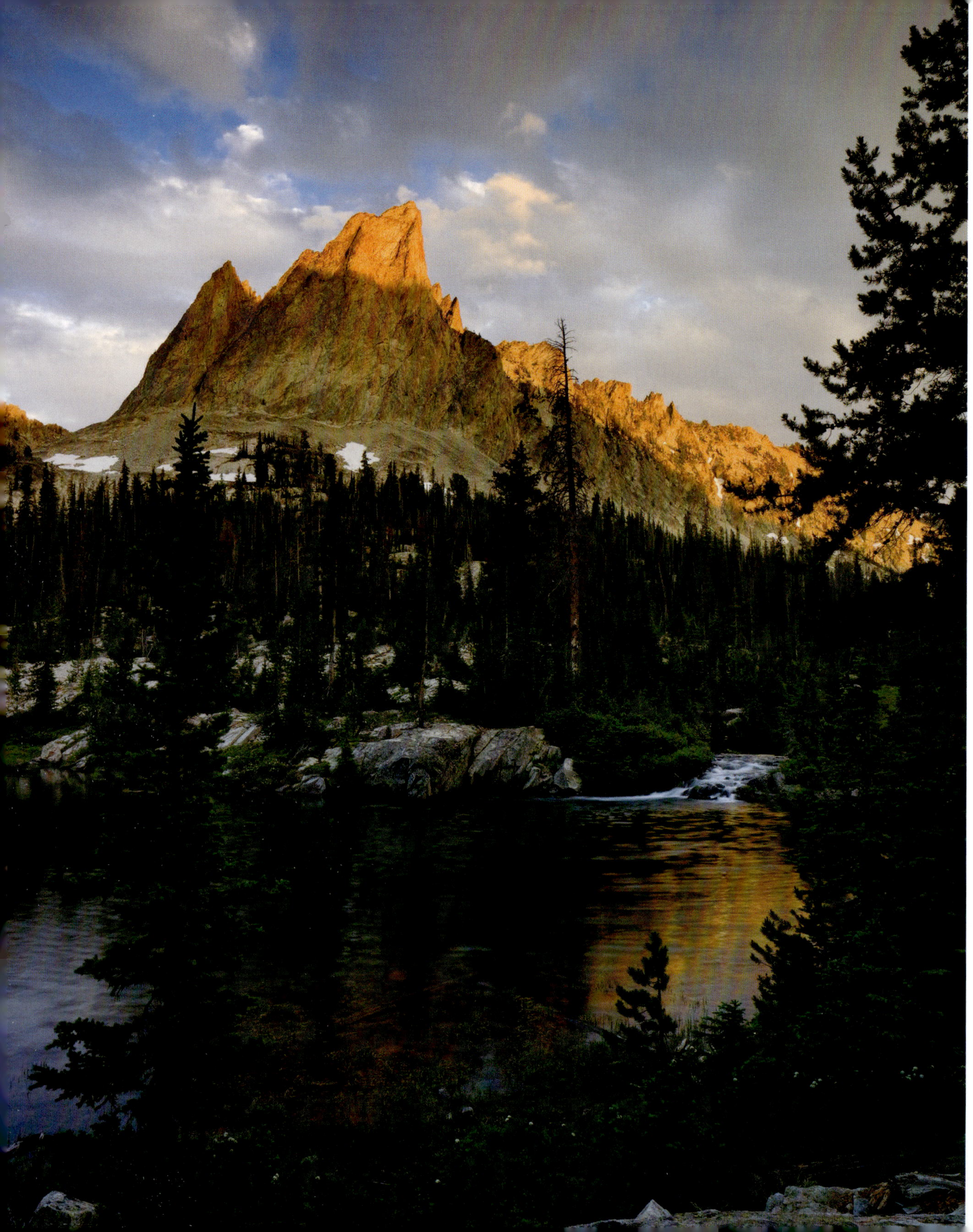

El Capitan Peak near Alice Lake
(Opposite) Sunset at Pettit Lake

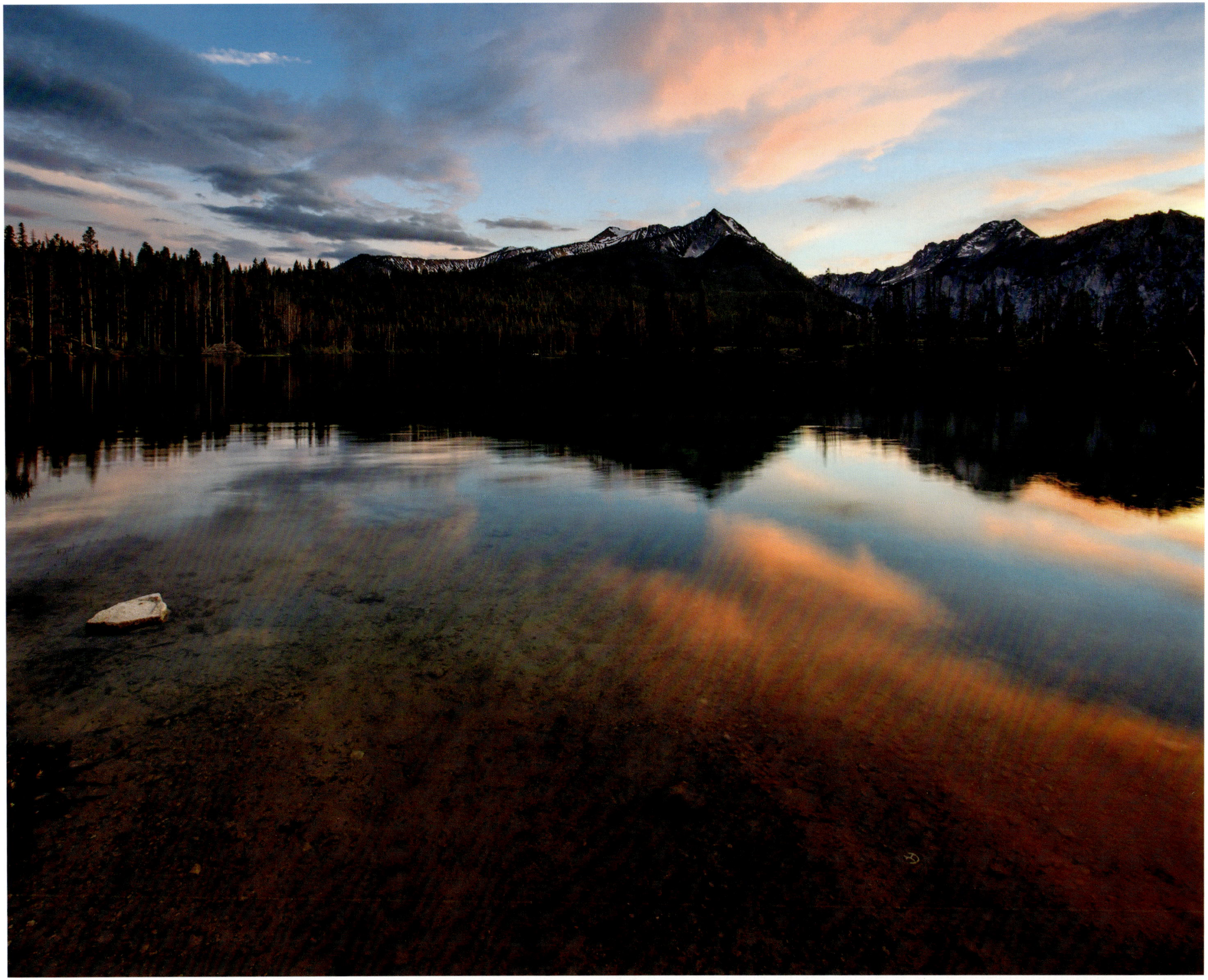

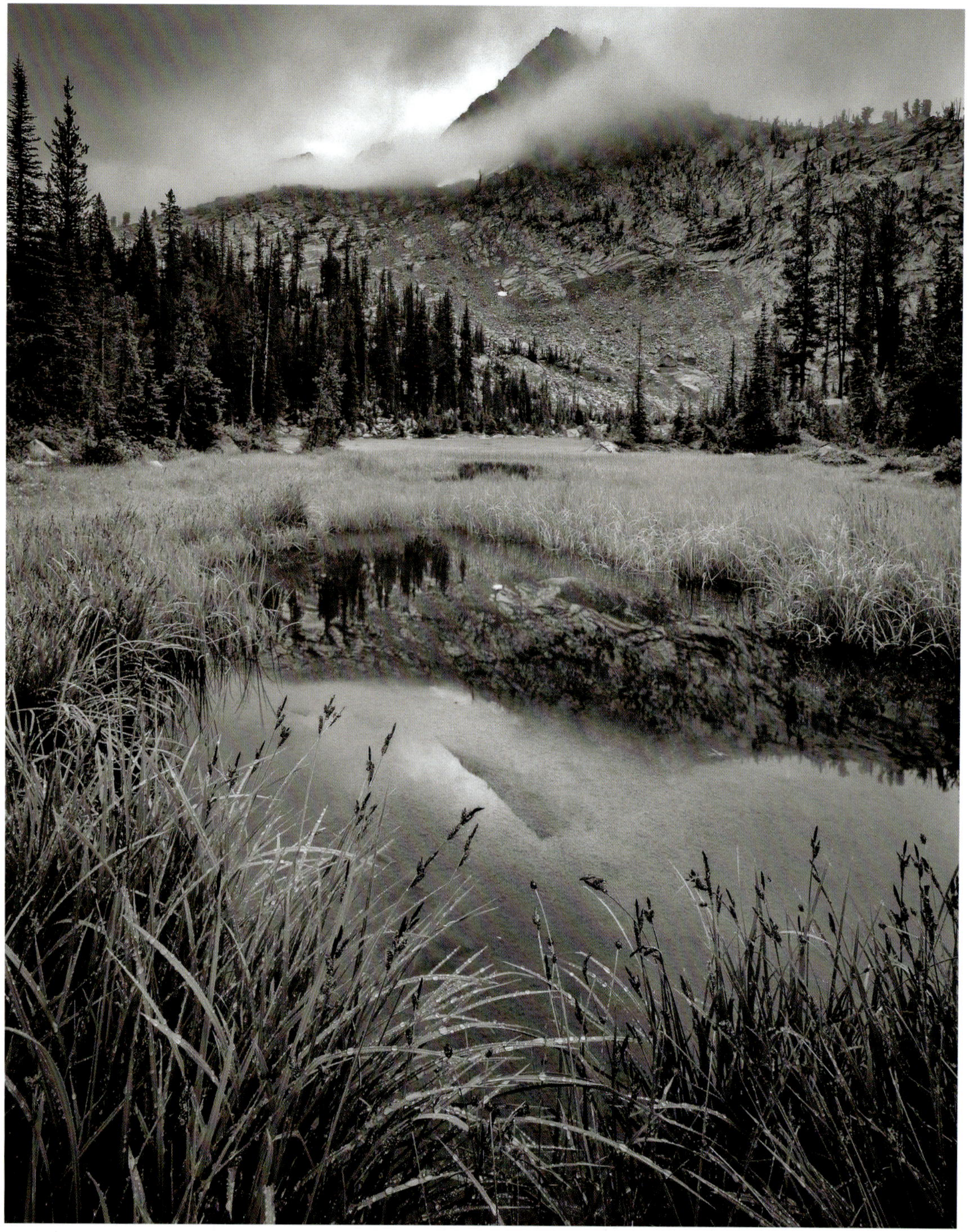

Fog engulfs Snowyside Peak
(Opposite) Rugged peaks above Alice Lake

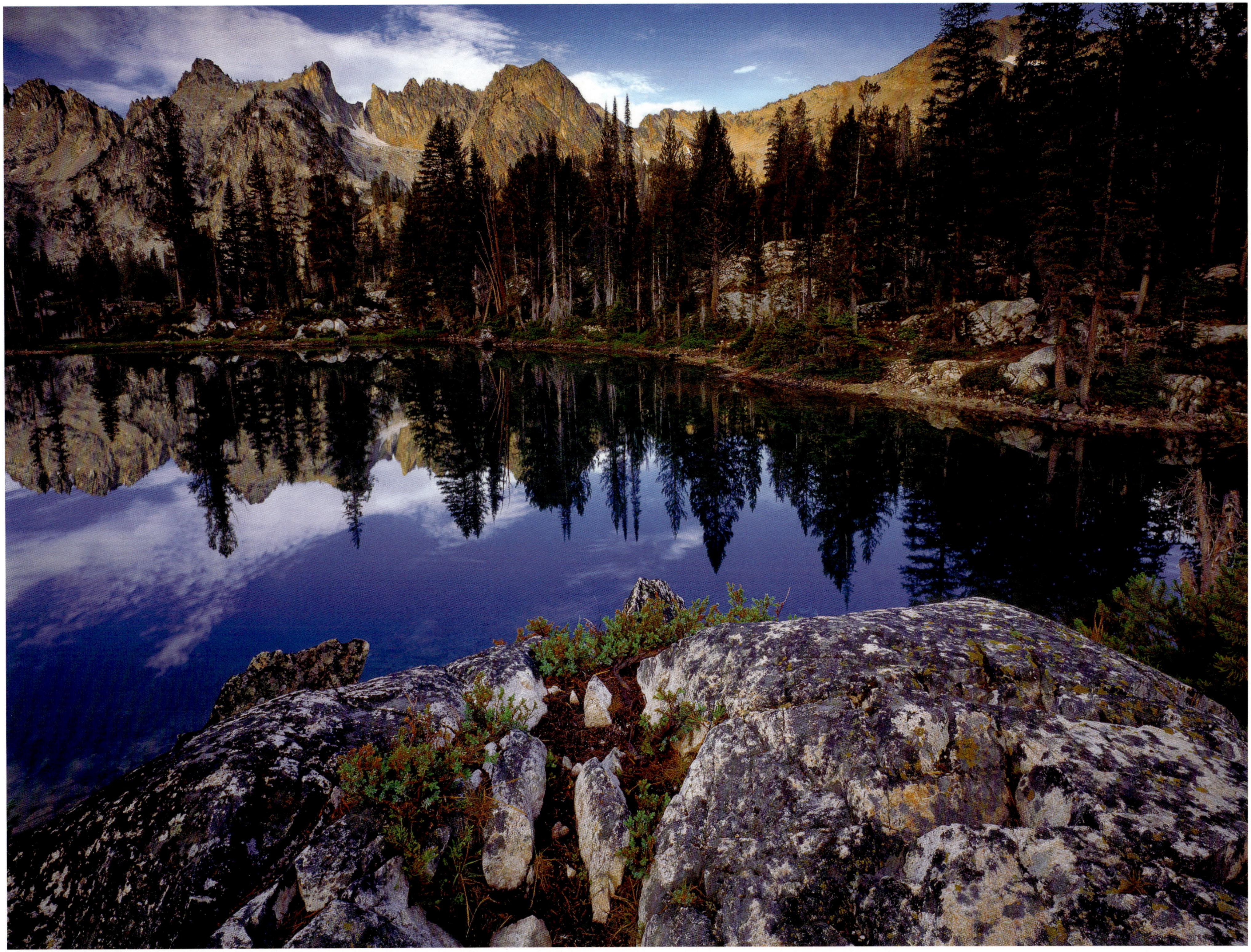

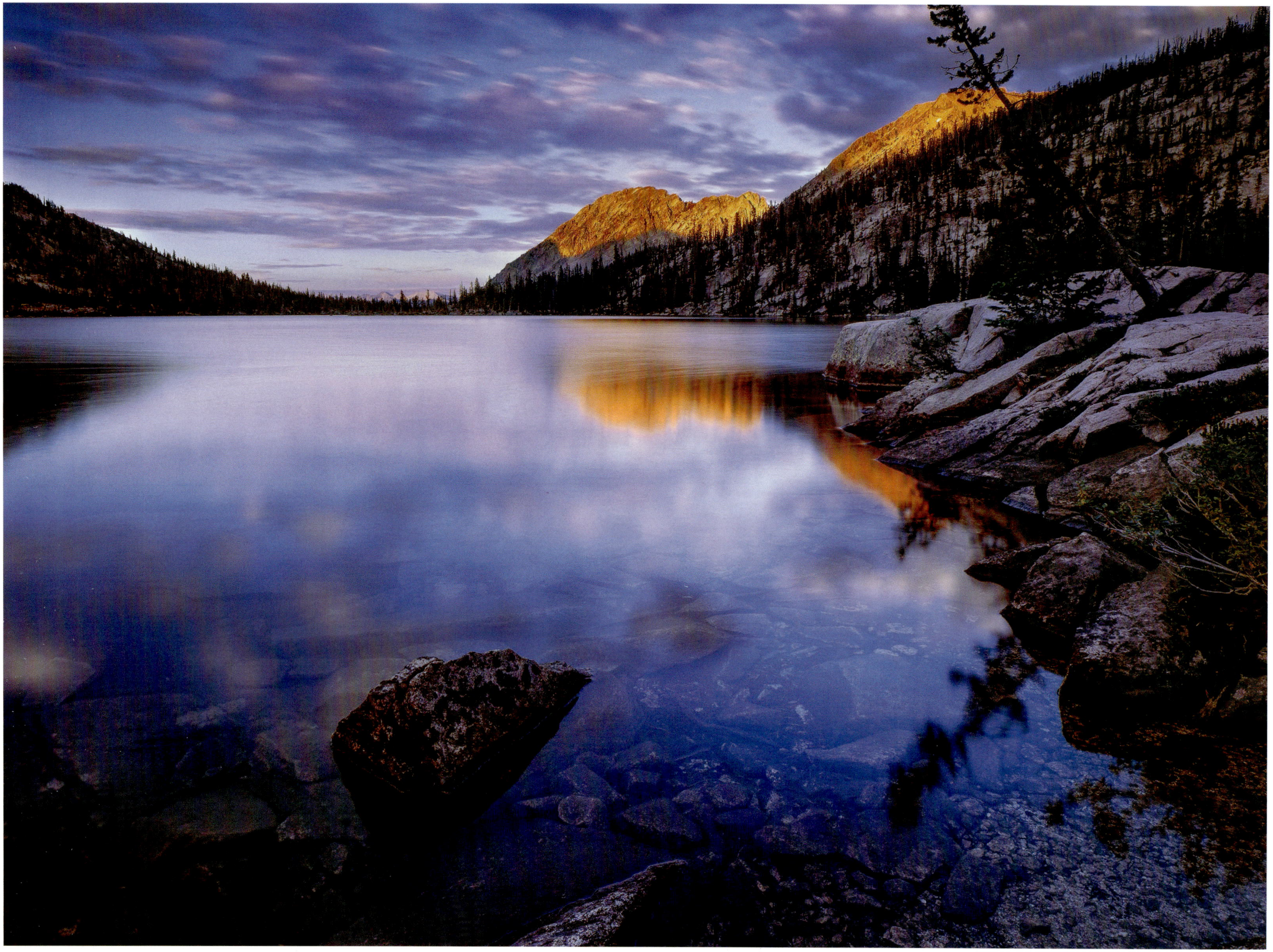

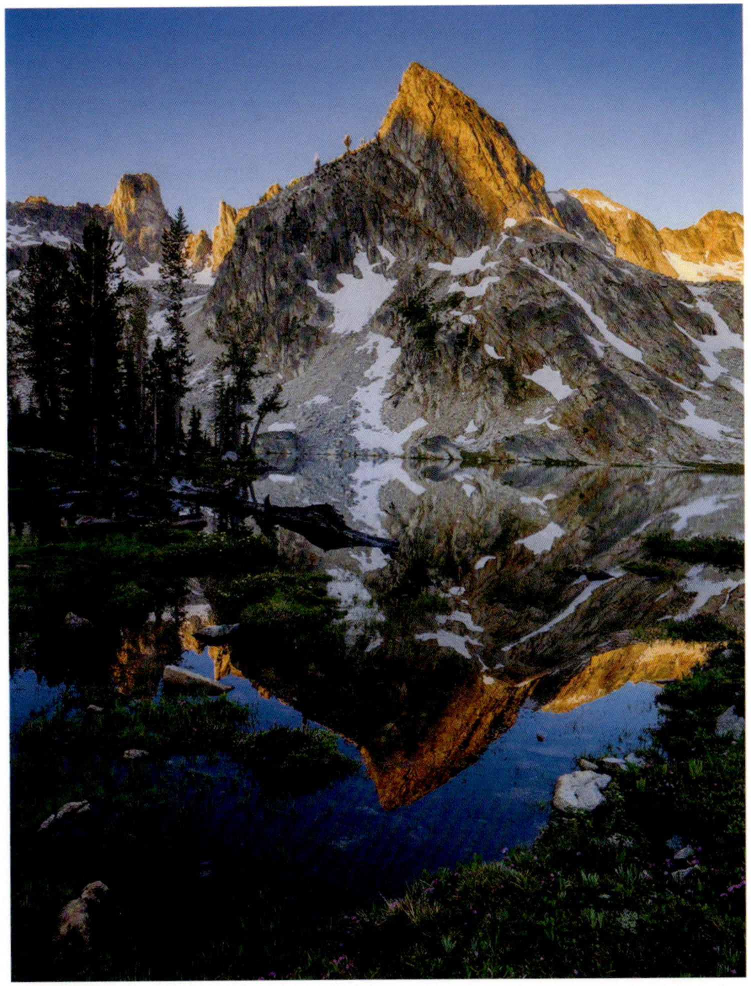

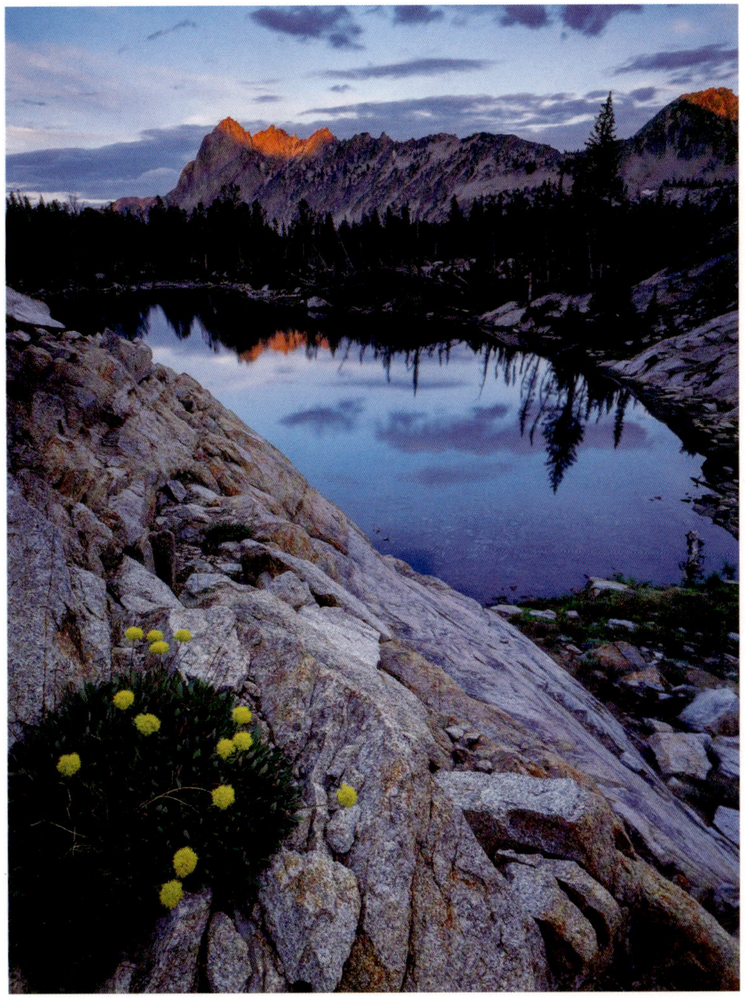

The Twin Lakes hug the base of rugged Sawtooth peaks

(Opposite) Toxaway Lake is one of the most popular of the high alpine lakes in the Sawtooths Wilderness.

Looking east toward El Capitan Peak from Twin Lakes

Alturas Lake

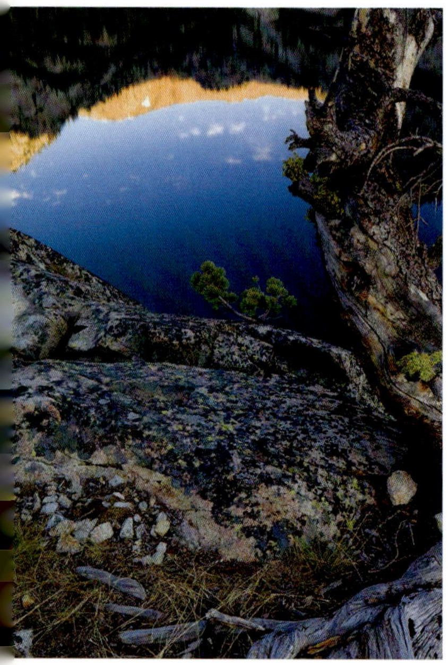

Alpine Creek Left Fork
Alpine Creek Right Fork
Unnamed Lakes

WE DON'T ALWAYS LEAVE THE BEER BEHIND. Precious few cans left cooling in the waterfalls of Alpine Creek or one of the countless unnamed lakes, become a weighty elixir that settles the evening like a blanket of light. We huddle in the glow of the stove. The roar of gas in blue flame stills the mosquitos. But we don't wait for sunrise, we pry ourselves from warm bags into the frost-tinged morning, fingers stiff, day packs hurriedly stuffed with clothes and food and gear. And we may climb, leaving the trails for rock and sky. One step, one breath, we can climb forever. But the peak runs out and we are there on Snowyside's pinnacle, pulling the log book from a can to look for names. We turn back round and pick our way through boulders or dance down a face of scree. There, great bodies of water lie nameless. And in our love and vanity we name the lakes for ourselves: hoping we can carry that moment on the rim of the world with us forever, or, futilely wishing that the lake itself noticed our passing, felt our feet in its rocks, our hands in its water, somehow.

(Detail) Unnamed Lake, Left Fork of Alpine Creek
Unnamed Lake, the first lake in the Left Fork chain of Alpine Creek.

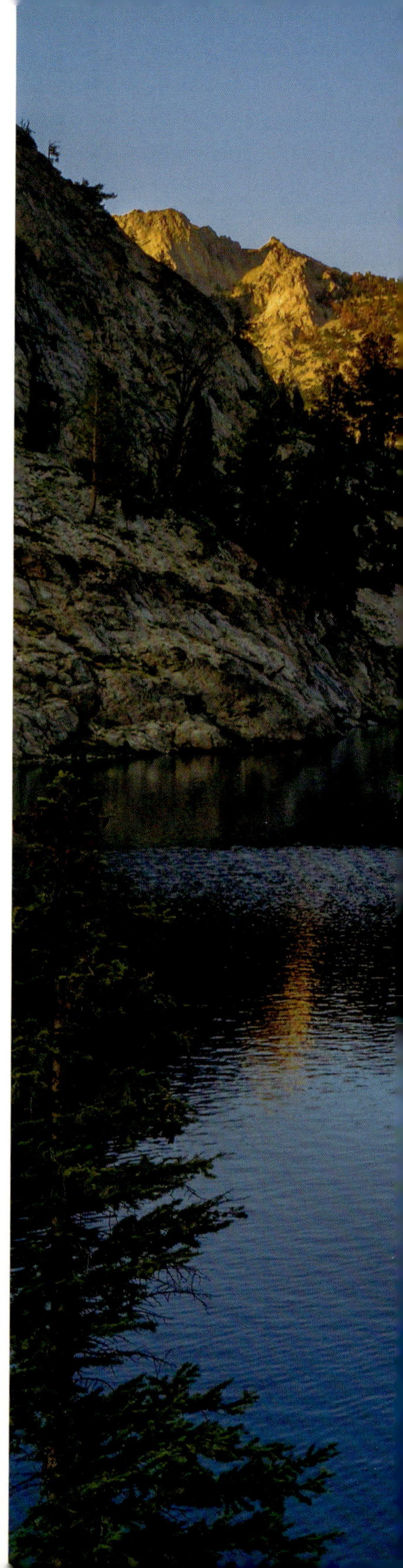

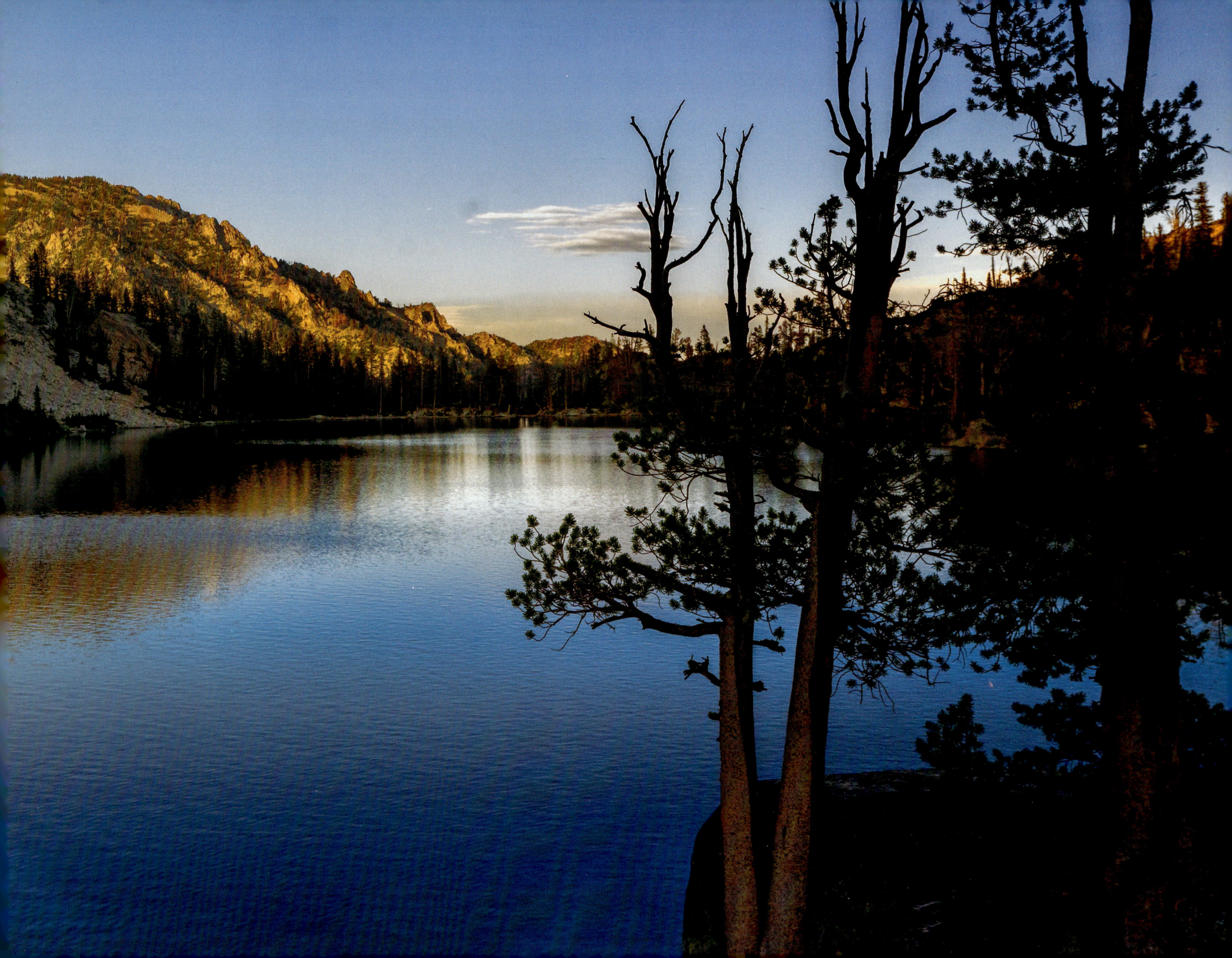

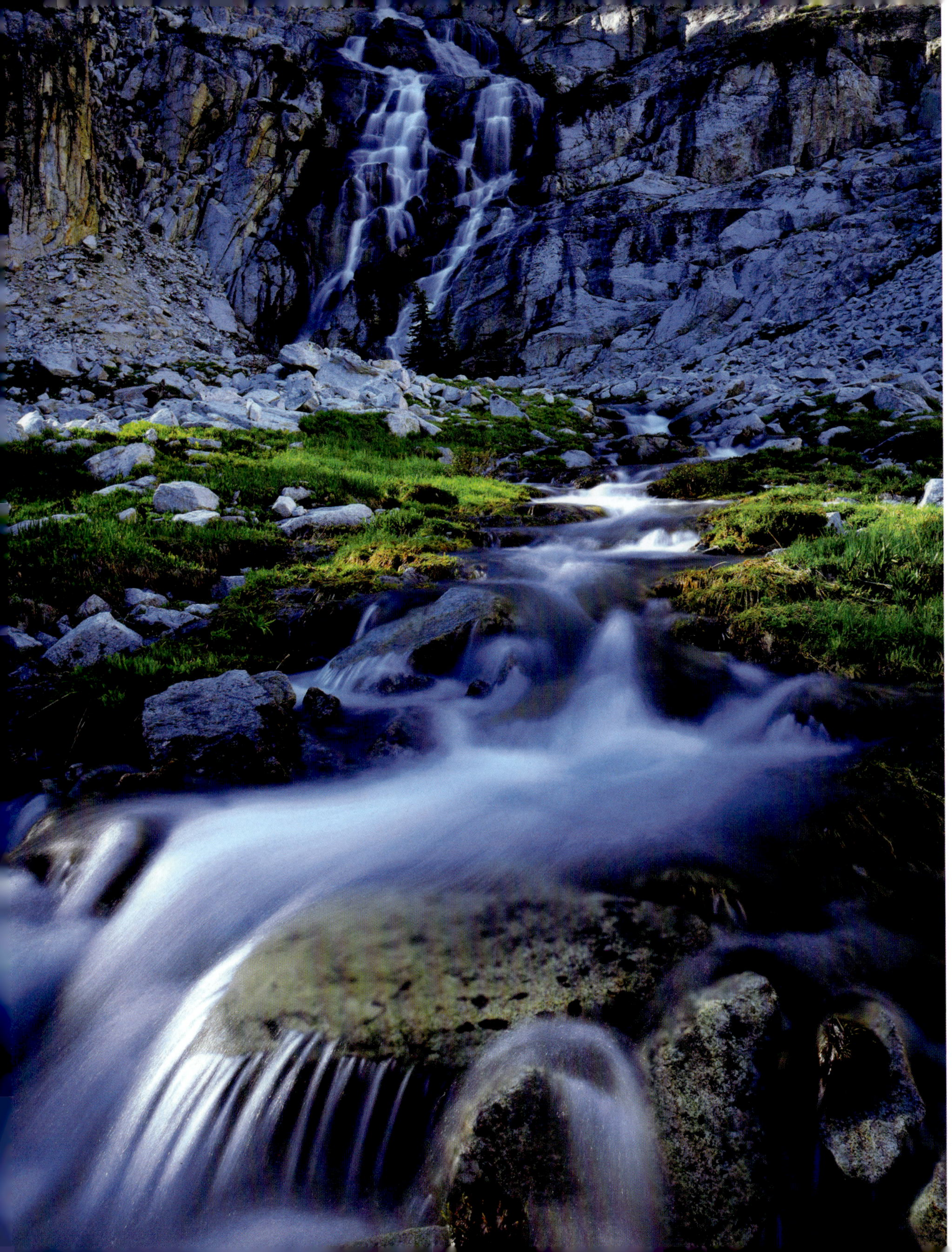

Water fall Alpine Creek
(Opposite) An unnamed lake - Right Fork of Alpine Creek

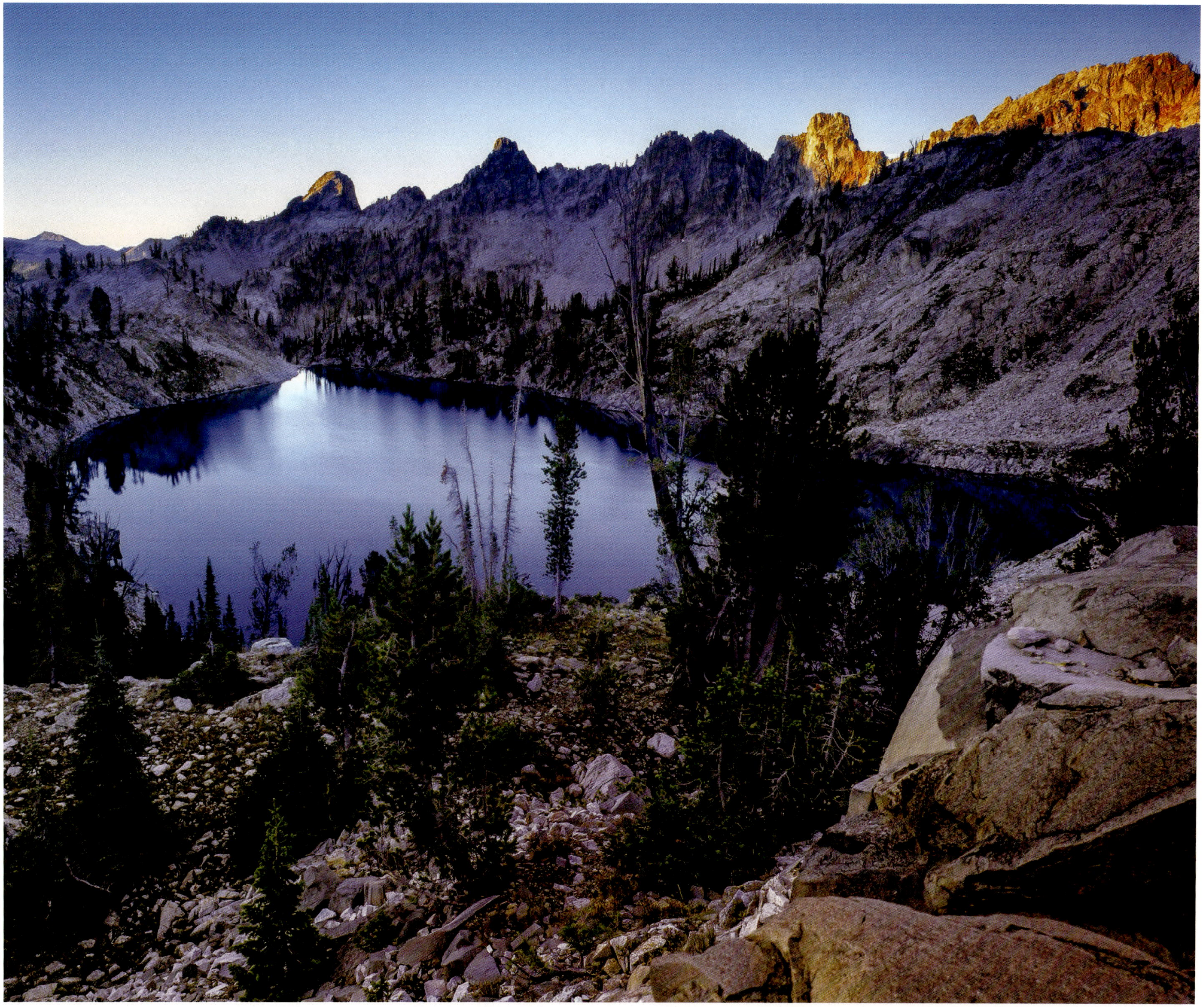

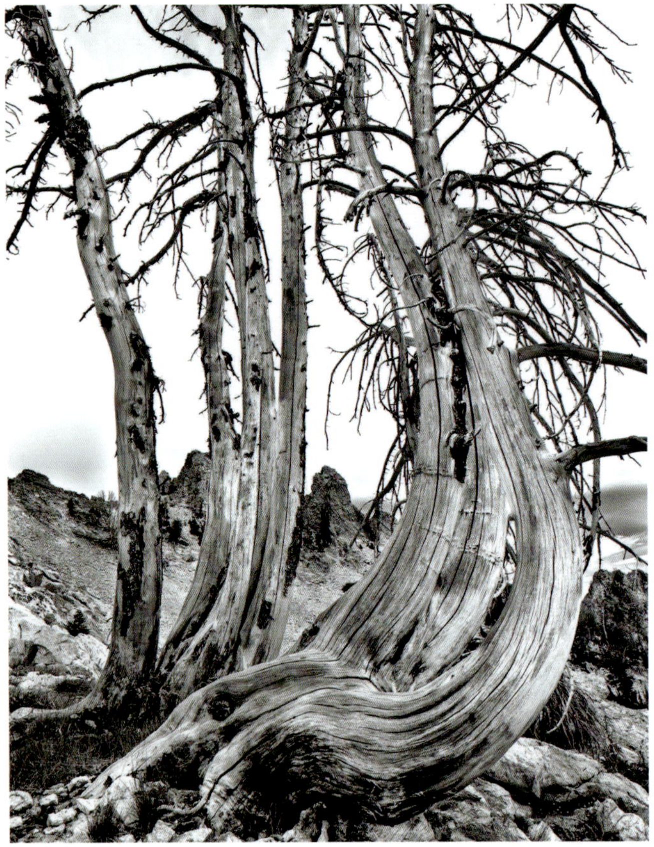

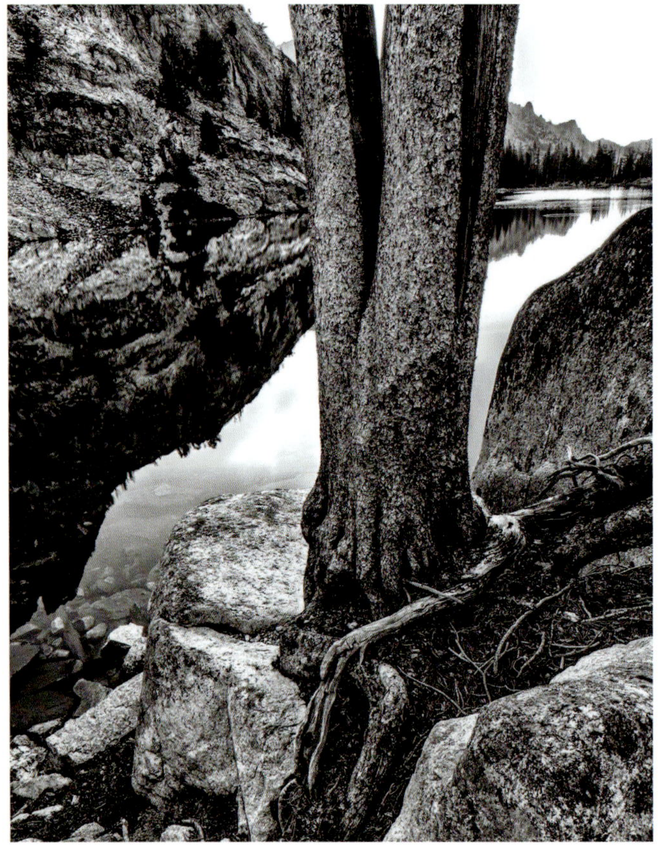

Pine skeletons on the ridge line of Snowyside Peak

Inlet of one of the unnamed Alpine Creek Lakes

(Opposite) Waterfall - Alpine Creek

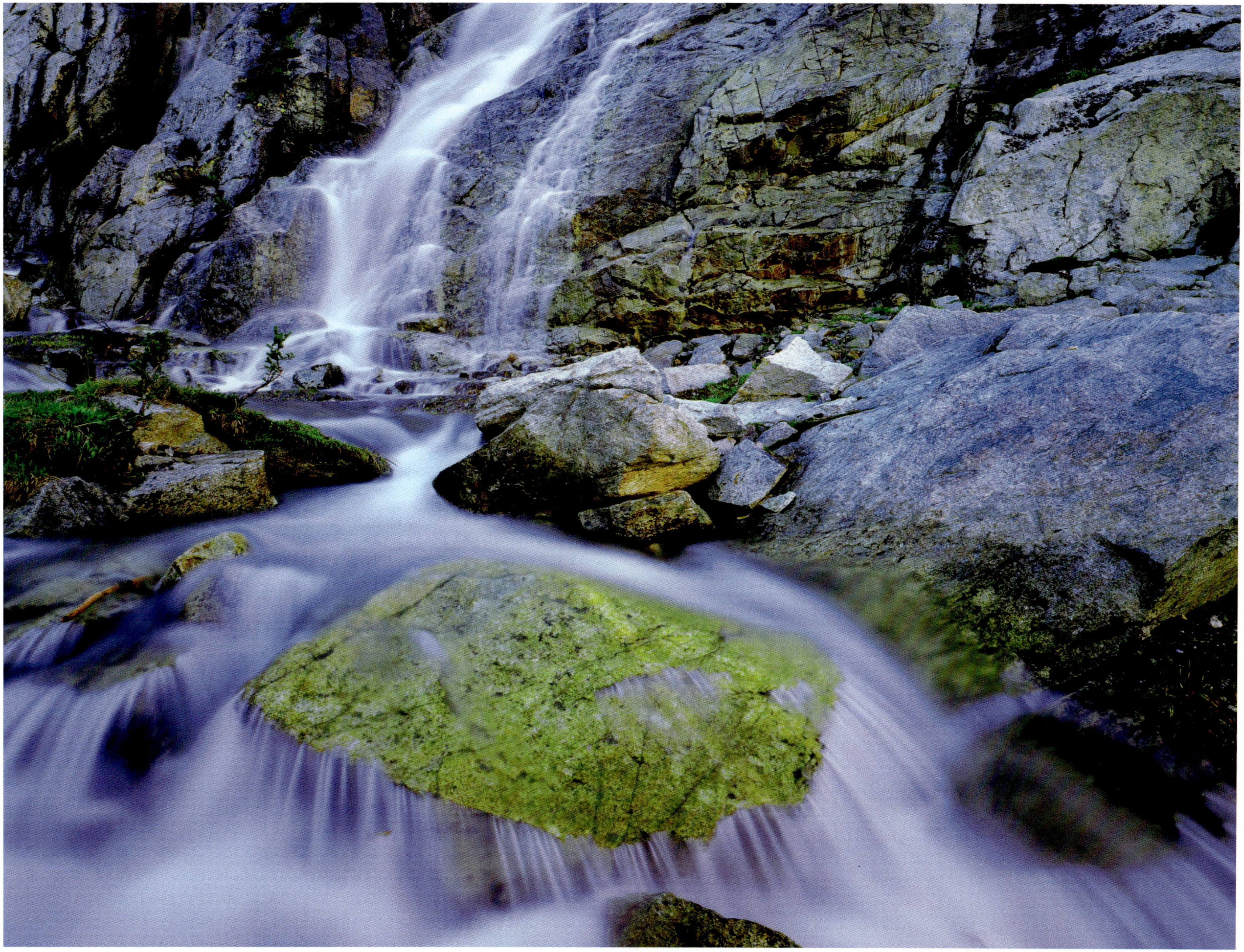

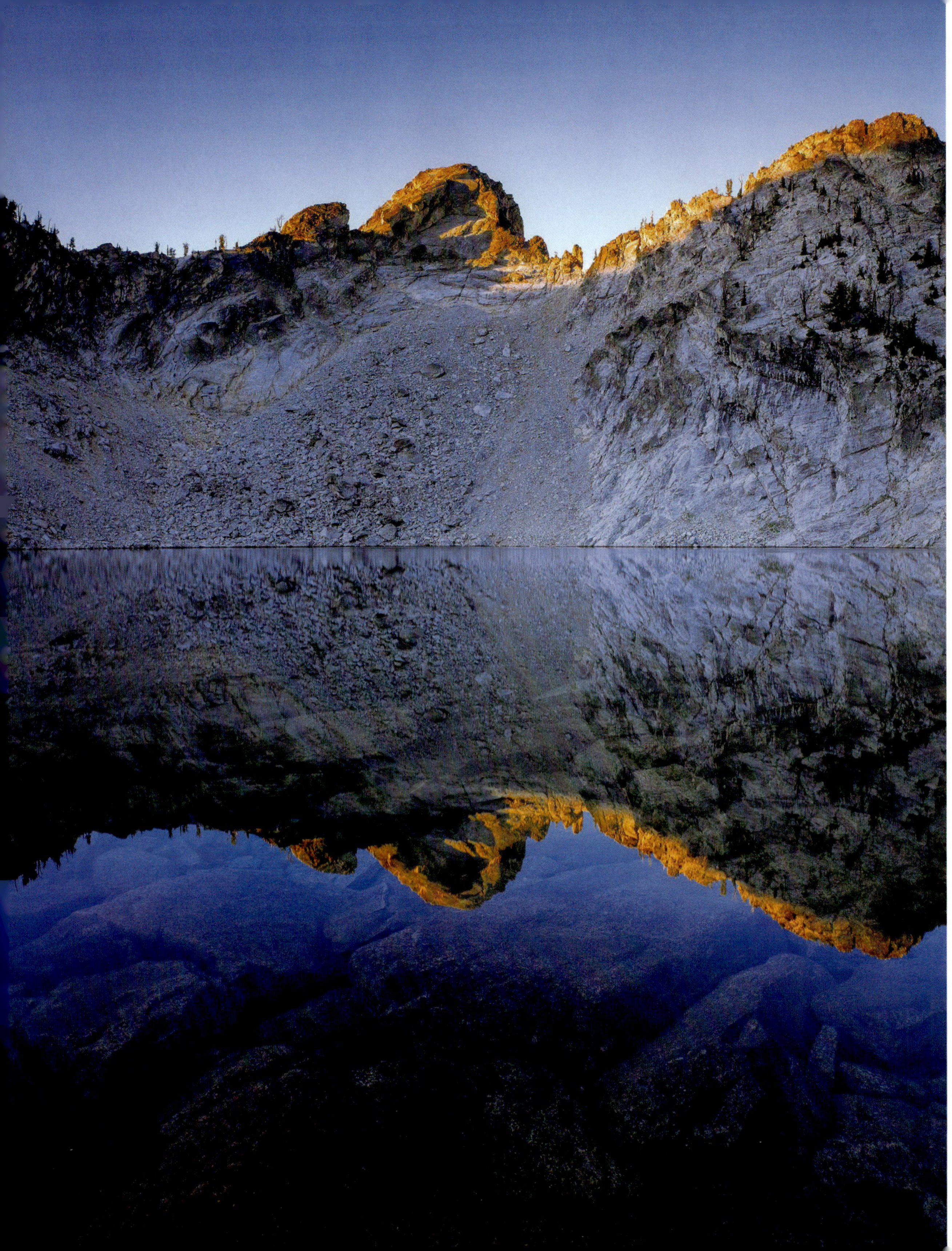

Deep blue reflections in an unnamed lake we call Puddin Slayer
Pines create graphic shapes along one of the Left Fork Lakes

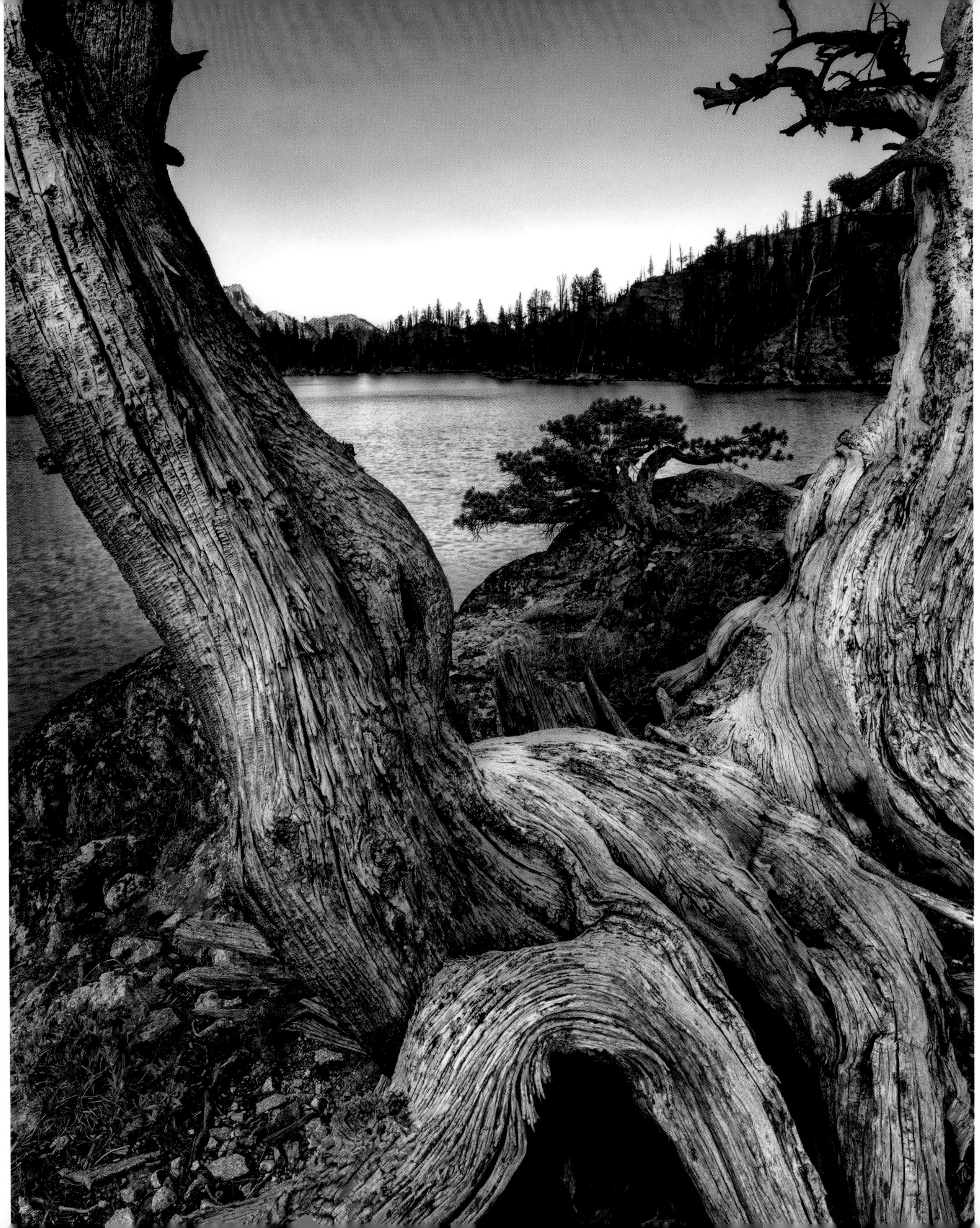

Grand Jean

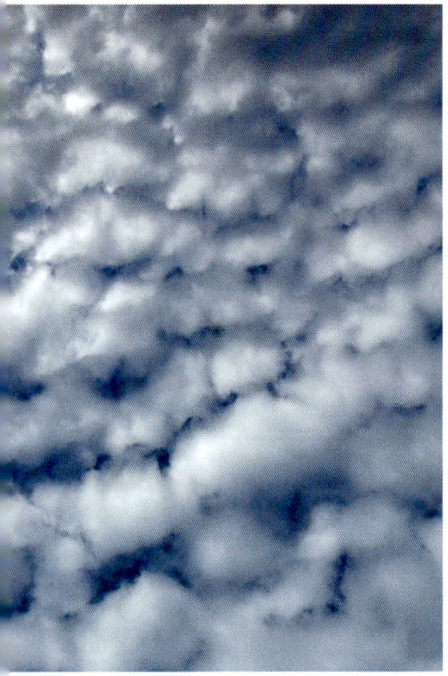

Baron Lakes
Mount Verita
Feather Lakes
Bead Lake

CLIMBING THE TRAIL ALONG THE SOUTH FORK of the Payette without the light, the Sawtooths wouldn't rise; the faces of Mt. Regan and Baron Peak wouldn't hang in evening colors flanked with snow. Without the light, the walk from Grand Jean would be a dry maze of sage, creeping up into pine, the scent of scarlet gillia, sweet drops of nectar squeezed from delicate trumpets onto the tongue. Without the light, Baron Lakes would be painfully frigid water and smooth flat granite, polished softer than marble, cool against the cheek. Without the light, the air instead would fill with the racketed calls of stellers jays, the whoosh of flicker wings, the whirr of hummingbirds and the jackhammer percussion of woodpeckers. Without the light, night time would be a journey though pools of moist and scented air, moss and mushroom, the cow-like stench of elk, the musk of lion, threads of wood smoke and rotting logs, the acrid alarm of ants, the scent of lacewing and dust of moths. Without the light, the sound of feet on the trail would rise from high scraping gravel to the low hollow beat of roots over hidden lakes and underground streams. Without the light, the Sawtooths speak in smell and texture, the sound of rockfall, hooves and bear turning logs.

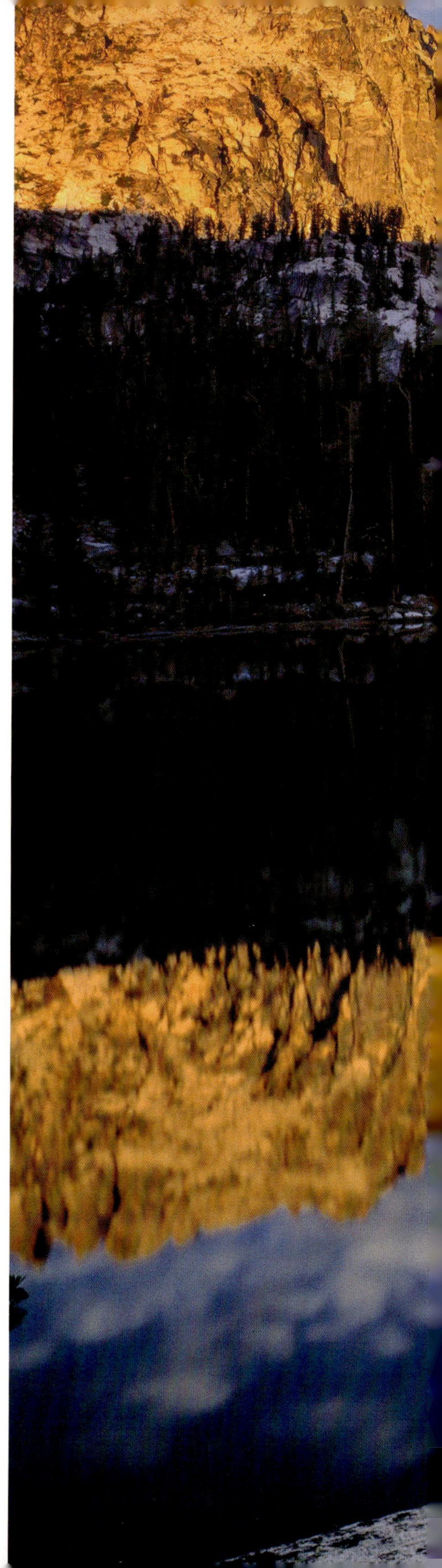

Beautiful cloud formations reflect into Upper Baron Lake

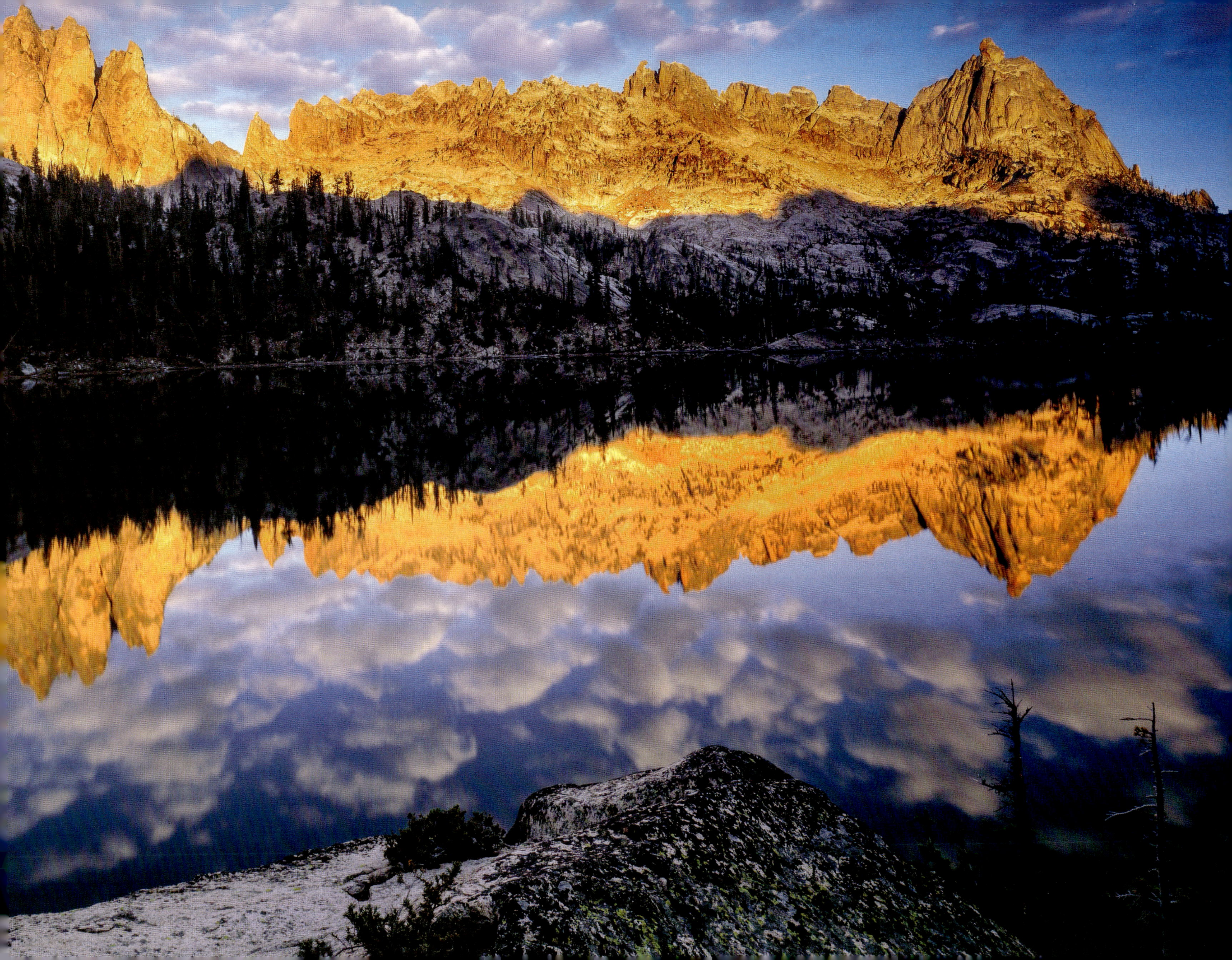

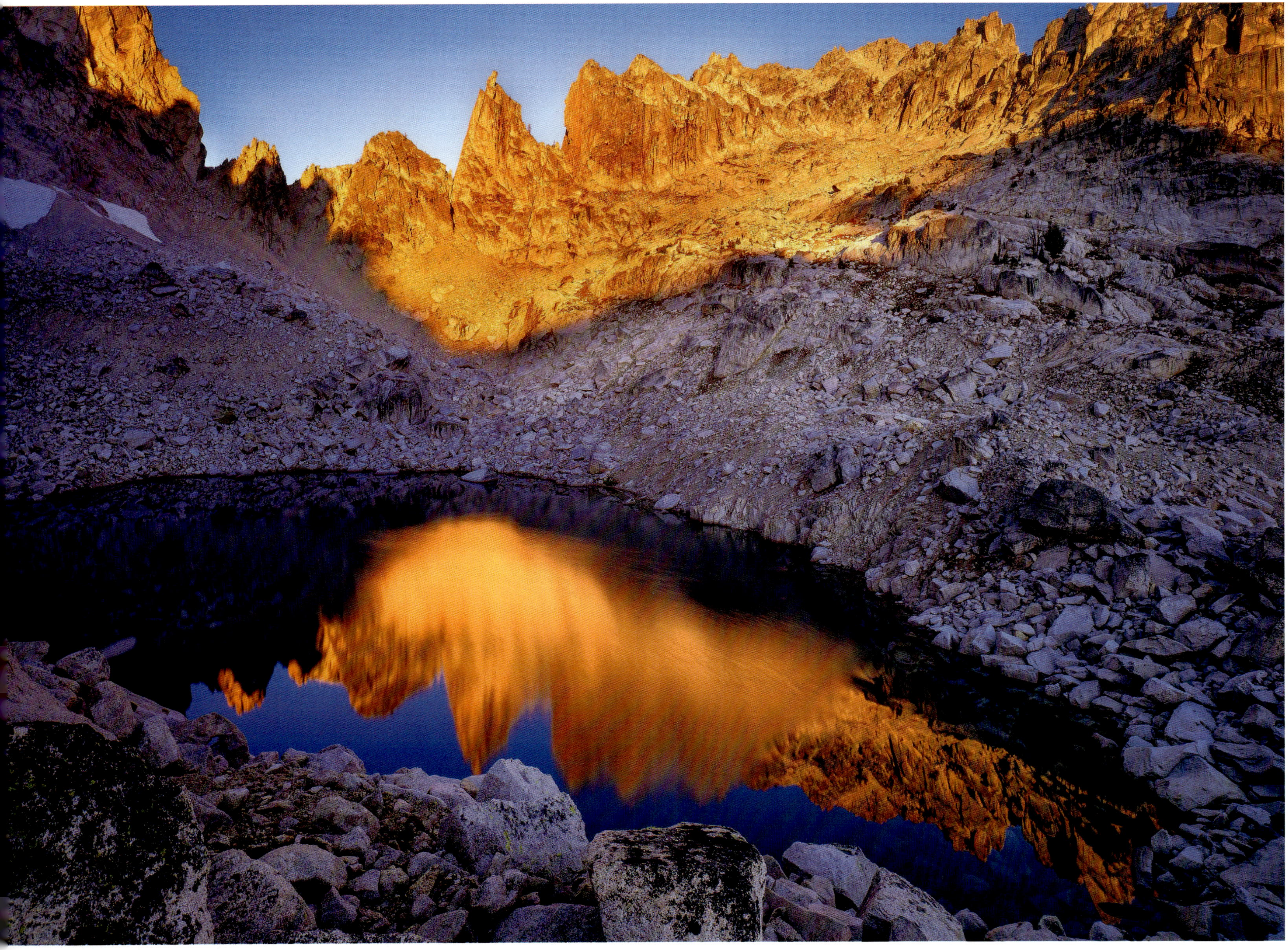

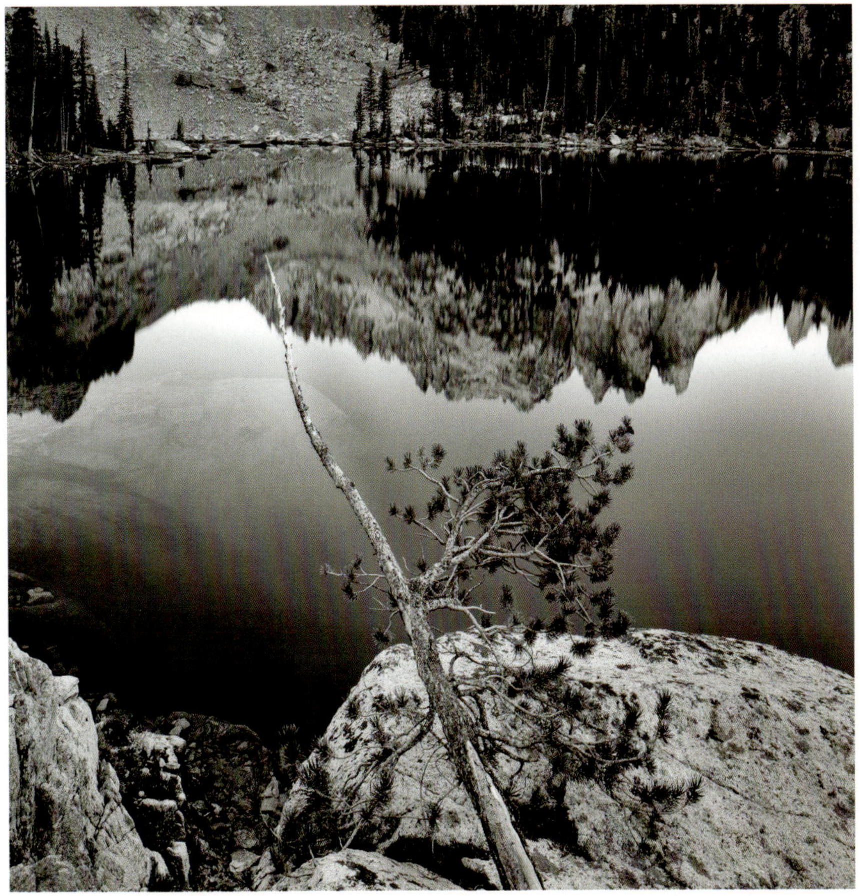

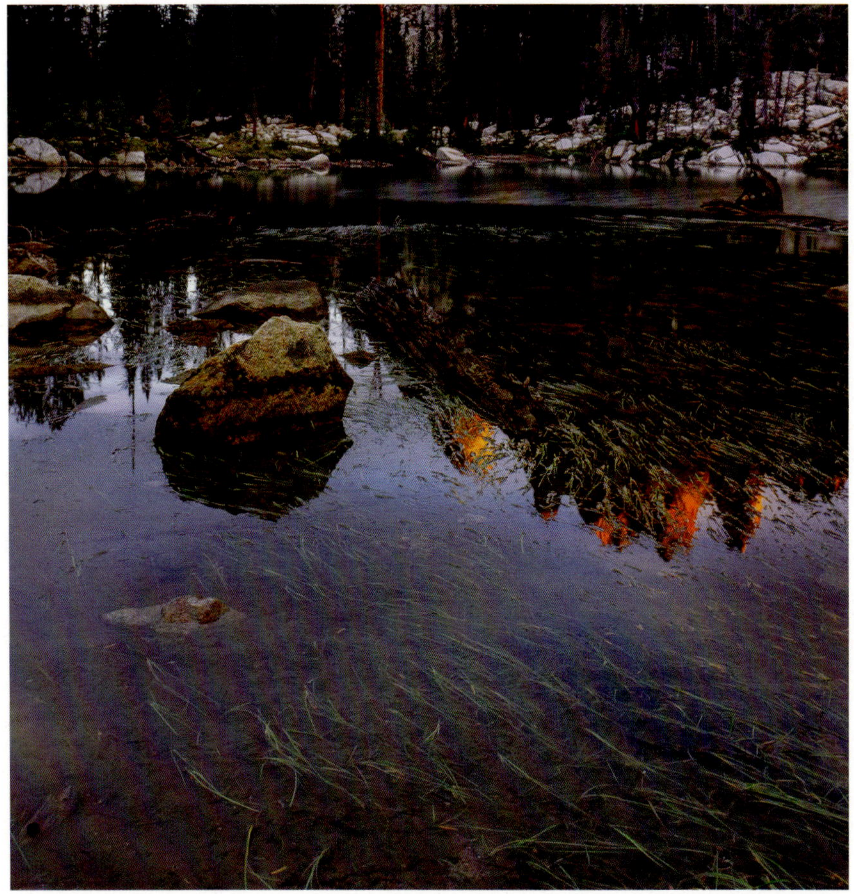

Graphic patterns reflect in Upper Barron Lake

(Opposite) Sharp granite peaks of Monte Verita

Warbonnet Peak reflects into Bead Lake

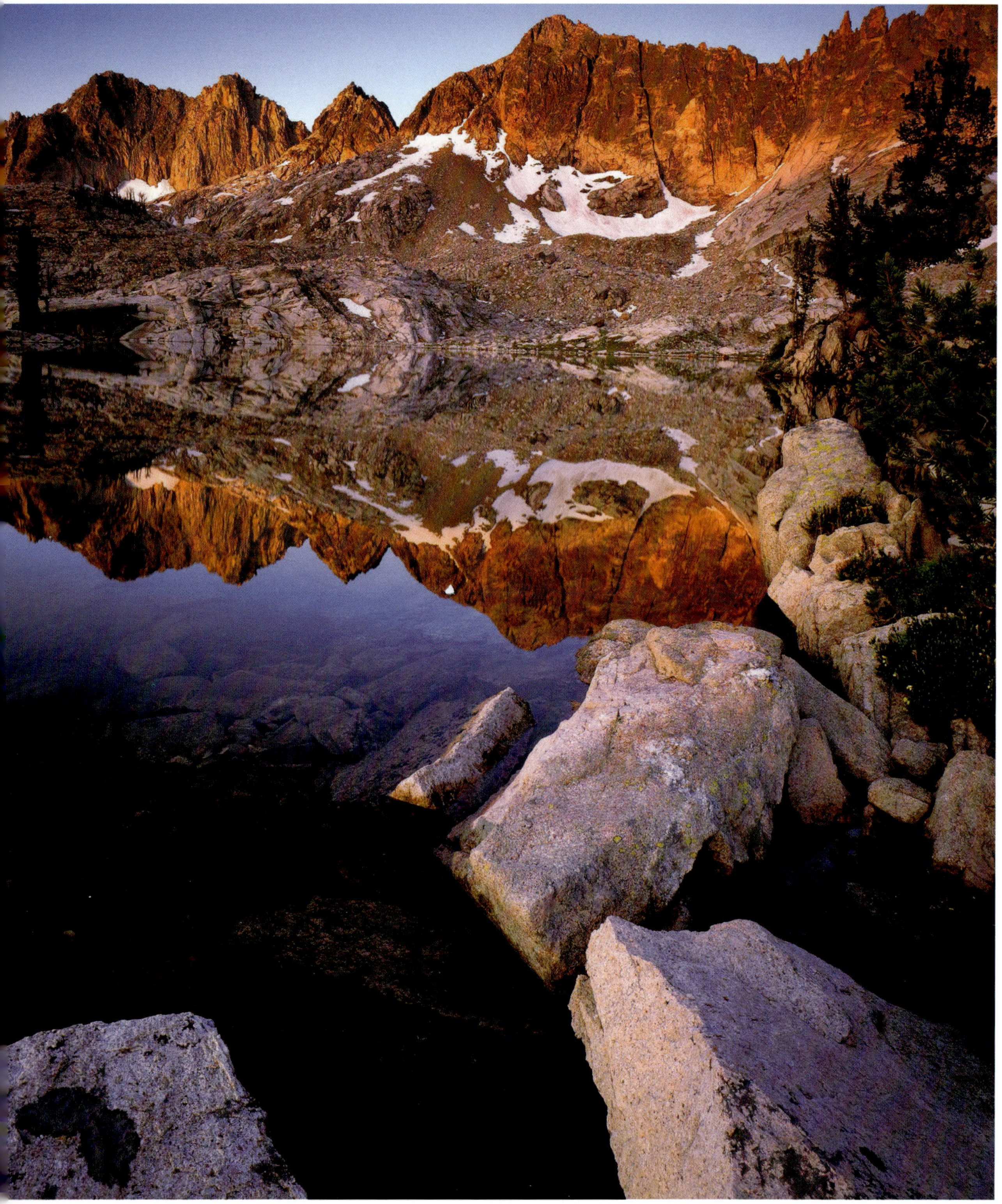

Sunrise on the peaks above Upper Barron Lake

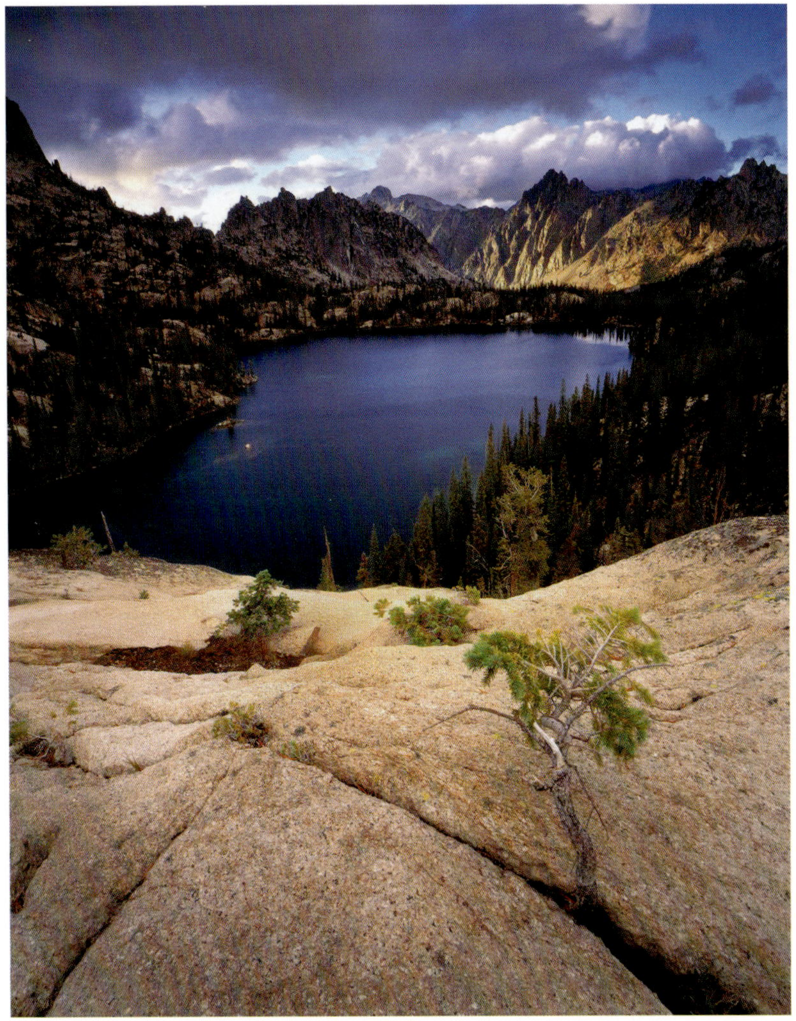

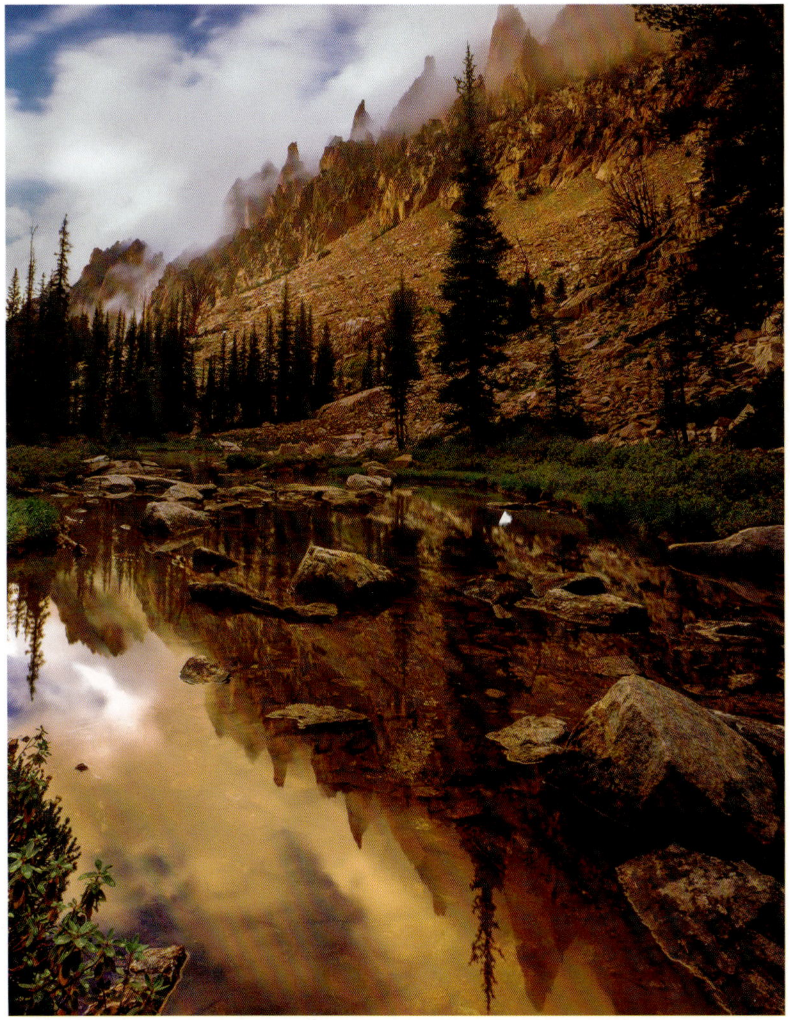

View from Middle Barron Lake

A storm breaks exposing Warbonnet Peak near Feather Lake

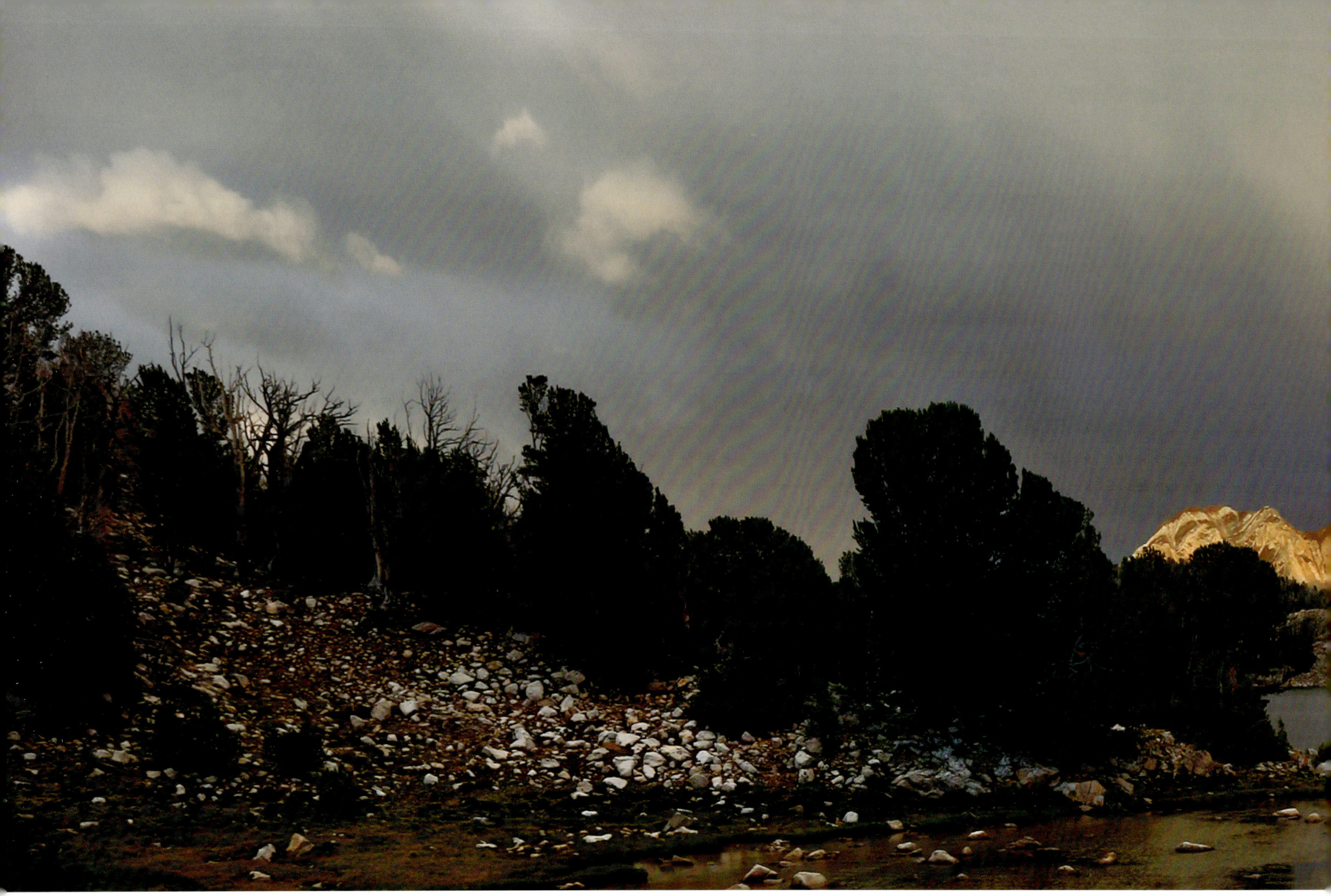

Slate Creek | Railroad Ridge | Big Boulder Chain | Little Boulder Chain | Castle Peak | Fourth of July Creek | Pole Creek-Boulder Mountains

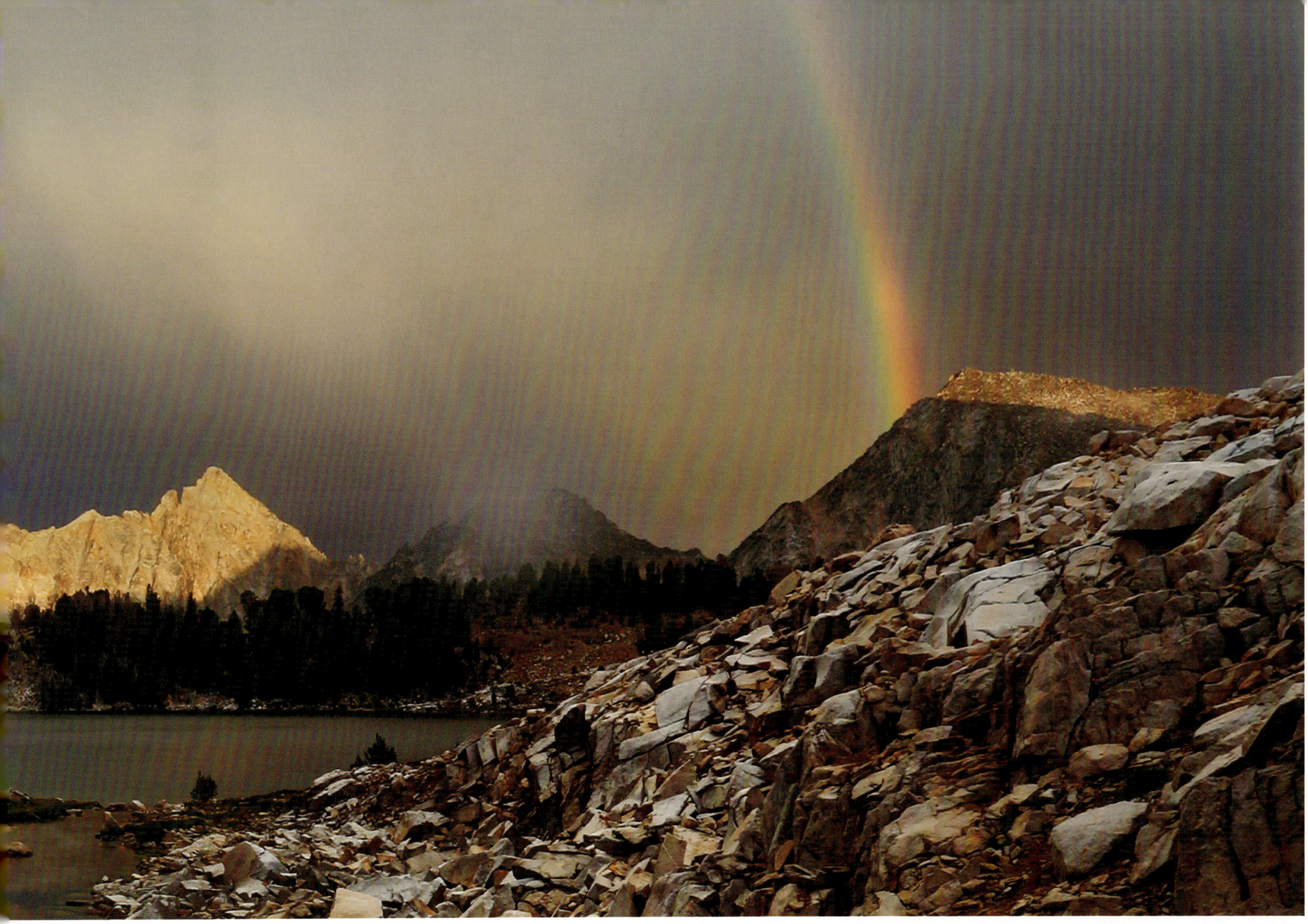

White Cloud Wilderness

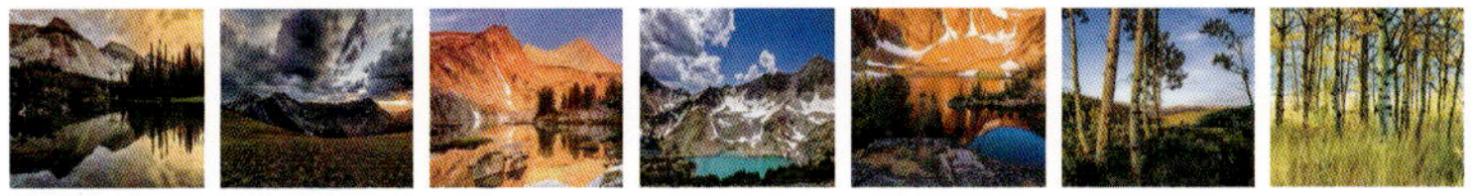

Slate Creek

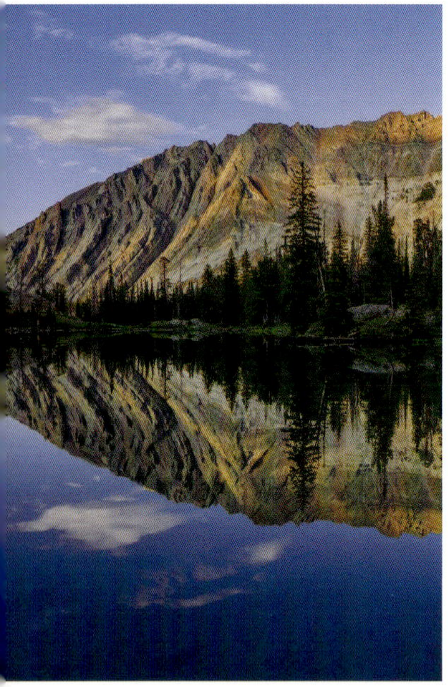

O'Calkins Lake
Big Horn Basin
HooDoo Lake

ONCE, WHERE THE WHITE CLOUDS STAND

a shallow ocean stretched deep, sediment rich with the skeletons of tiny plankton. Ground to powder, they lay, layer on layer, buried deep until the volcanos came, spewing ash and steam to the south and west. Vast miles of tectonic plates melted from below and rose through crust. Red liquid stone formed a granite dome, cooled grey, flecked with iron and lead. And at the edges, the bones of the ocean cooked to metamorphic limestone until the glaciers carved them, slicing soft rock into white peaks and walls, hollowing the sides into cirque basins, round and perfect lakes. The crenelated heights of O'Calkins Peak were dug by a tower of ice, it stands, a pyramid in a line of peaks shiny against the sky. What was once dark lava and ash melted in the Chinese Wall. Heat warped layers and stone fractured until hard spires rose. And now Slate Creek falls wearing a channel through sharp black rock. Lava fingers heat springs and boulder grinds against boulder, wearing smooth, washing the dust to the sea, shaping stone, emptying valleys dug by glaciers. High up, water gathers, filling lake after lake with melted snow.

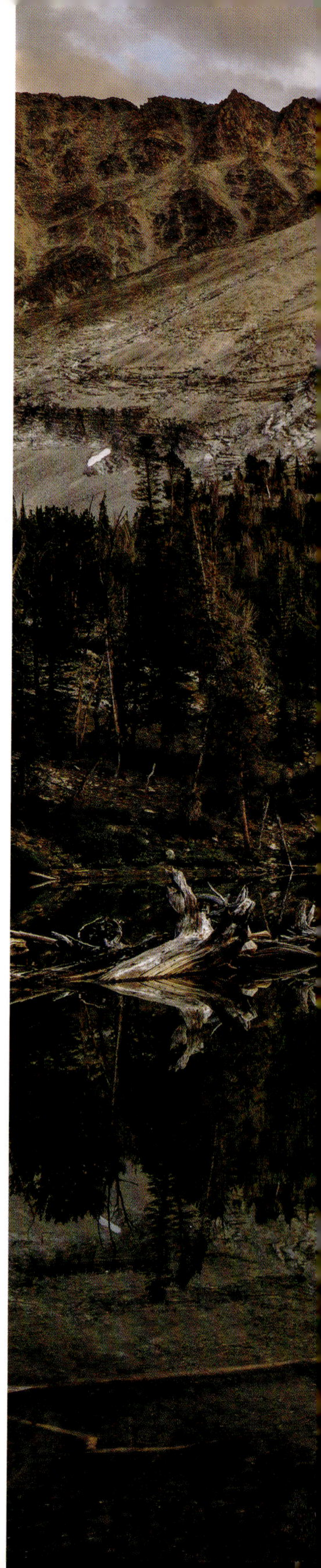

(Detail) The Chinese Wall - O'Calkins Lake
O'Calkins Peak - 11,487 Feet

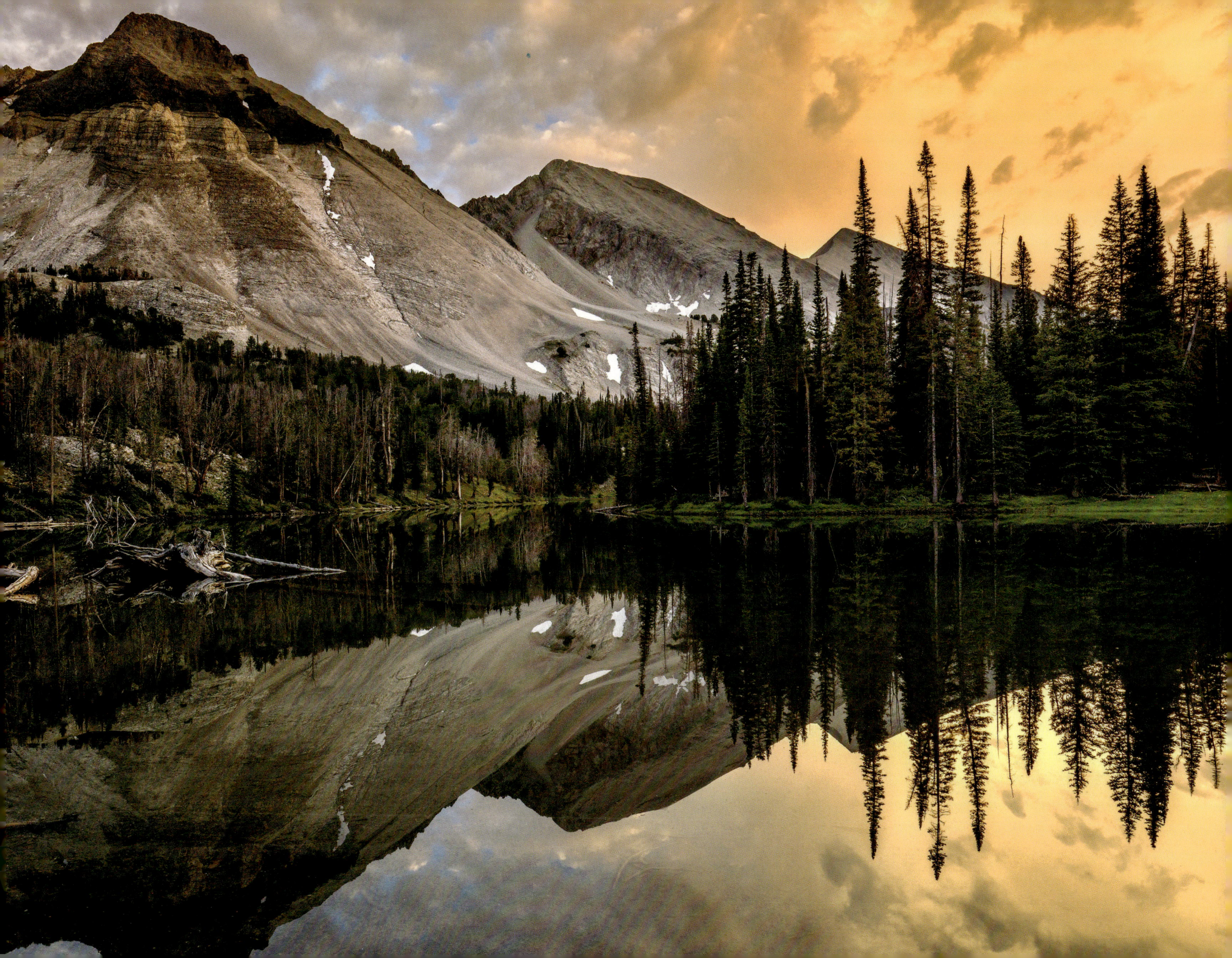

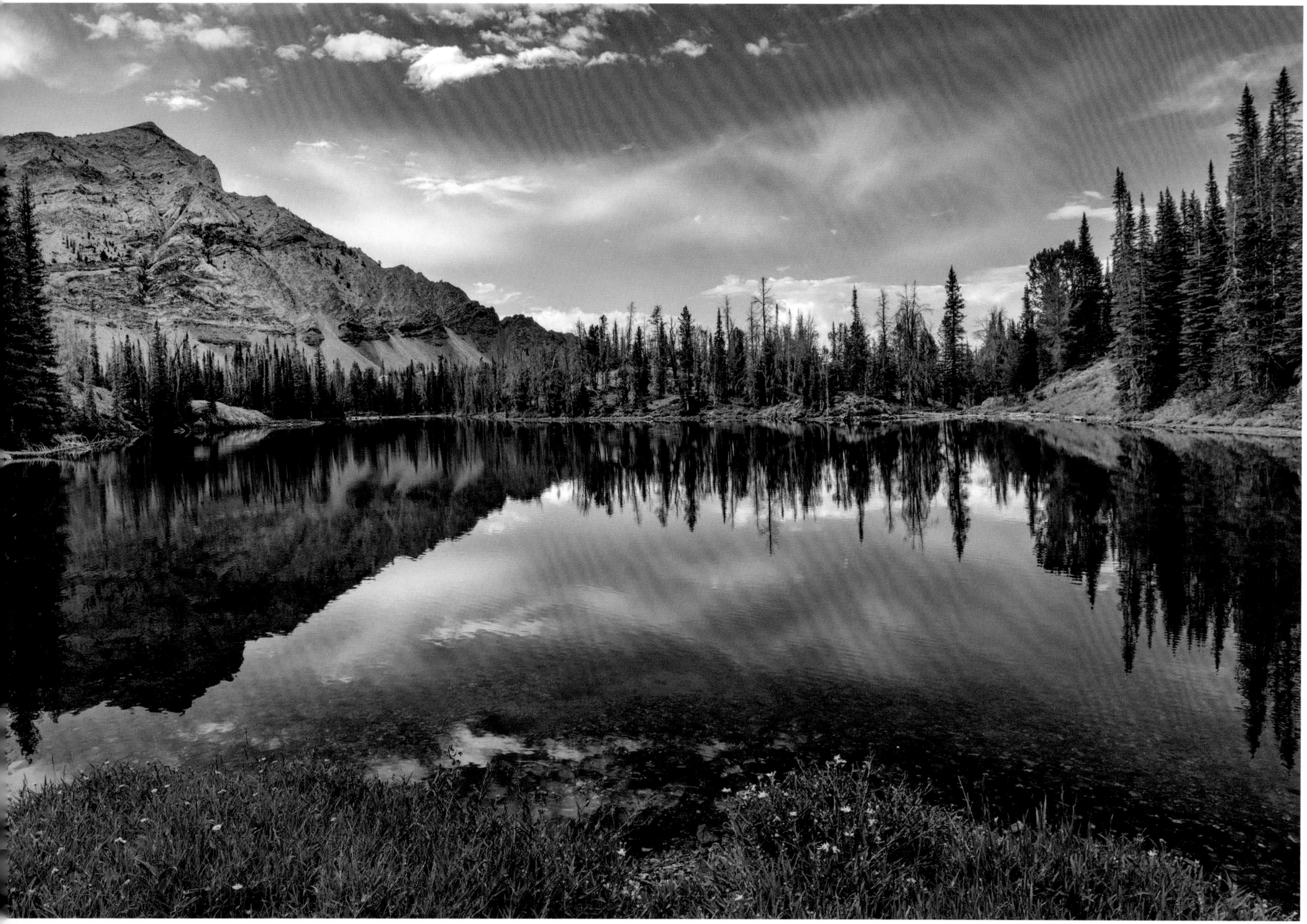

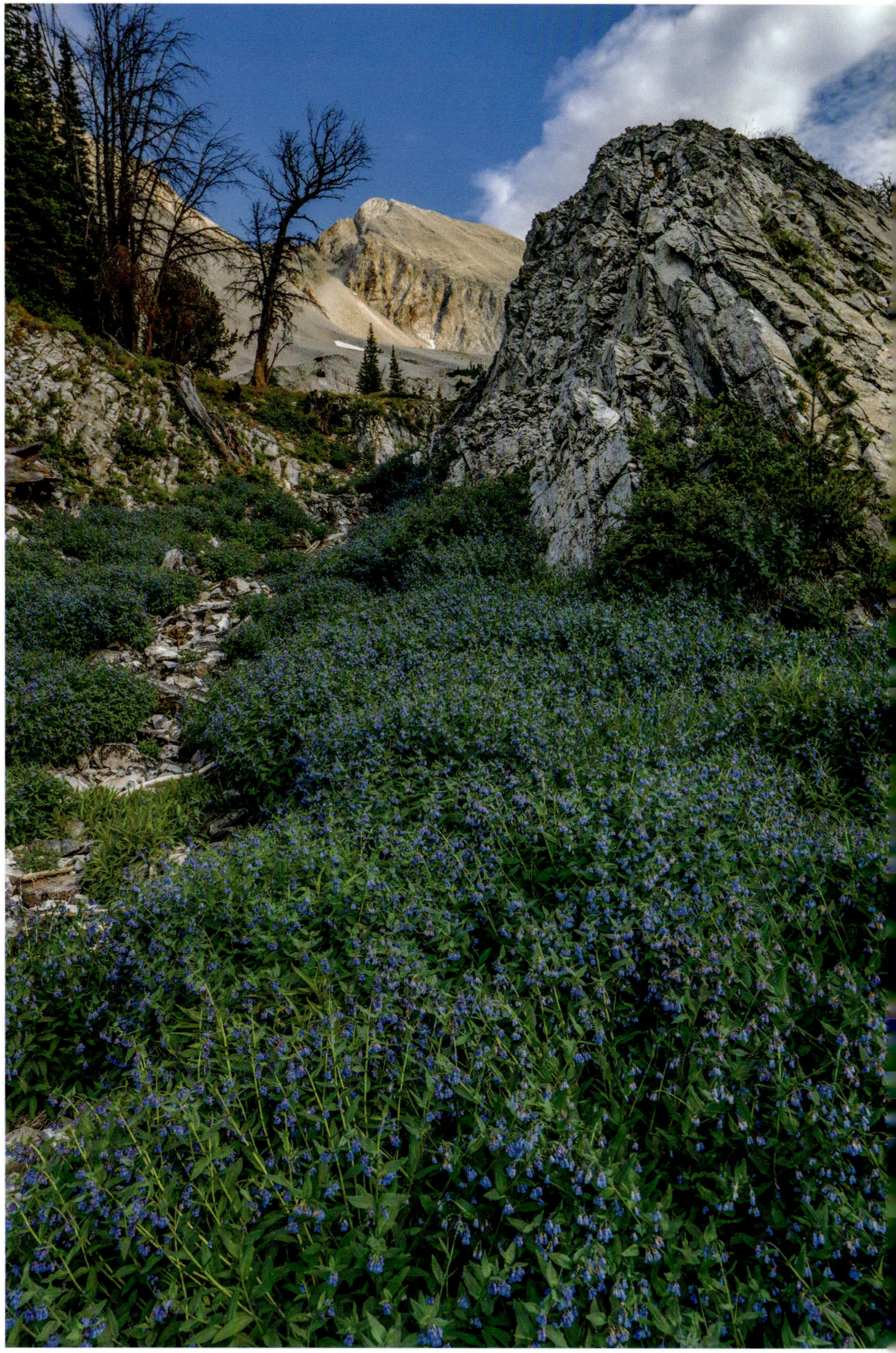

O'Calkins Lake - 9000 feet in the northern edge of the White Clouds Wilderness

Blue bells bloom in the aptly named Sheep Basin

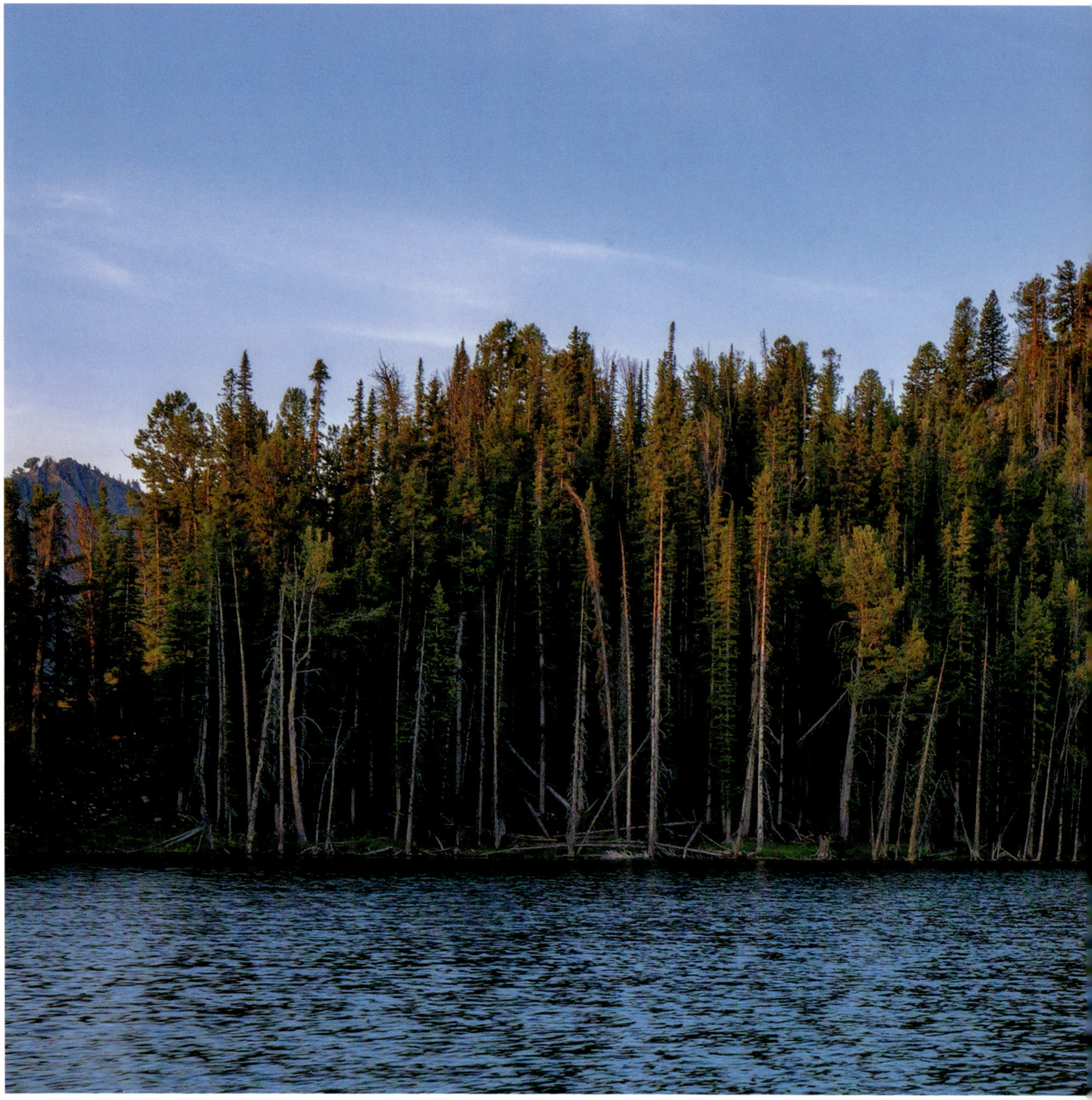

Logepole pine blanket the shore of Hoodoo Lake

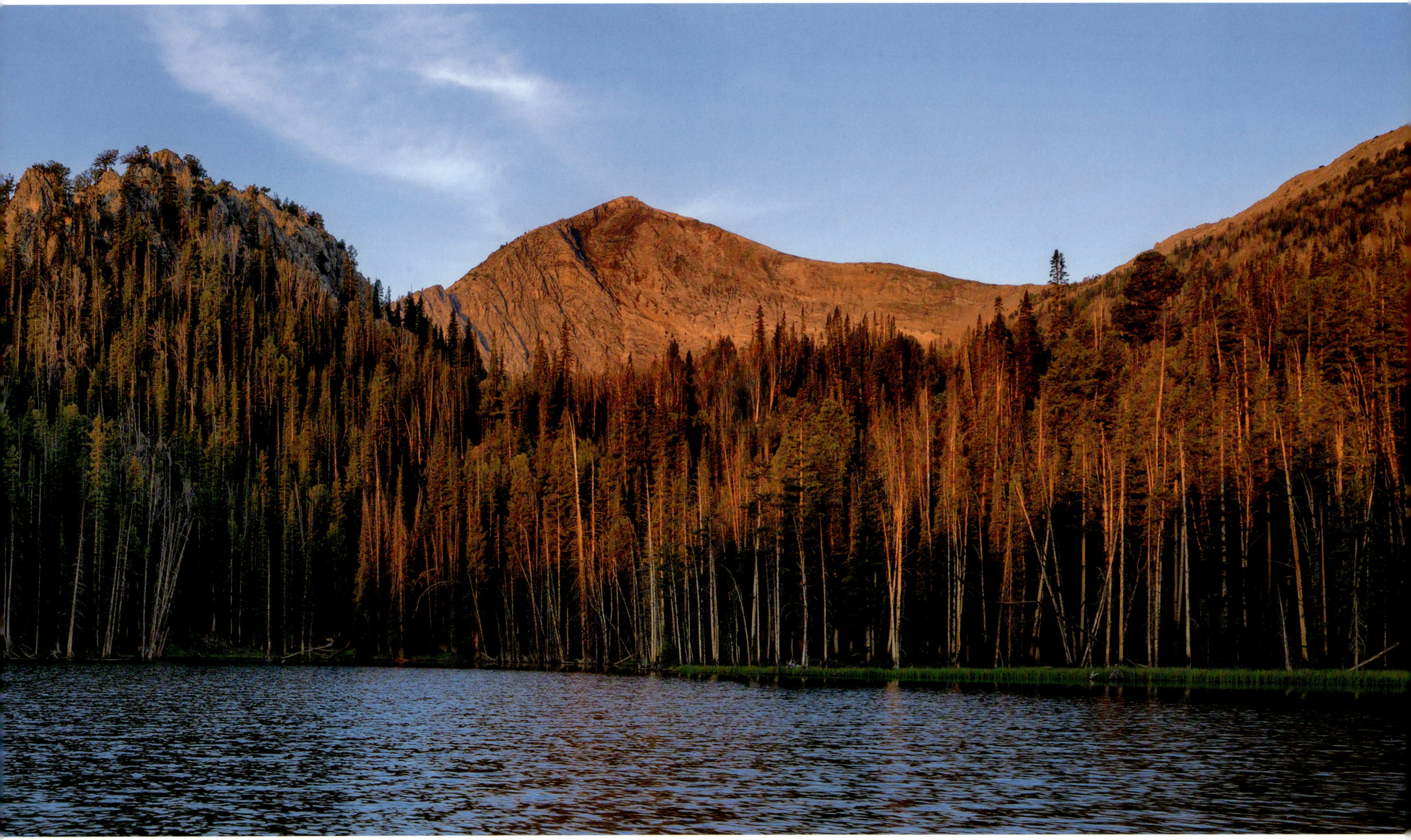

Railroad Ridge

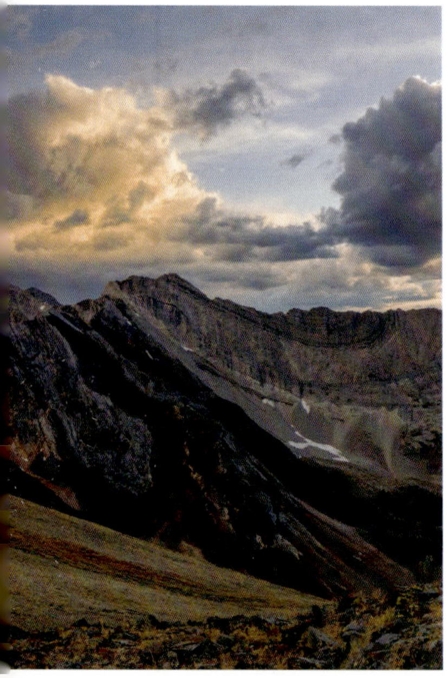

Railroad Ridge
Tin Cup Lake
Gunsite Lake
Quartzite Lake

FROM THE DRY CANYONS OF THE SALMON RIVER FAR BELOW,

warm air rises and a golden eagle circles black over the rounded back of Railroad Ridge. Jeep tracks cut lines that fade into the clouds. White peaks rise, stark beside the dark stone of the ramparts above the Gunsight. Water is a mirage: streaks of snow on crystalline limestone in the shadows. A raven calls. Sun falls heavy and warm. Mice curl in burrows. Tiny tufts of plants bloom in a multicolored proliferation, a forest or tundra only inches high. There, yellow stonecrop, white vetch, tiny onions and succulents, mounds of pink or white phlox, tiny purple lupine and spined sage grow. Deer browse, with antelope. Soft plants armor themselves with points and pungent oils. Their lacy roots cling, dug deep in fine soil, hidden beneath a layer of flat brown rocks. Wind sweeps up from the west. What is not anchored here, blows into the sky.

(Detail) Railroad Ridge, at 10,000 feet
Sunset from Railroad ridge, the The Chinese Wall

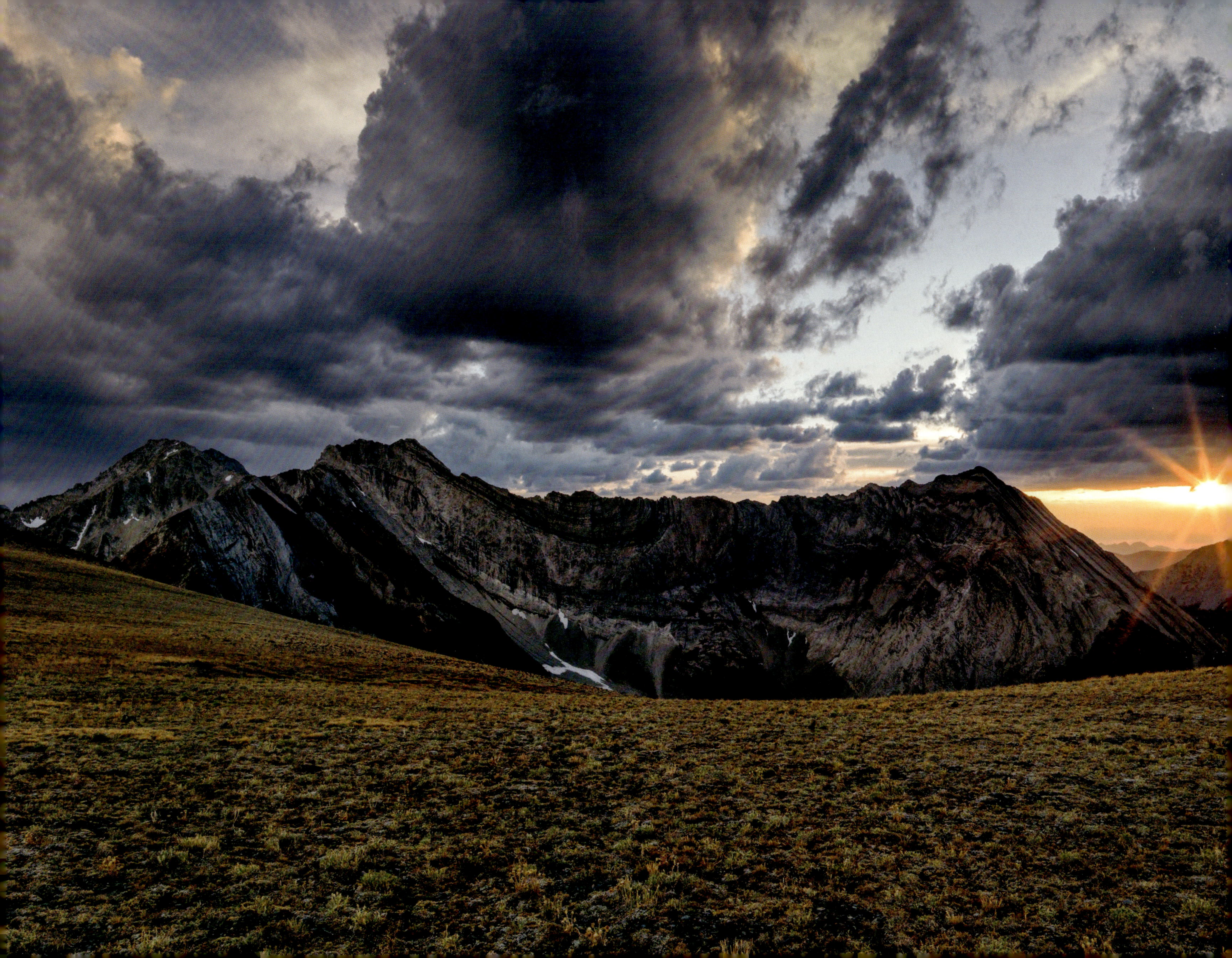

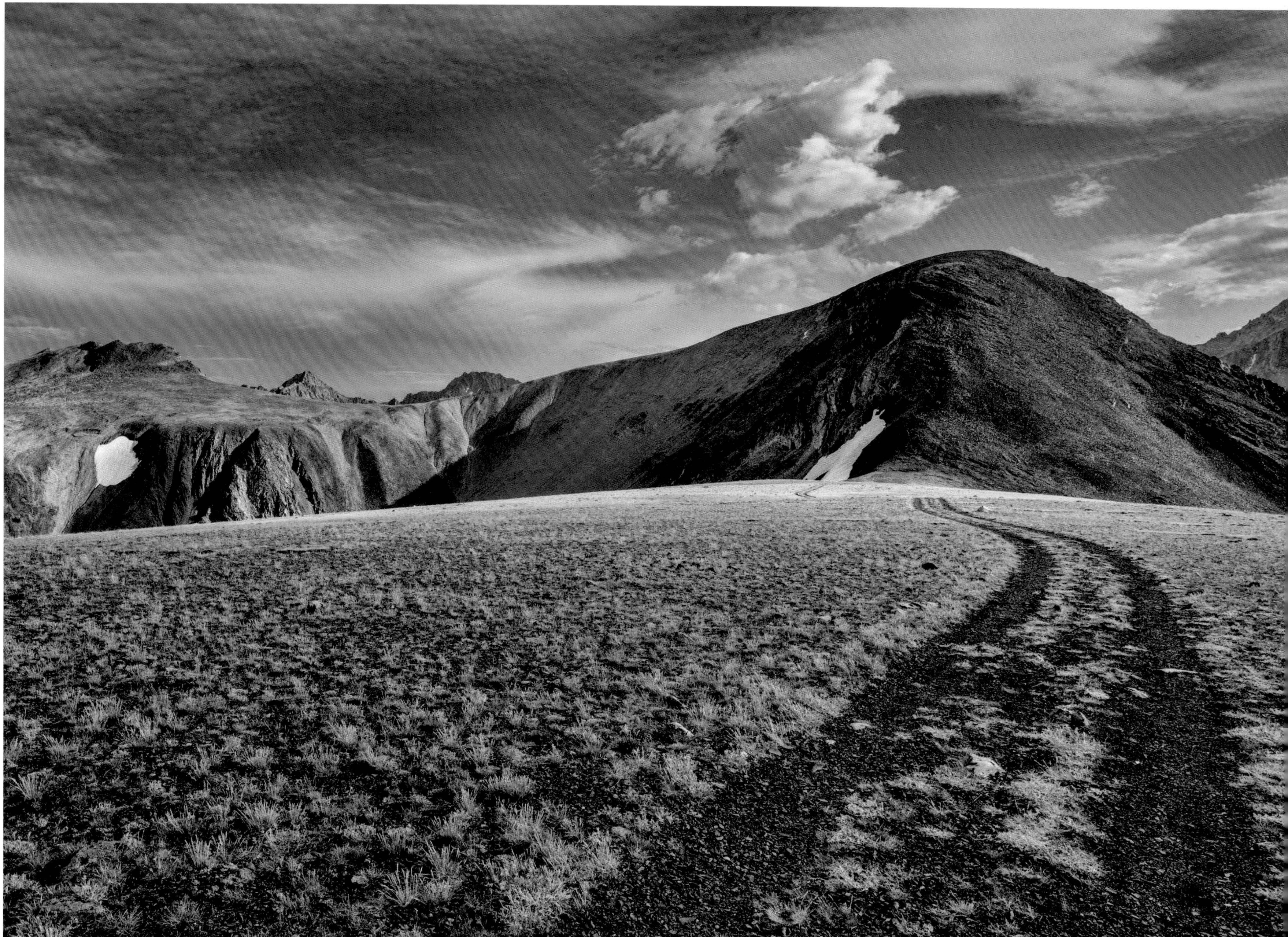

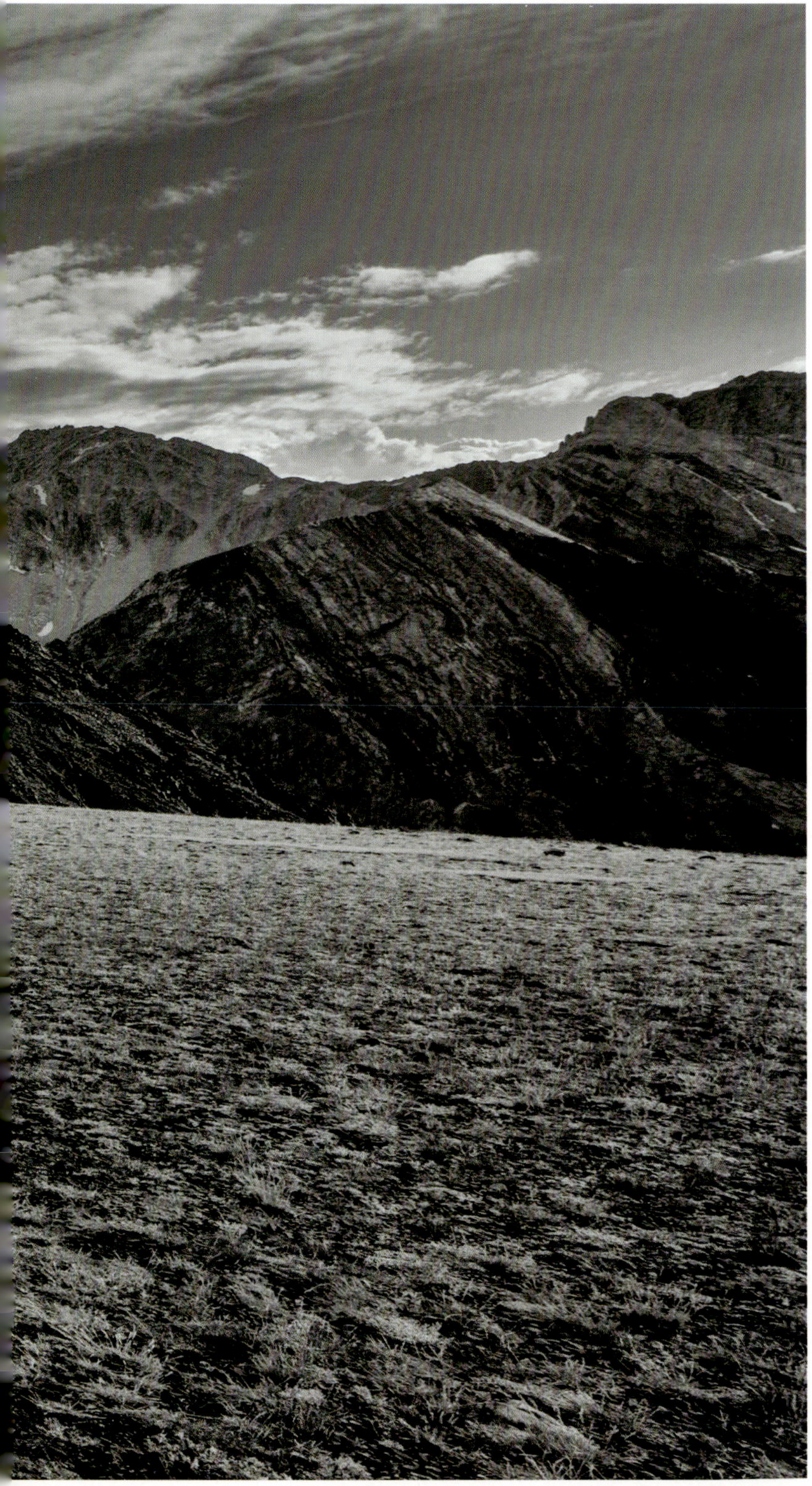

The highest road in the White Clouds at 10,000 feet - Railroad Ridge

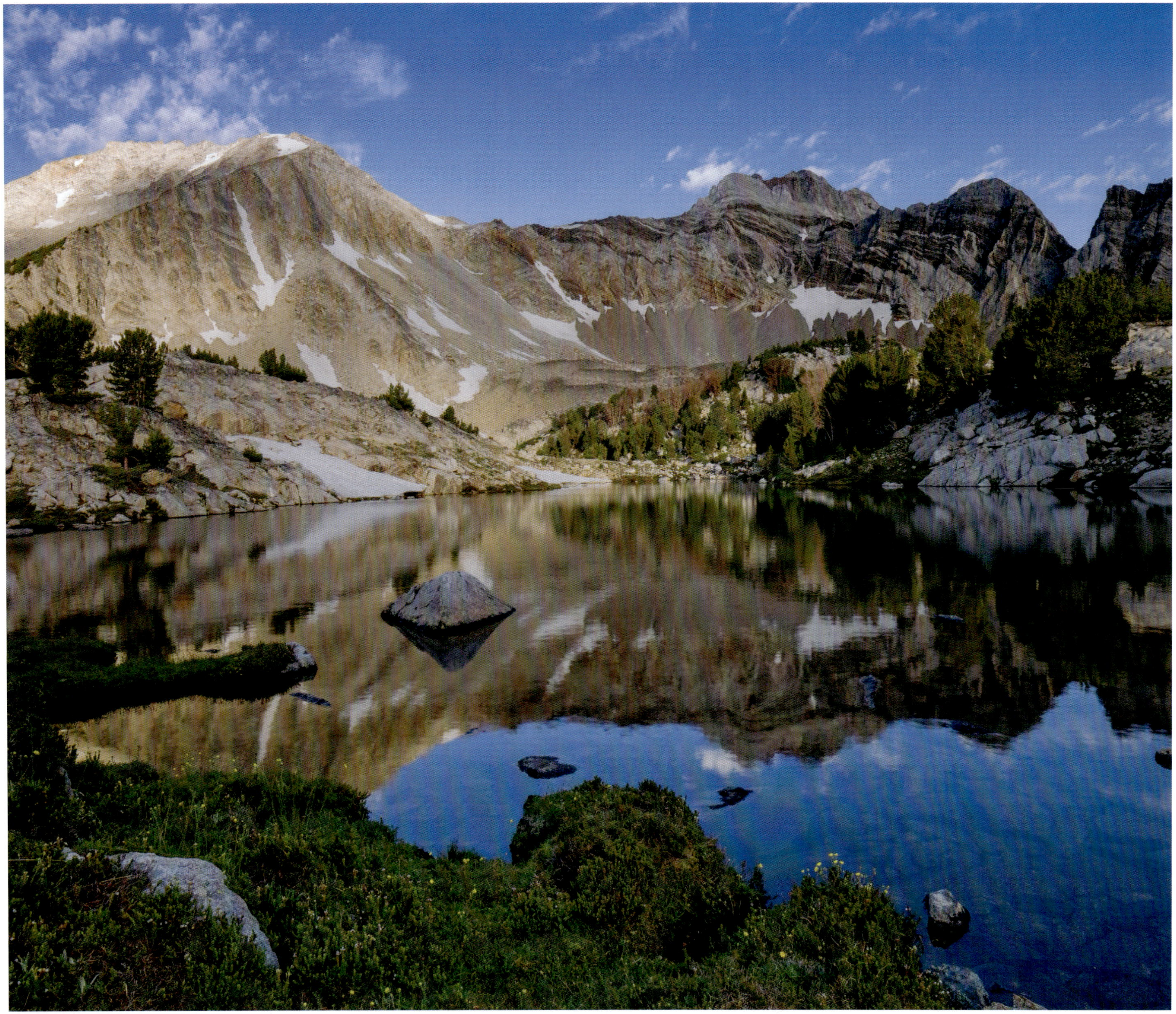

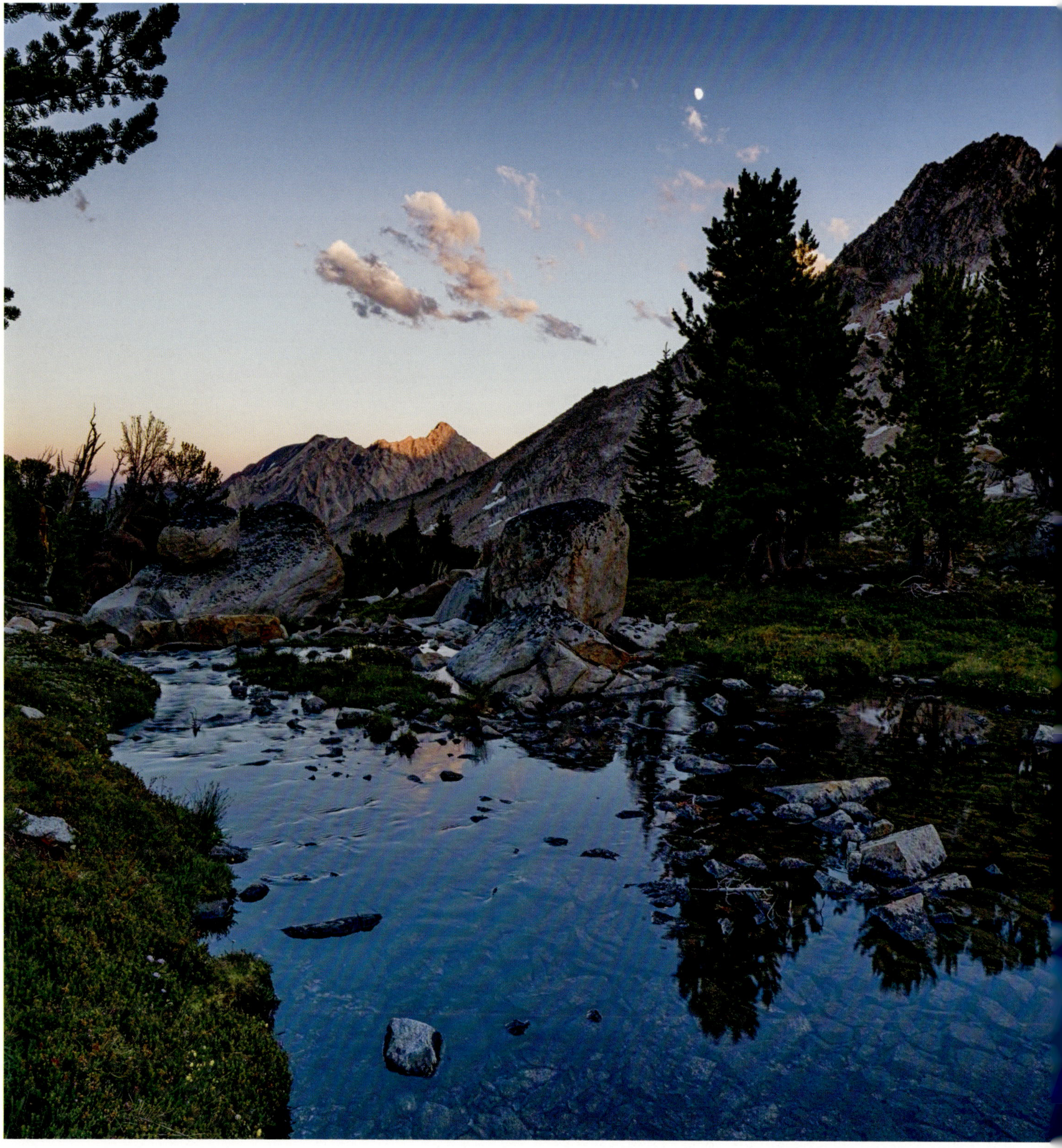

The Chinese Wall and Tin Cup Lake
Evening falls at the outlet of Quartzite Lake

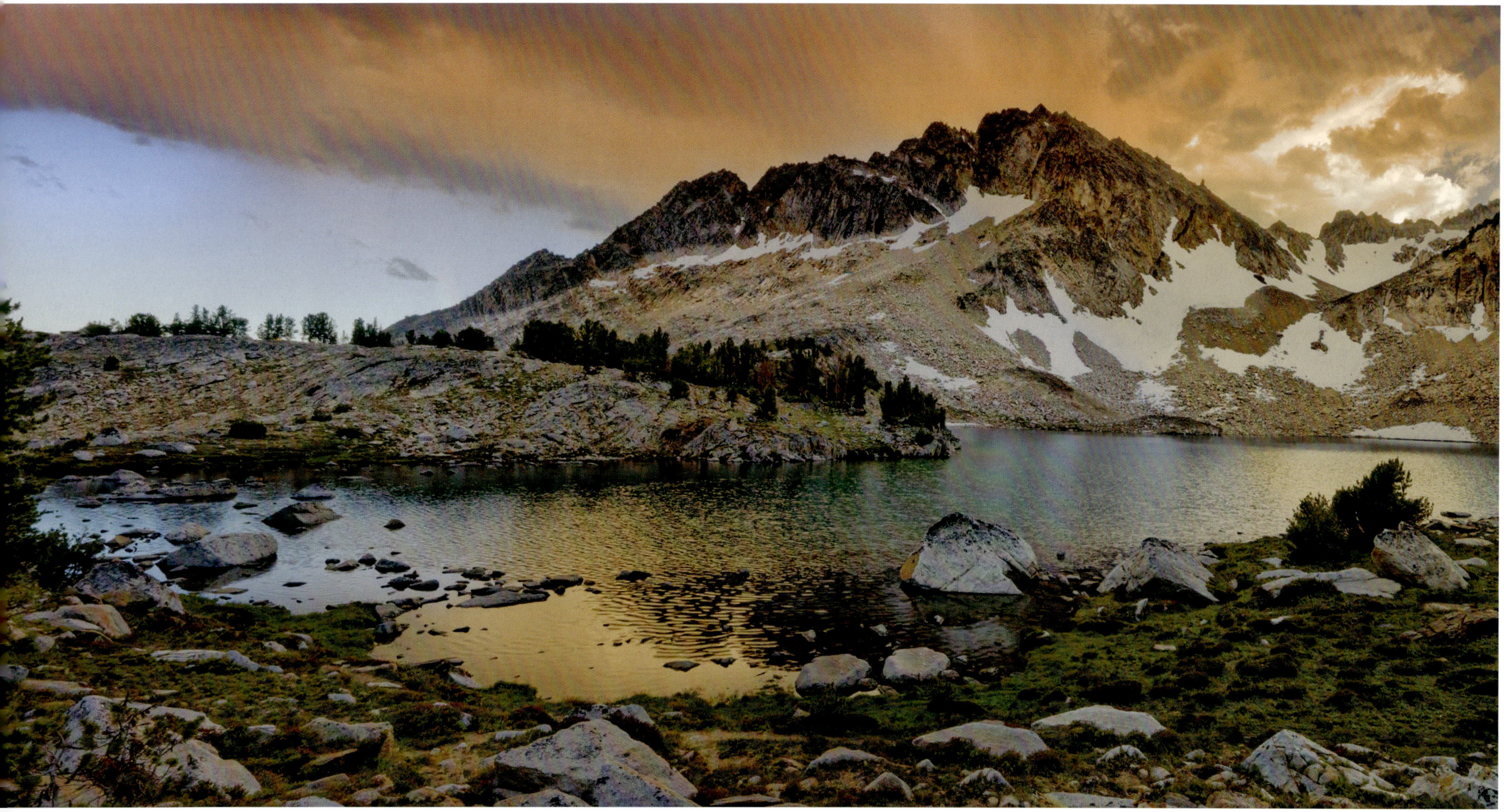

Storm Clouds over Quartzite Lake

(Opposite) White Cloud Peaks reflect into a small tarn near Gunsite Lake

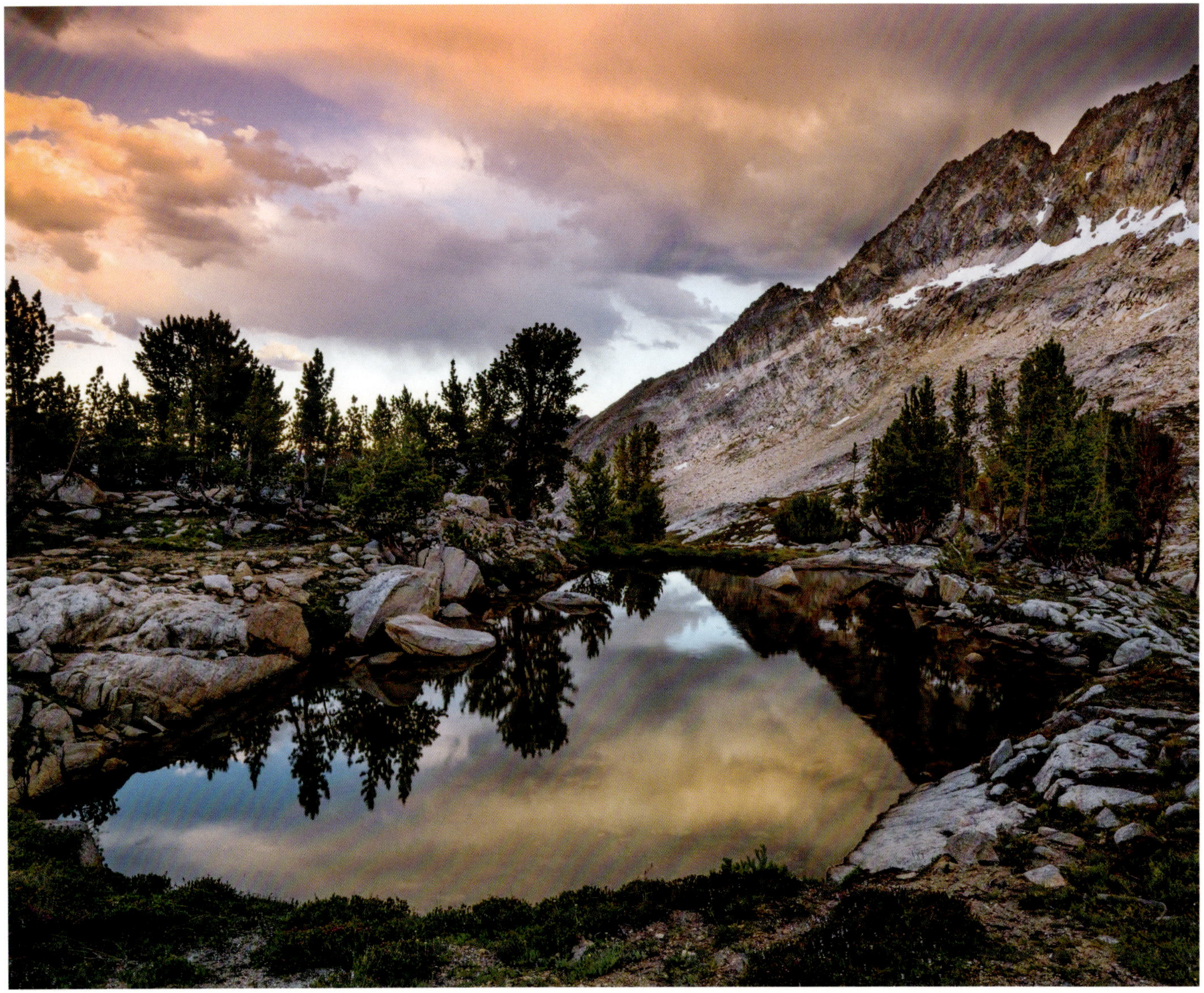

Big Boulder

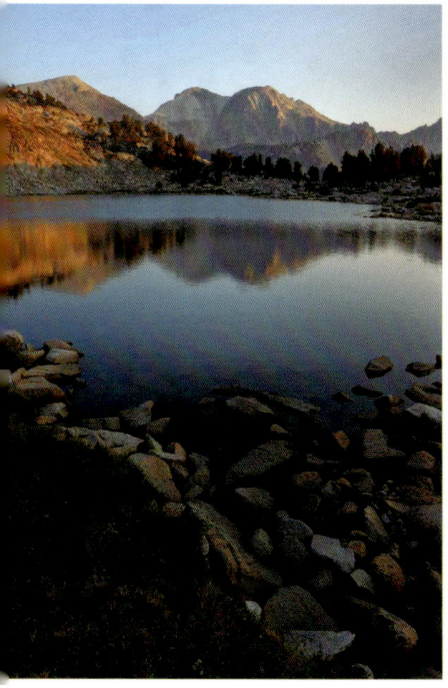

YOU CAN FOLLOW THE CREEK UP,

scramble boulder ladders until the water runs out, a green tread extinguished in a pool of glass or a stretch of pink tinged snow. There Cove Lake opens and the air thins, hold your breath and listen where goats leave tufts of fur, rounded prints in bits of dirt, black clots of dung. Swaths of meadow hold the imprint of their bodies, grass clipped by yellowed teeth. Their dark eyes hang somewhere in the rock above, steady, great beards tangled, horns polished curves of ribbed obsidian. Their stomachs moan, hooves shift, great shoulders heave as they silently climb. Be humble on this rock, the path to the sky is made of air.

Island Lake
Walker Lake
Cove Lake
Sapphire Lake
Cirque Lake
Snow Lake
Slide Lake

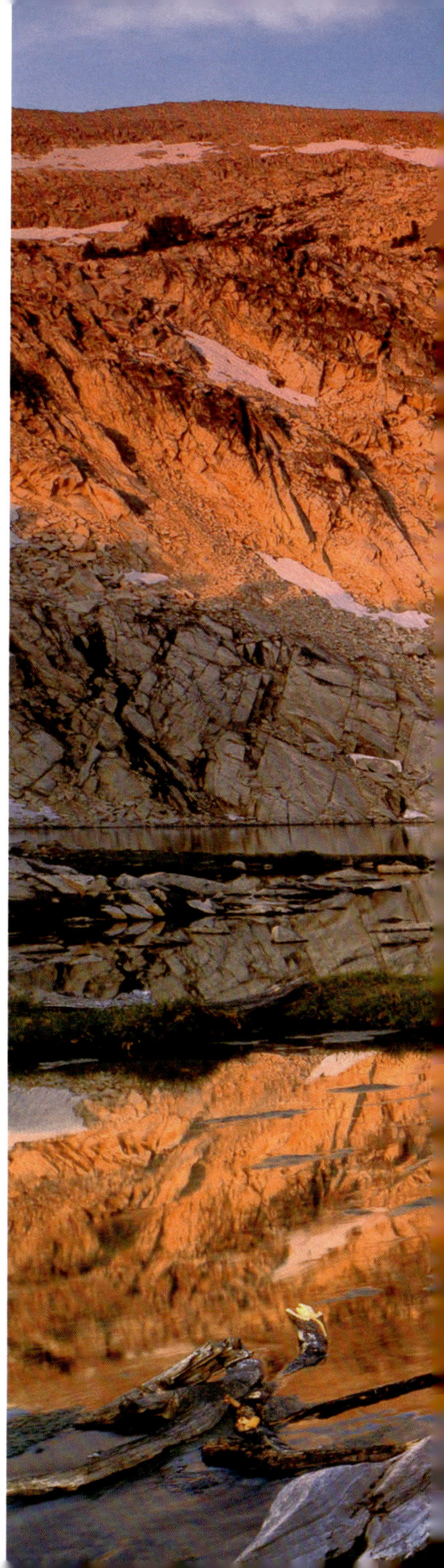

(Detail) Boulder Lake, sits at the top of Big Boulder Lakes
Sapphire Lake, and D.O. Lee Peak

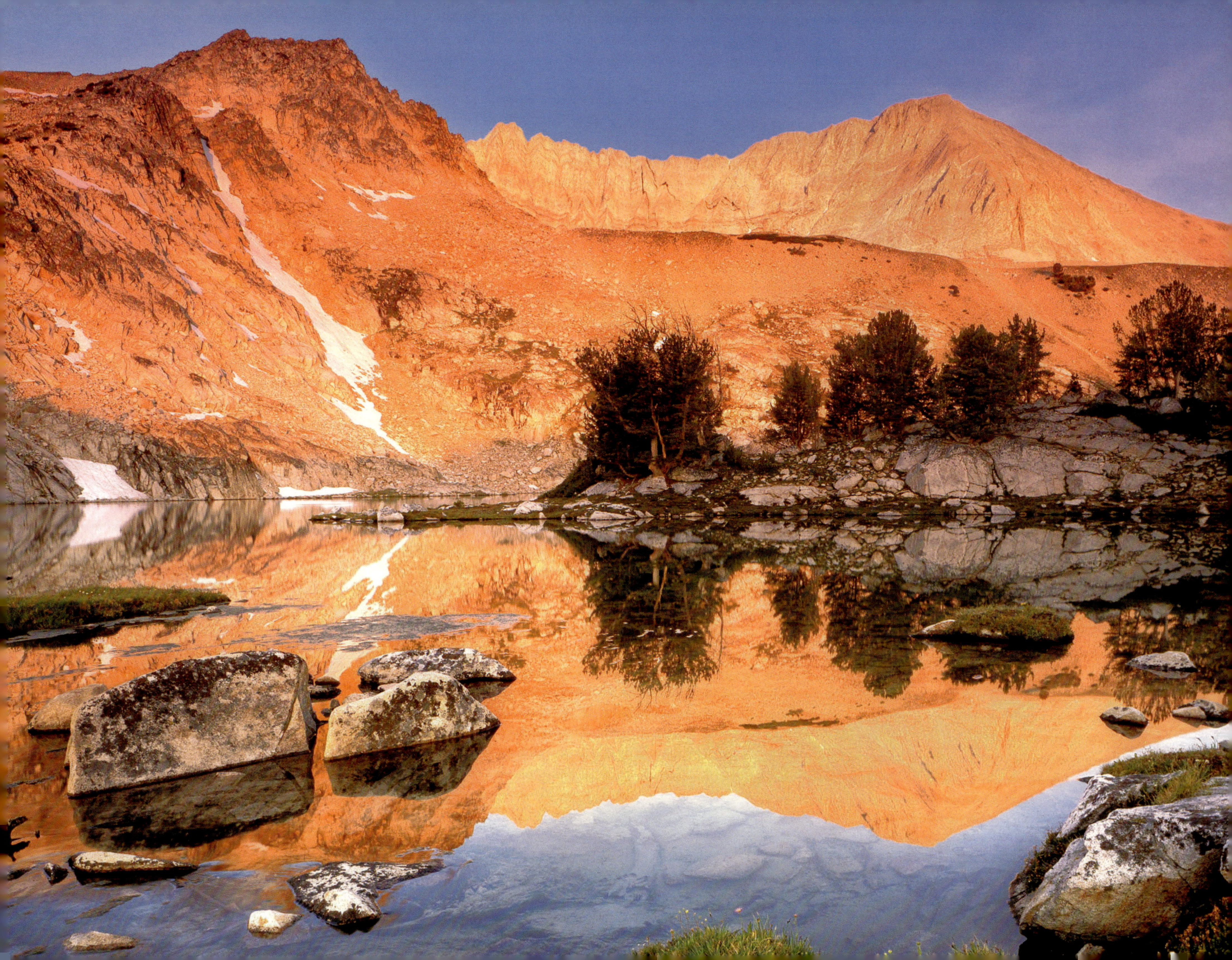

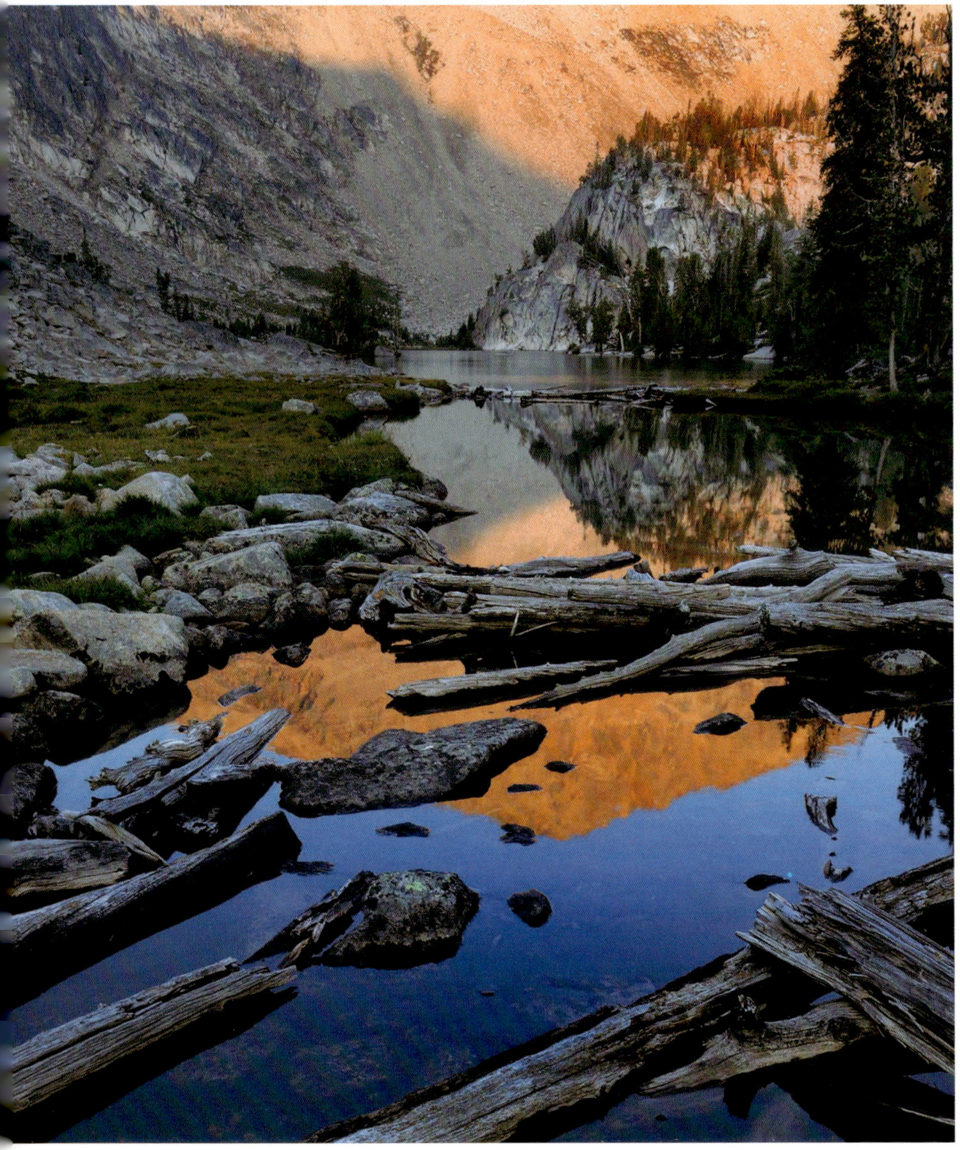

Perfectly still water at the outlet of Island Lake

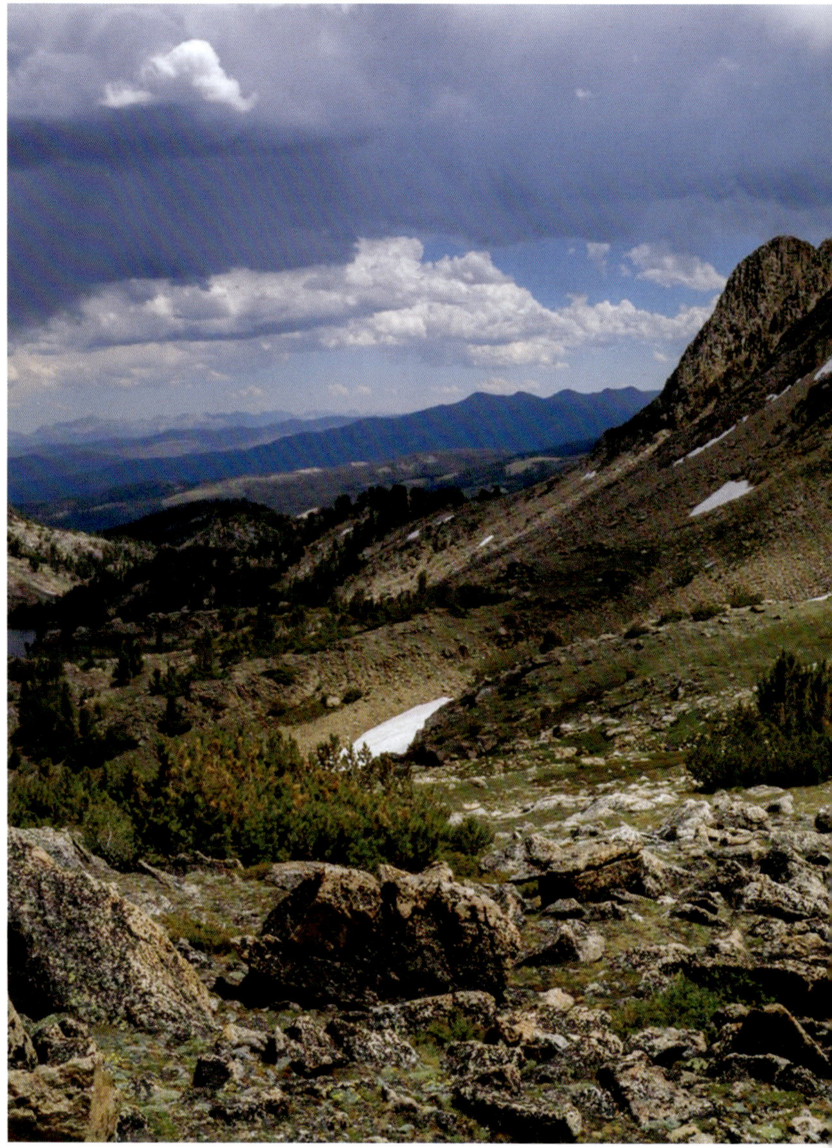

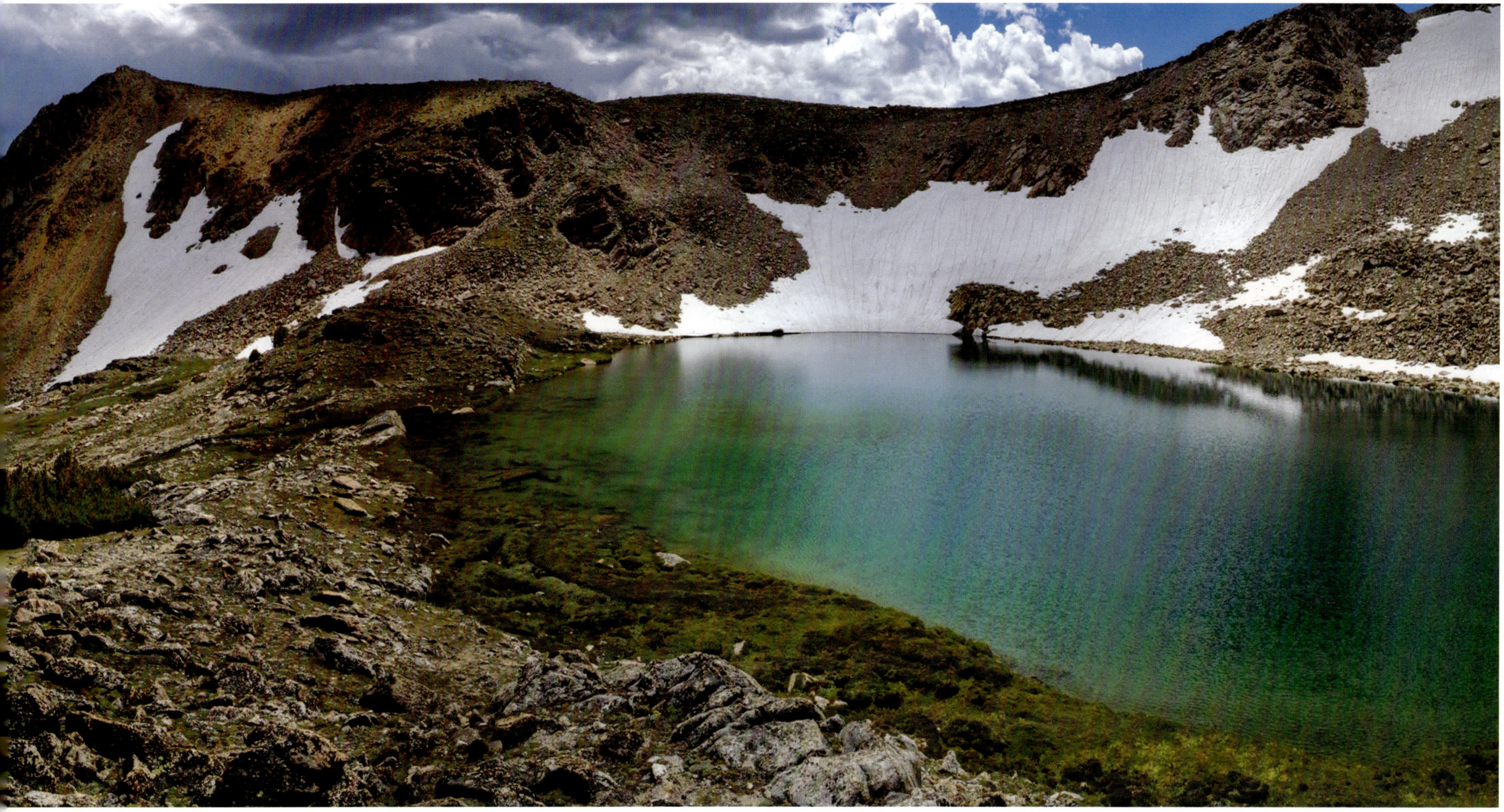

Slide Lake balances on the edge at the top of Big Boulder Creek

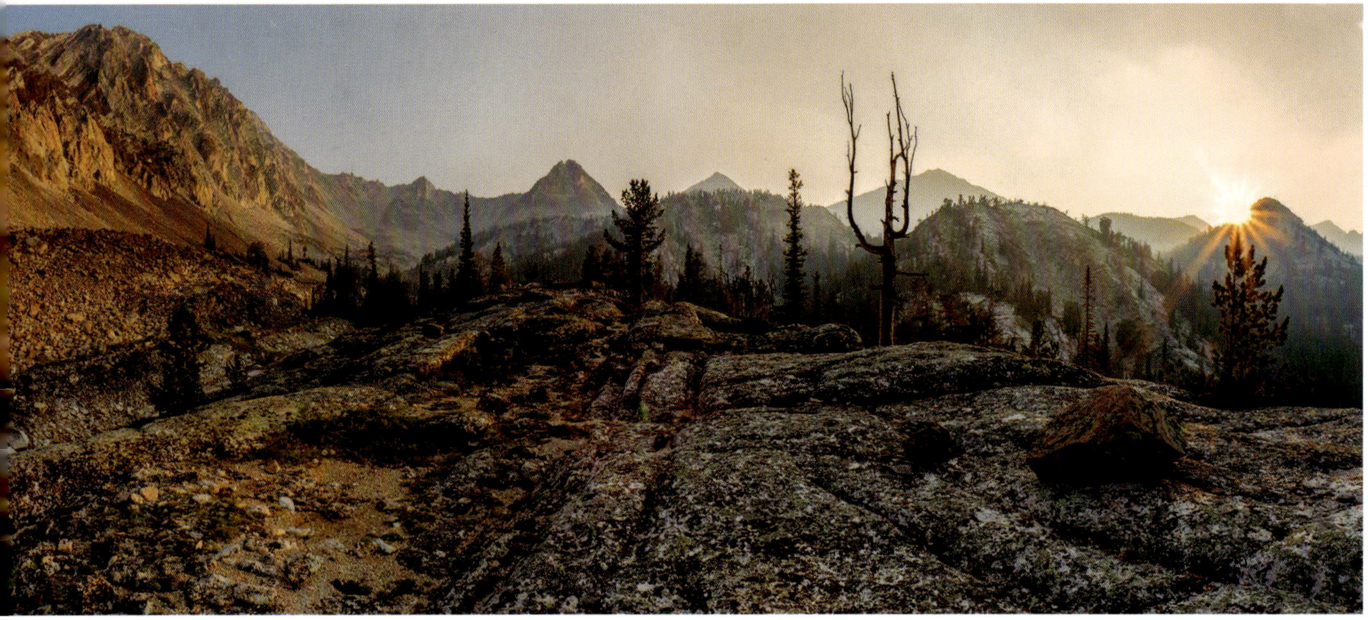

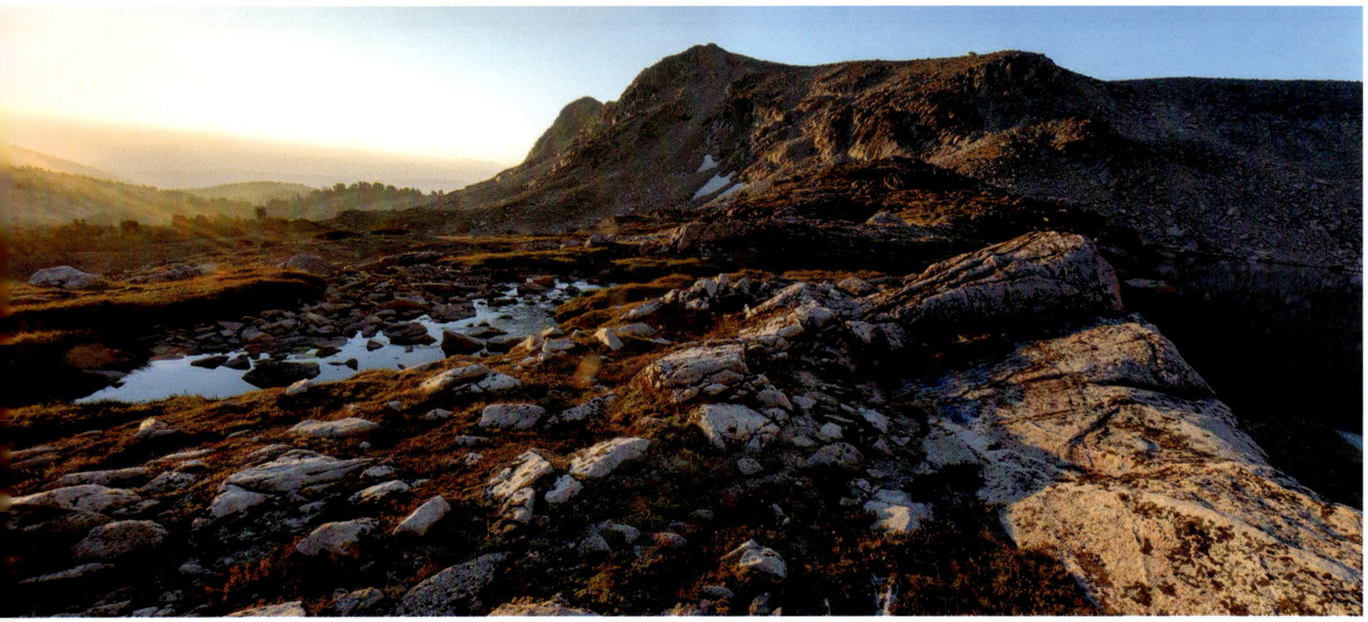

Smoke fills the sky along Goat Lake ridge during the summer fire season
Smoke from a nearby fire settles into the valleys of Big Boulder Creek

Aqua-blue melt water from The Kettles at Cirque Lake

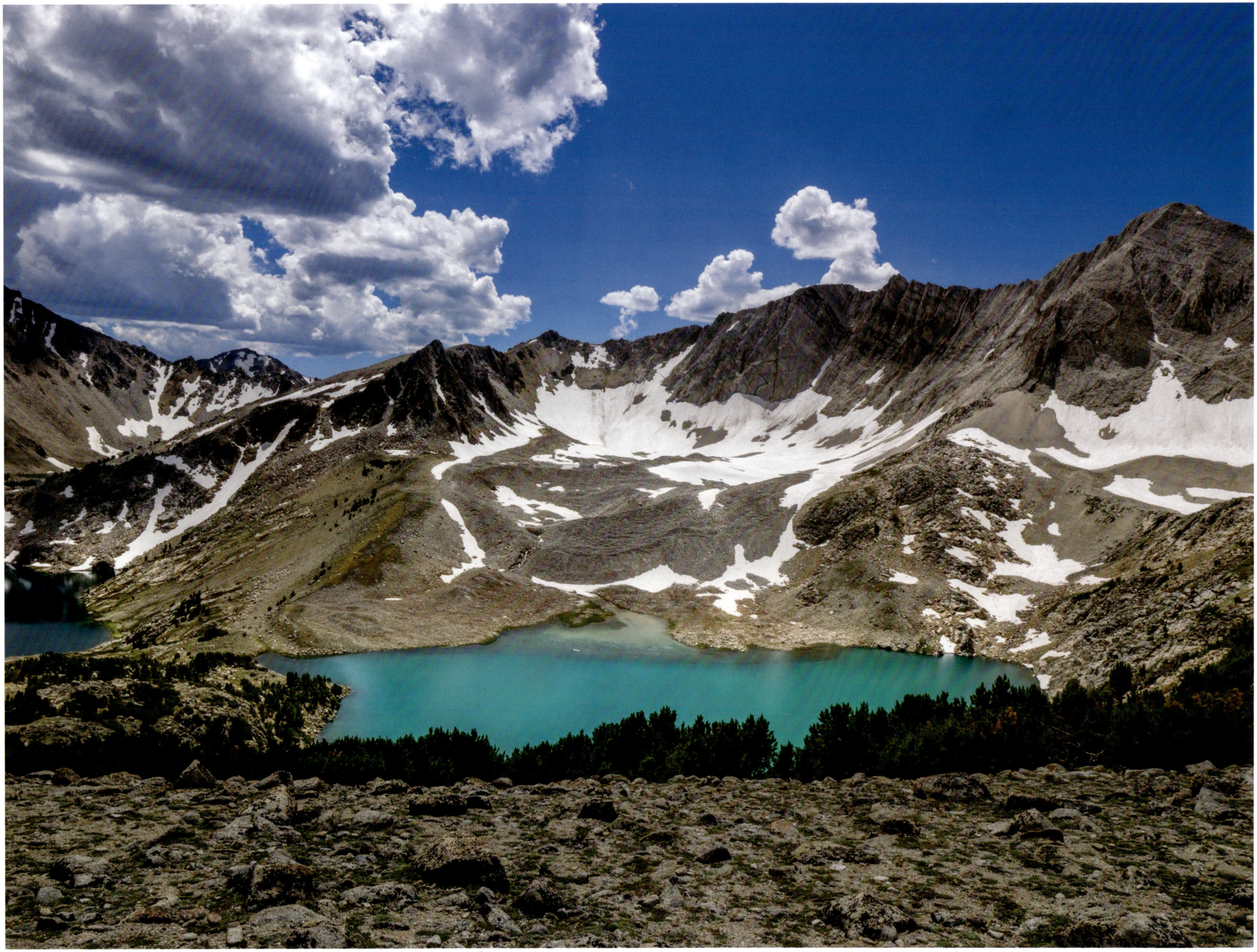

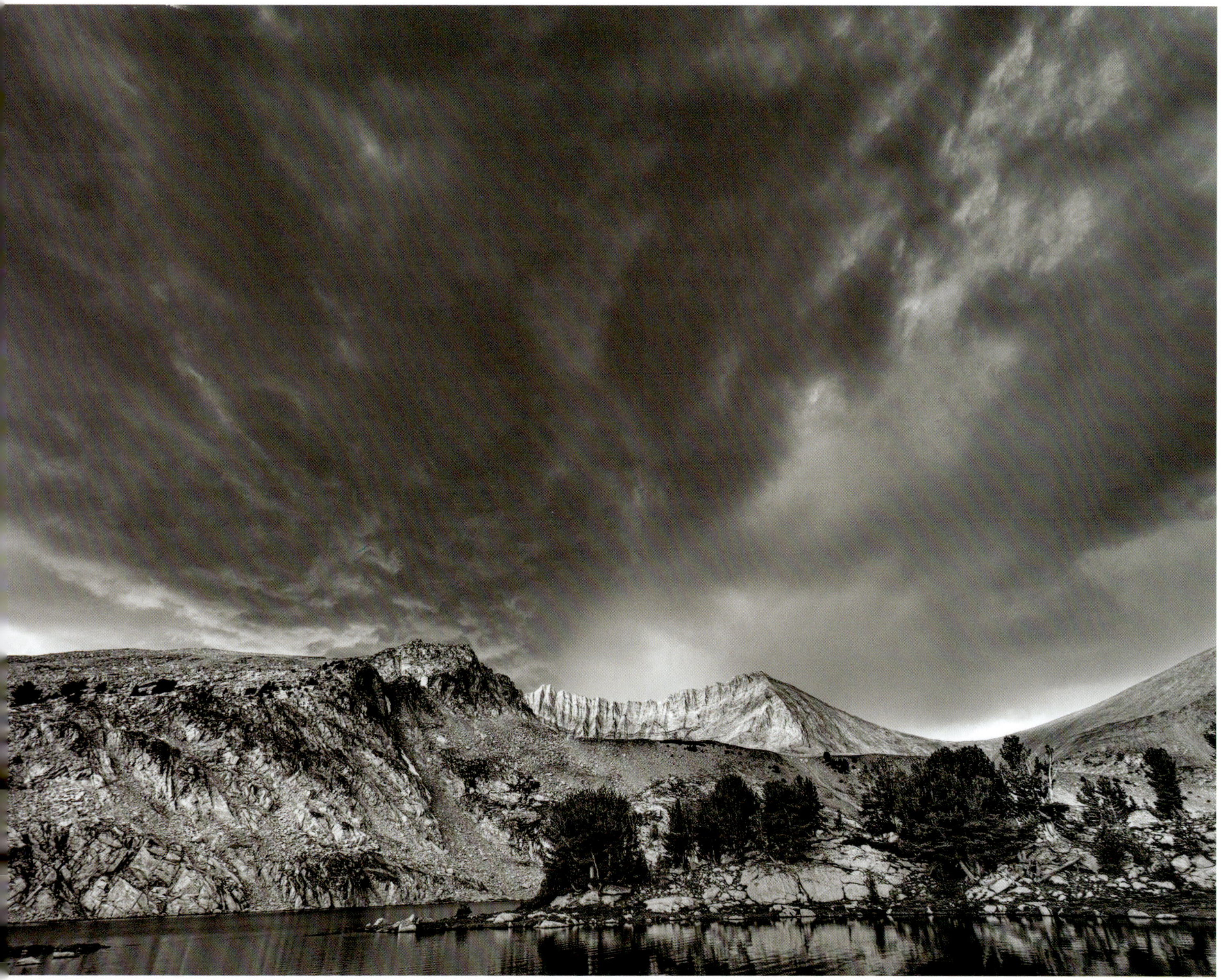

Summer thunderheads over Lee Peak

(Opposite) The milky-way and millions of stars are visible during the new moon at Gentian Lake

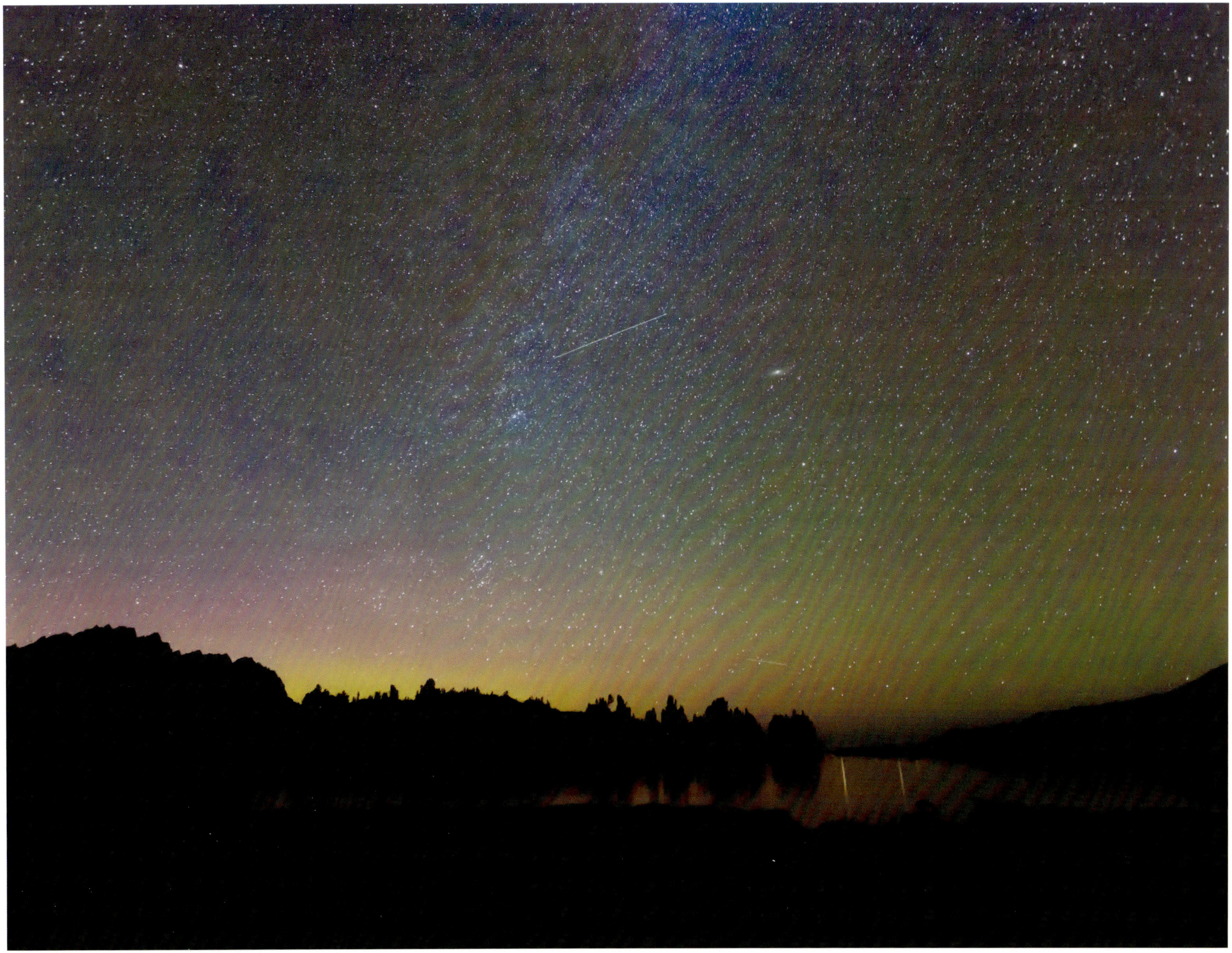

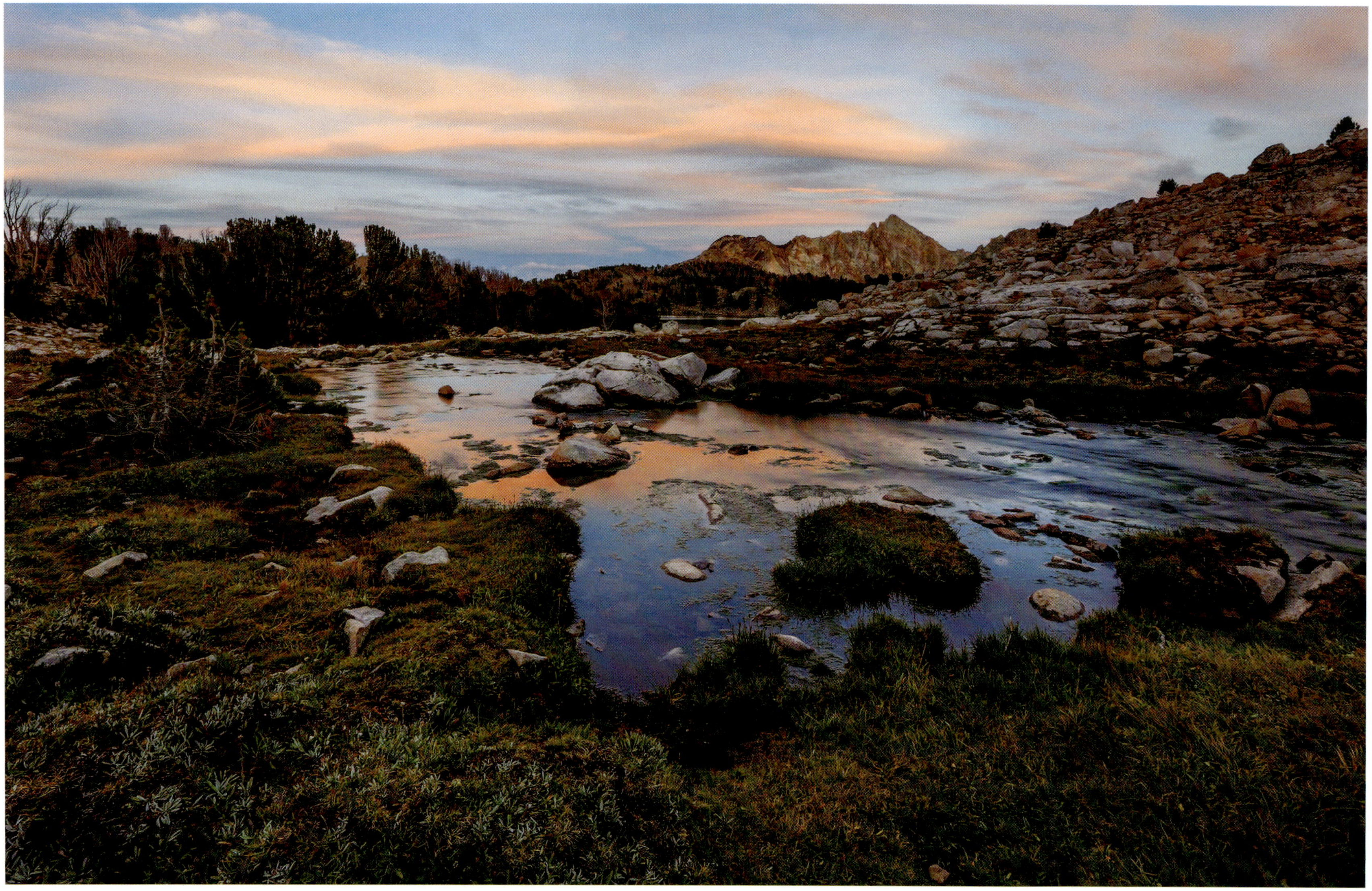

Warm summer clouds illuminate the creek between Sapphire and Cove Lakes

(Opposite) Classic stark white peaks above Cove Lake

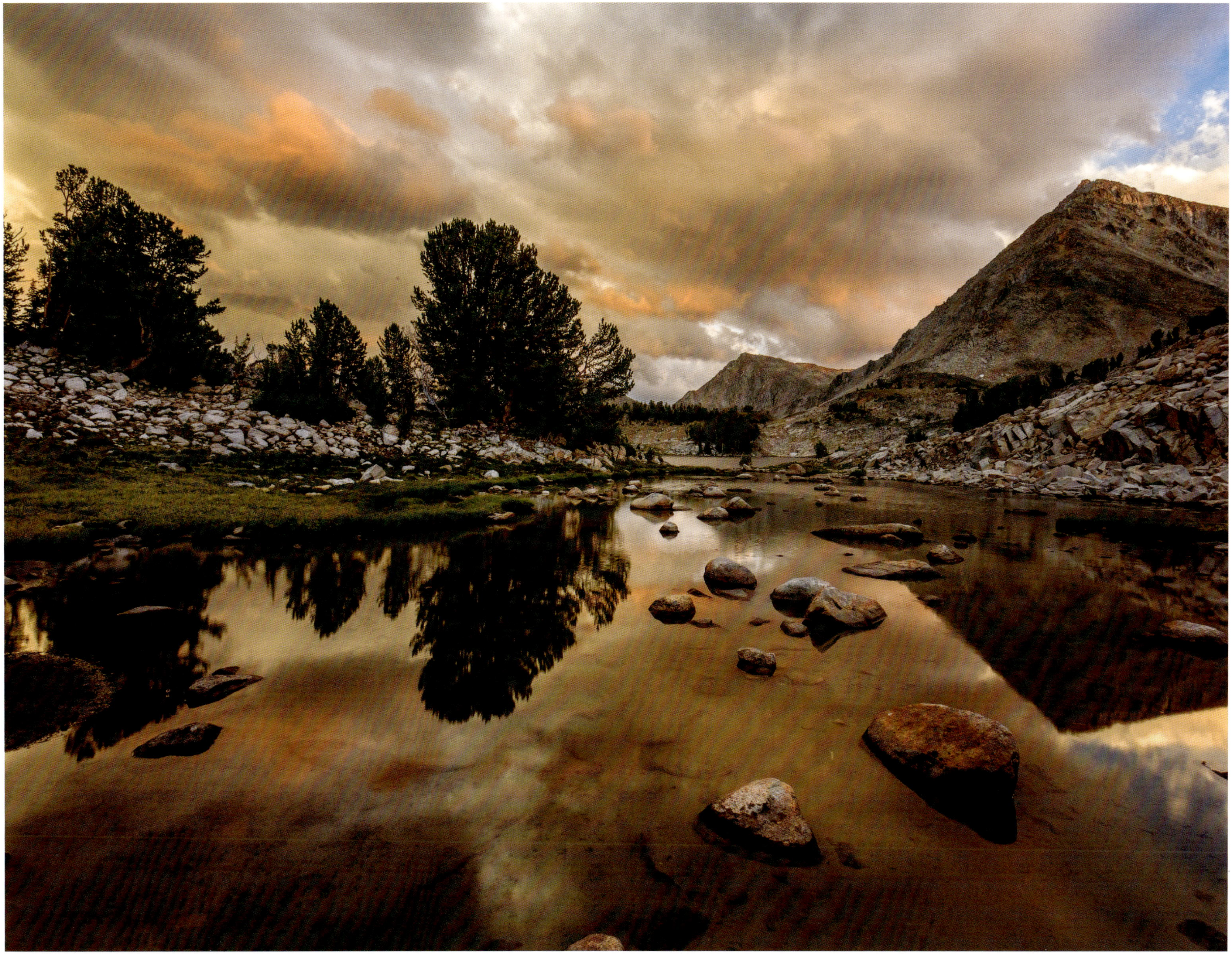

Boulder Chain

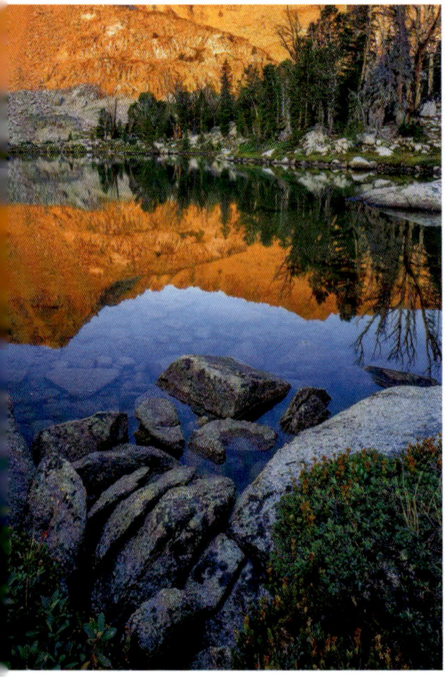

Slide Rock Lake
Lodgepole Lake
Hour Glass Lake
Hidden Lake
Lonesome Lake
Scoop Lake

BY THE PARKING LOT RASPBERRIES RIPEN IN THE ROCKS,

their scent sweet as they shrivel and dry. Higher up, along Little Boulder Creek, at the edges of lodgepole stands and in meadows, strawberries send red creepers from serrated trios of leaves. Pea-sized berries ripen from white to red. Tiny seeds form a pattern on their surface, sweet, intense, these are few but worthwhile. Climbing the trail out of the bottoms to Hatchet then Lodgepole Lake, whortleberry make a carpet of tiny green leaves dotted with miniature red berries. These are smaller than huckleberry which runs the north slopes in the pines. These berries ripen in late summer and the bears strip the leaves and fruit from the plants with their mouths, leaving bare stems on the carpet of green. Trout circle lazy, flesh poached or steamed just to warm. It flakes from the bones, rich grey, white to pink, skin a silvery wrapping strong and slick. In the woods, grouse lumber, heavy bodied, slow like fat hens. Deer and elk graze the meadows of the lower lakes. In the crevasses of the highest boulder-strewn ridges, wild sorrel grows. Clusters of lemon-flavored leaves send up spikes of disorderly pink flowers. All is delicate, enough for a mouthful, a taste in passing, leaving most for the animals and birds that struggle to fatten for winter when from Lonesome Peak and Castle the deep snow will come.

(Detail) Scoop Lake
Lonesome Lake, at the top of the world at 10,435 feet

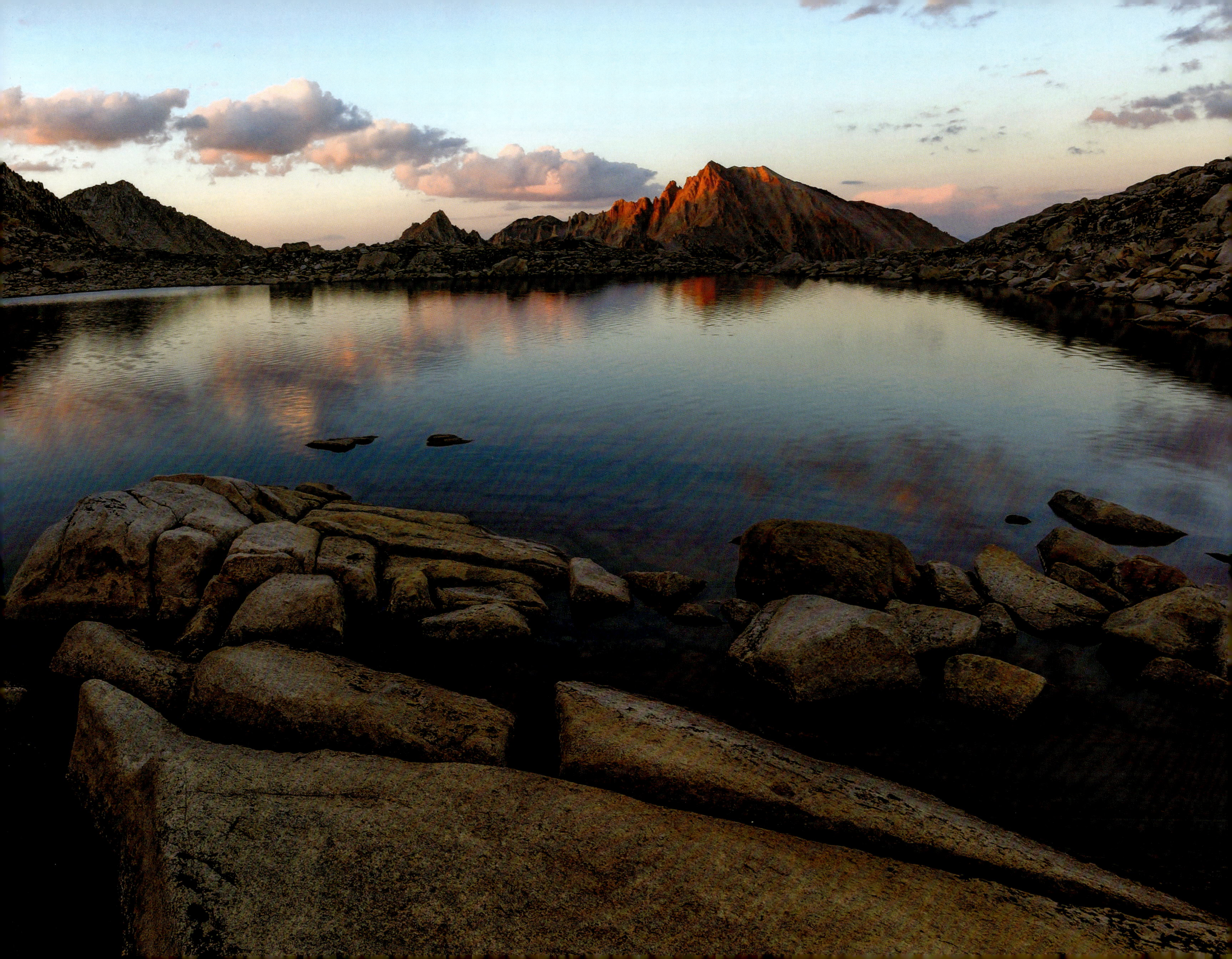

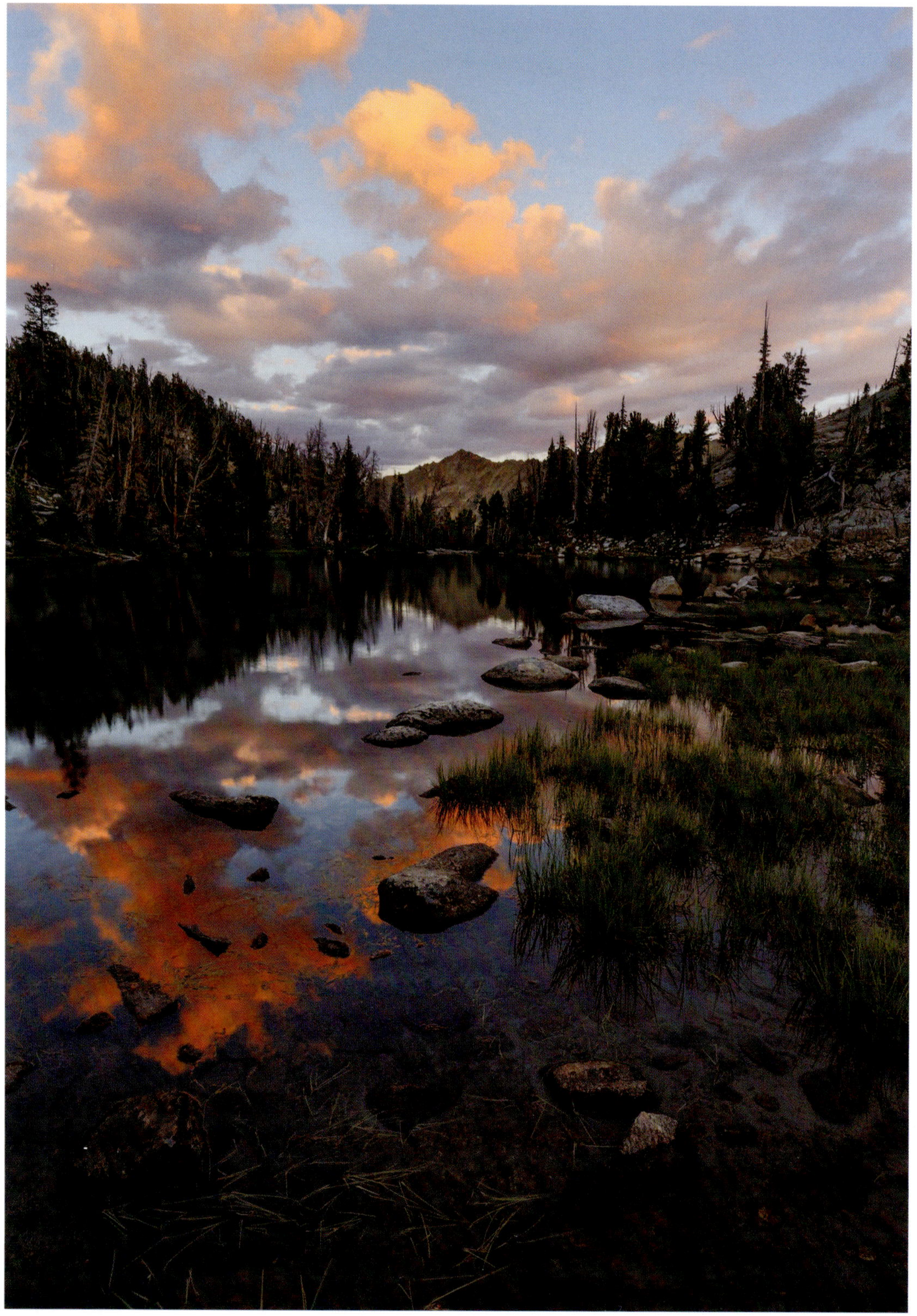

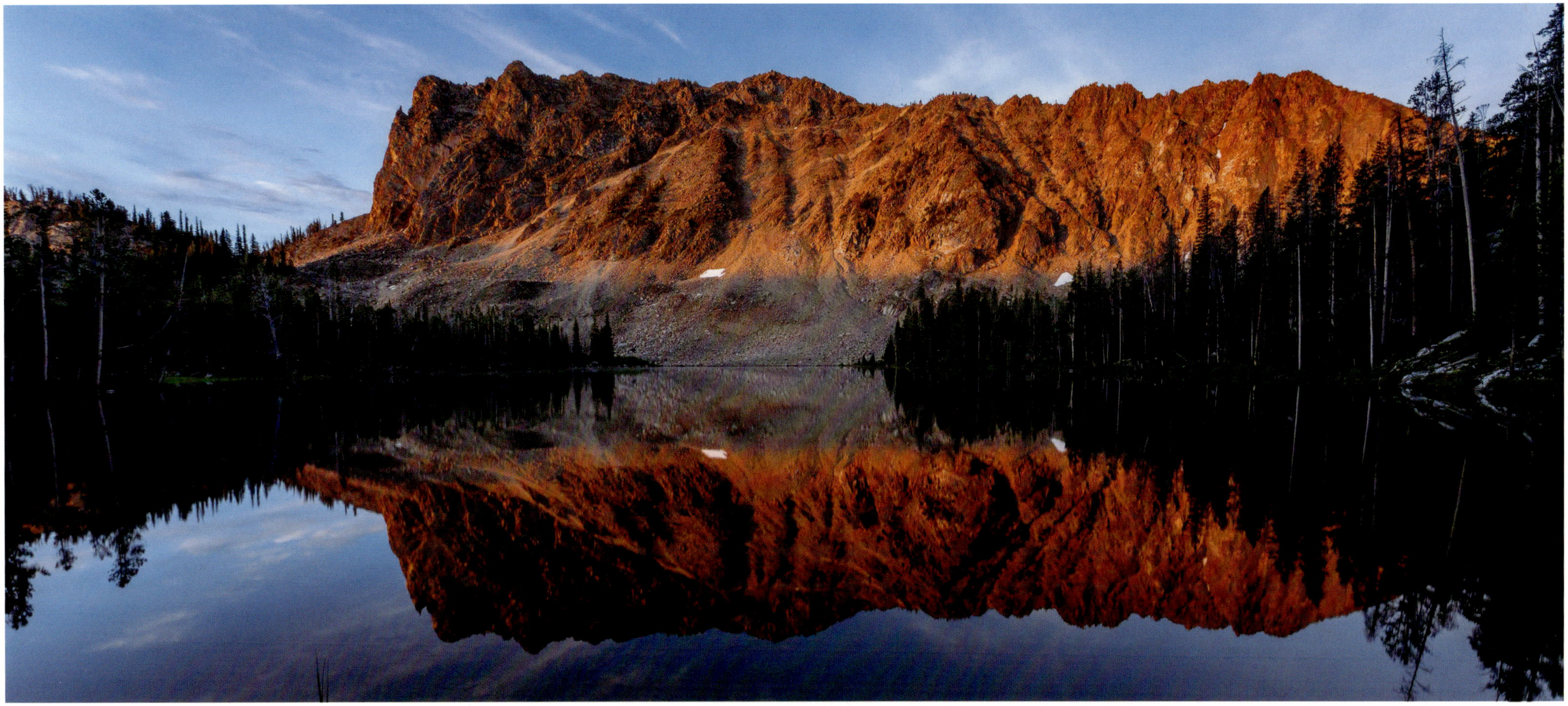

White Cloud Peaks tower over Slide Rock Lake

(Opposite) Moody clouds fill the evening sky at Hour Glass Lake

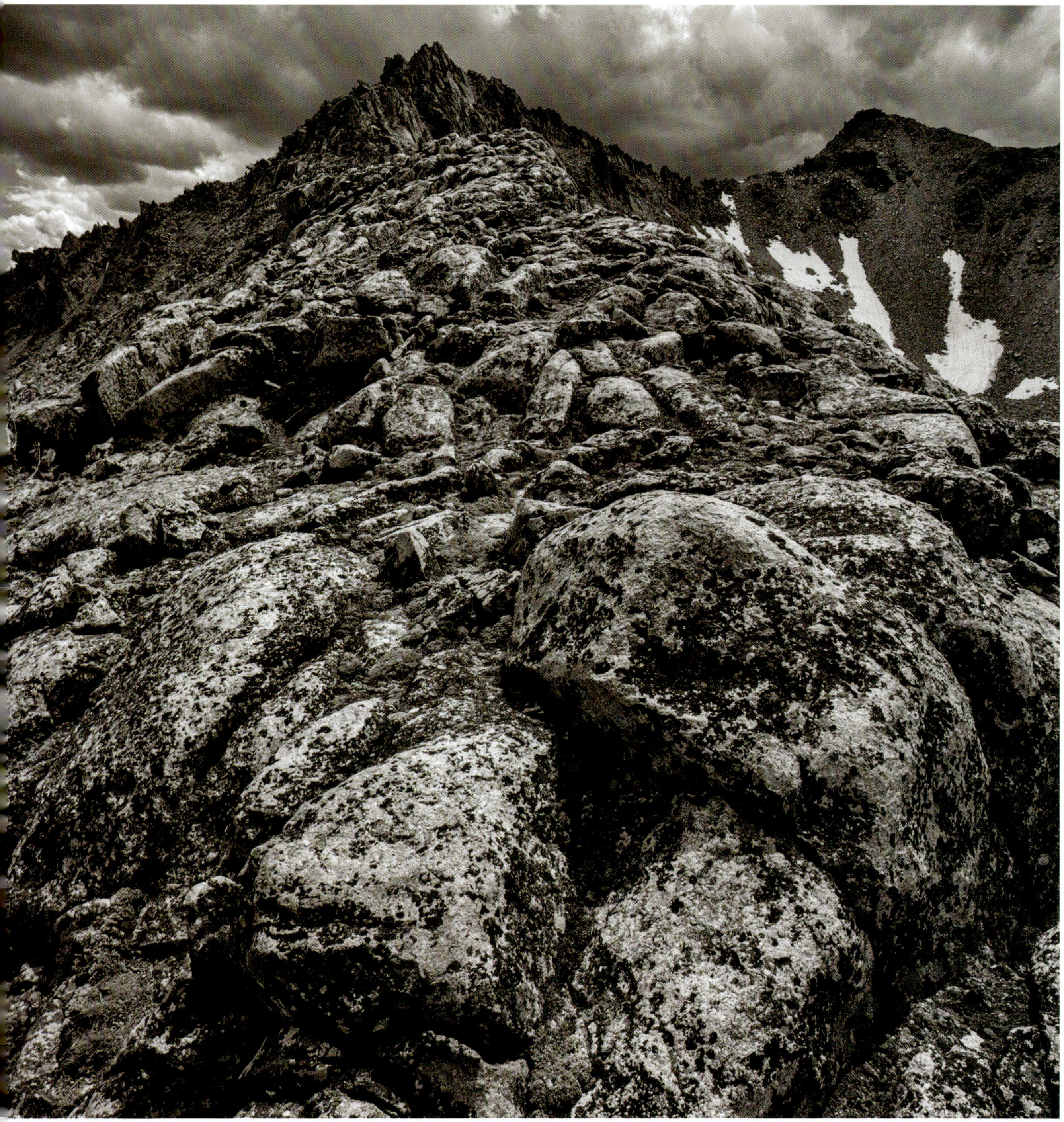

A boulder stairway to Lonesome Peak
(Opposite) Summer storms at Hummock Lake

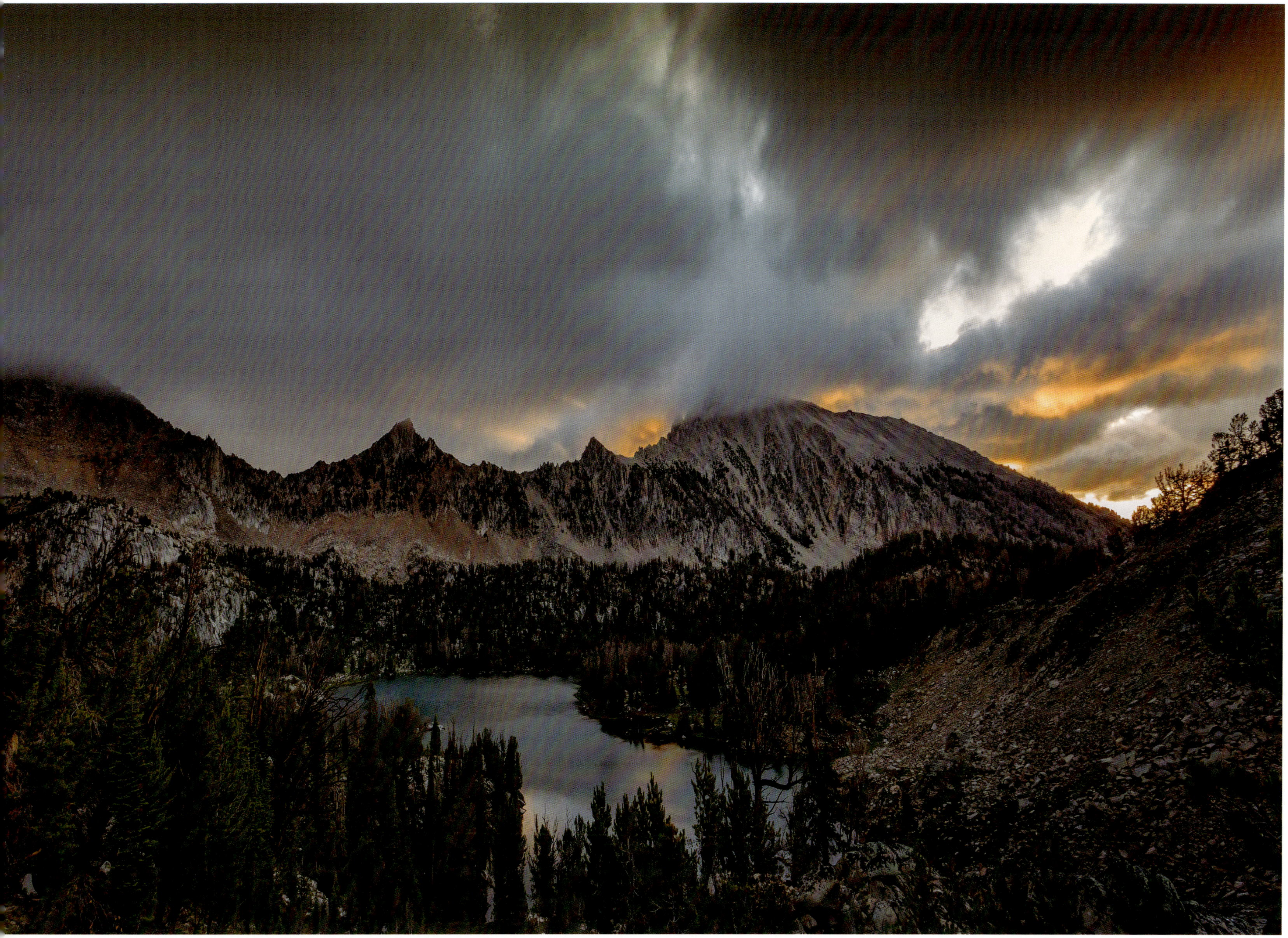

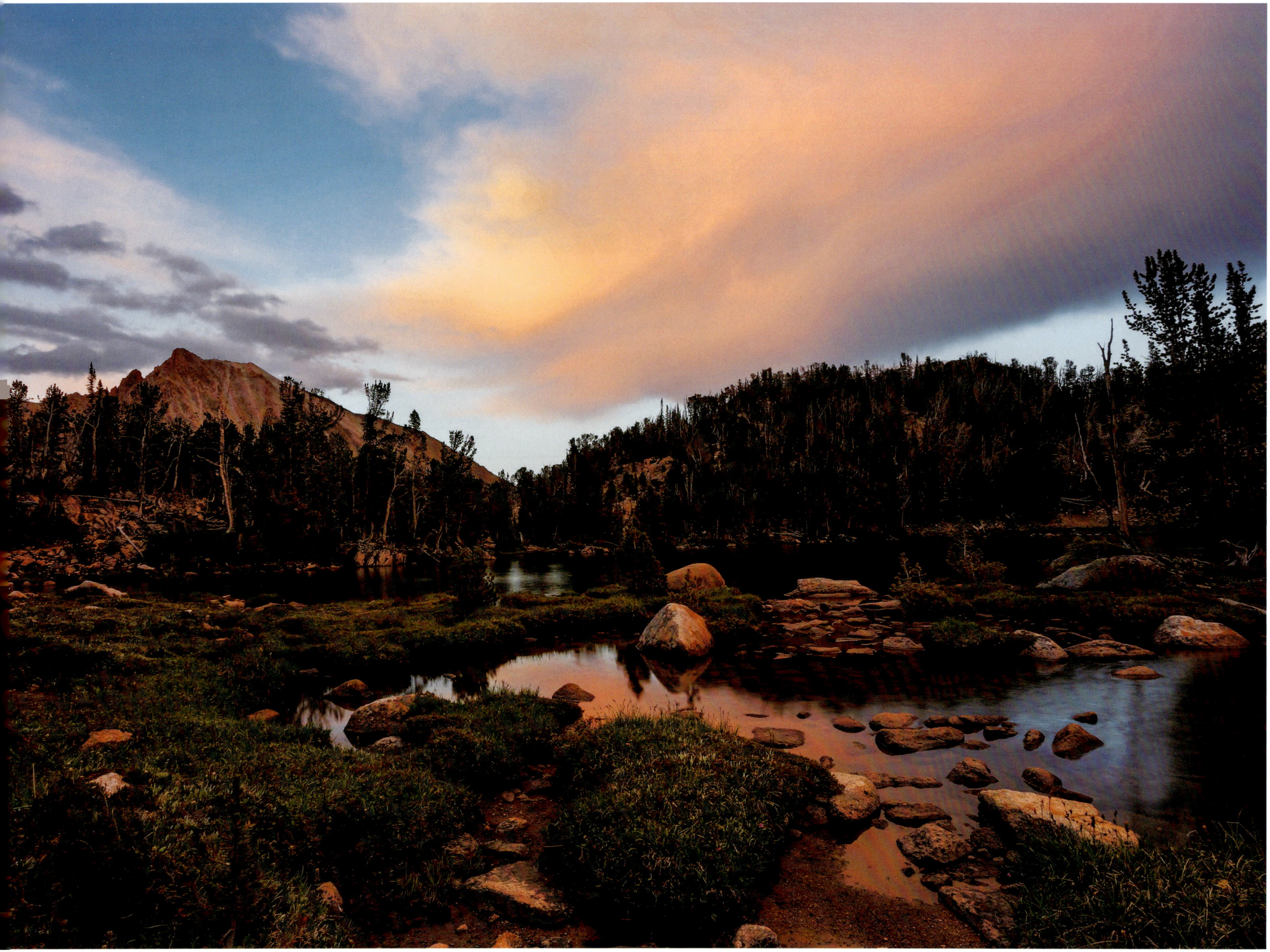

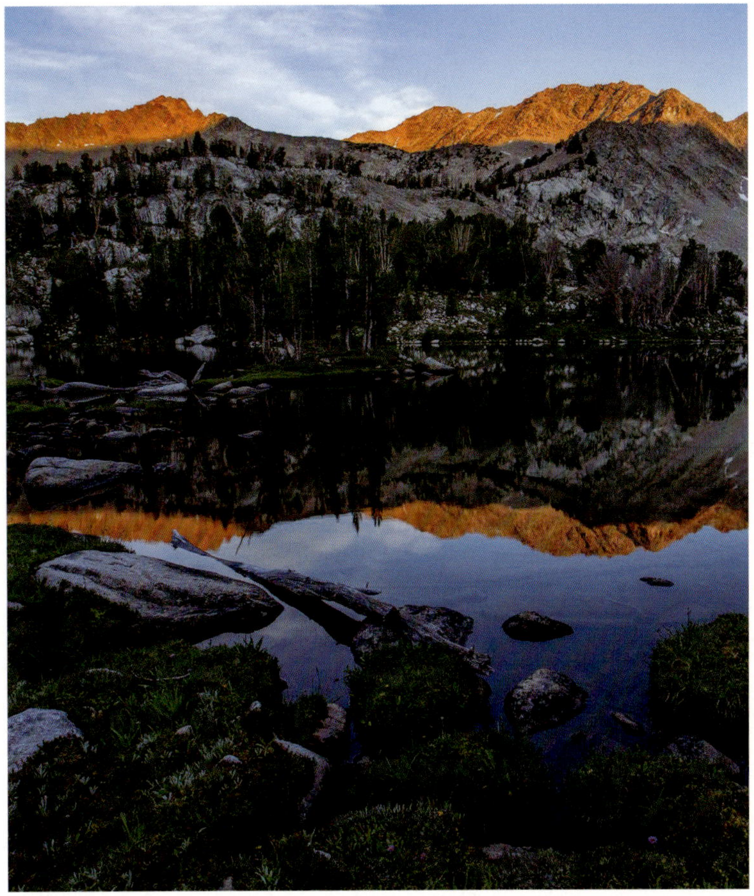

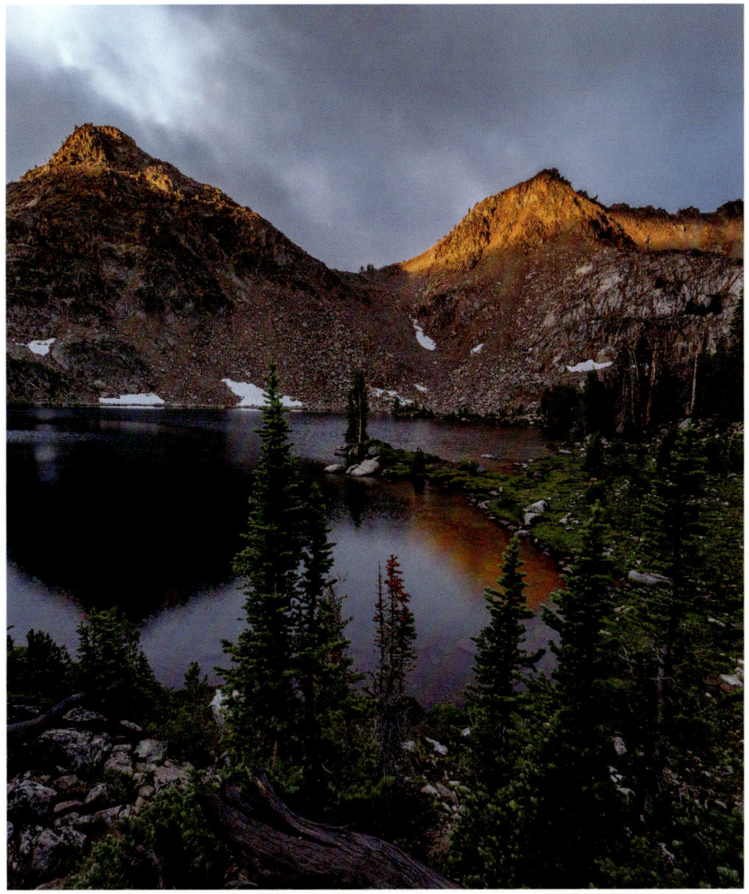

Hummock Lake - the central lake in the chain

(Opposite) Summer rain in the upper reaches of the Boulder Chain - Scoop Lake

Sunlight illuminates the tips of the White Cloud Peaks - Scoop Lake

Castle Peak Area

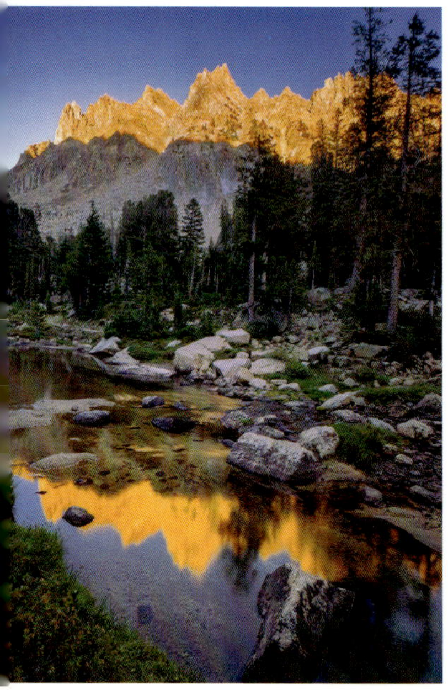

Chamberlain Basin Lakes
Four Lakes Basin
Castle Lake
Noisy Lake
Quiet Lake
Scree Lake

LIGHT FADES. CLOUDS GATHER.

Quiet lake lies wide in the valley, deep below the spires of Castle Peak. Rockfall punctuates the stillness where, in Noisy Lake below, water voices mumble and call, eerie in darkness and light. At dawn the image of Castle peak echoes back from lakes and puddles to the sky, a mountain multiplied by light and water. Warmed stone shines next to snow fields, a sky huge above the trees. And clouds boil into cumulus and nimbus. Lenticulars hang stationary in the wind. Alto sirus "mares tails" call storms and changing weather, high up they form in feather-like plumes. In the calm of evening, puffy rows of white roll-like waves, a quilt of white pinned to a sky.

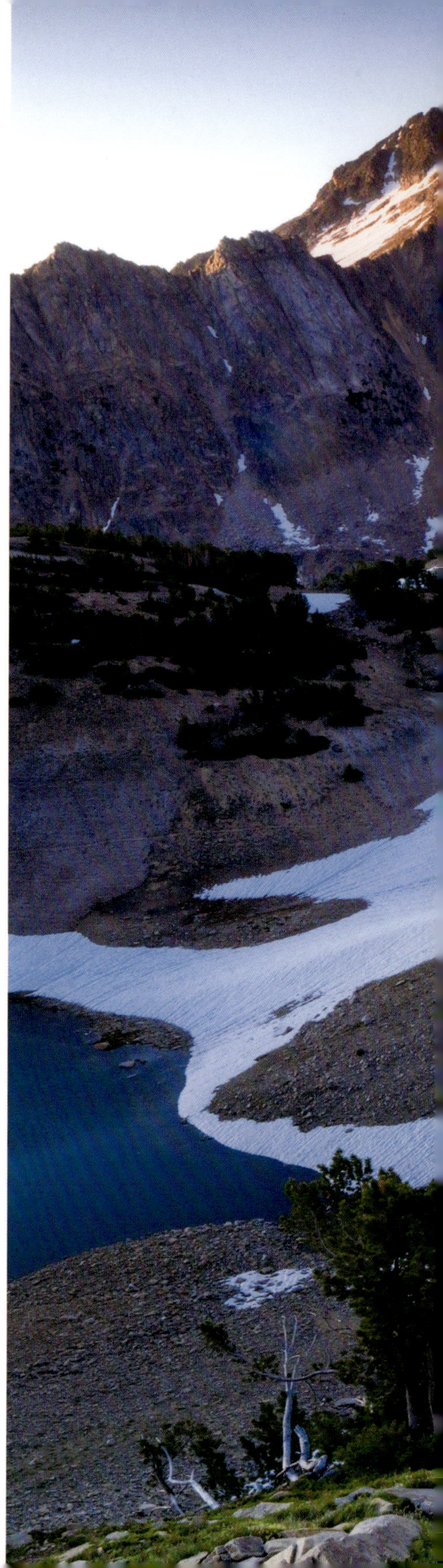

(Detail) Serrate Ridge reflects in the inlet of Quiet Lake
Ice cover the lakes on Four Lakes Basin well into July

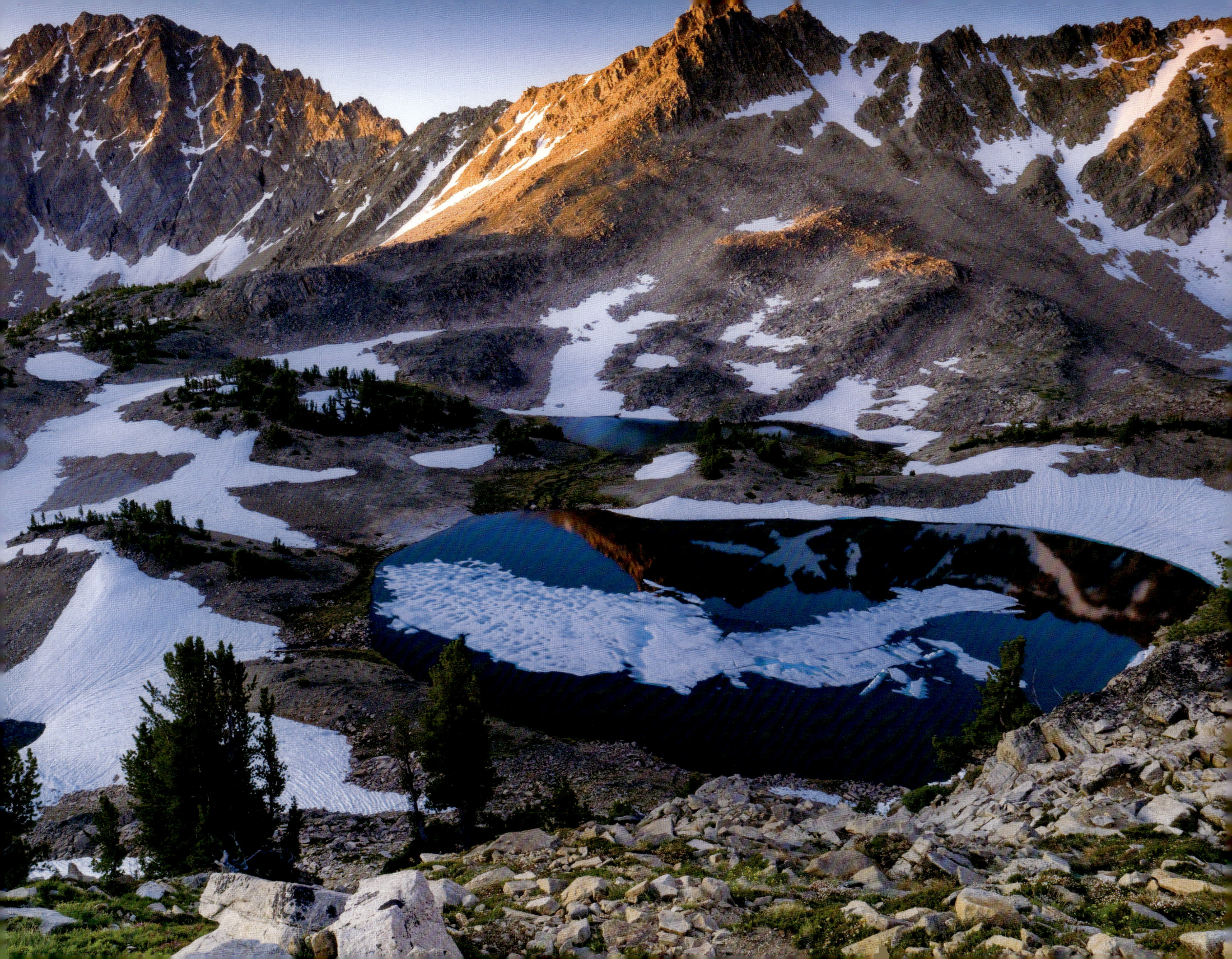

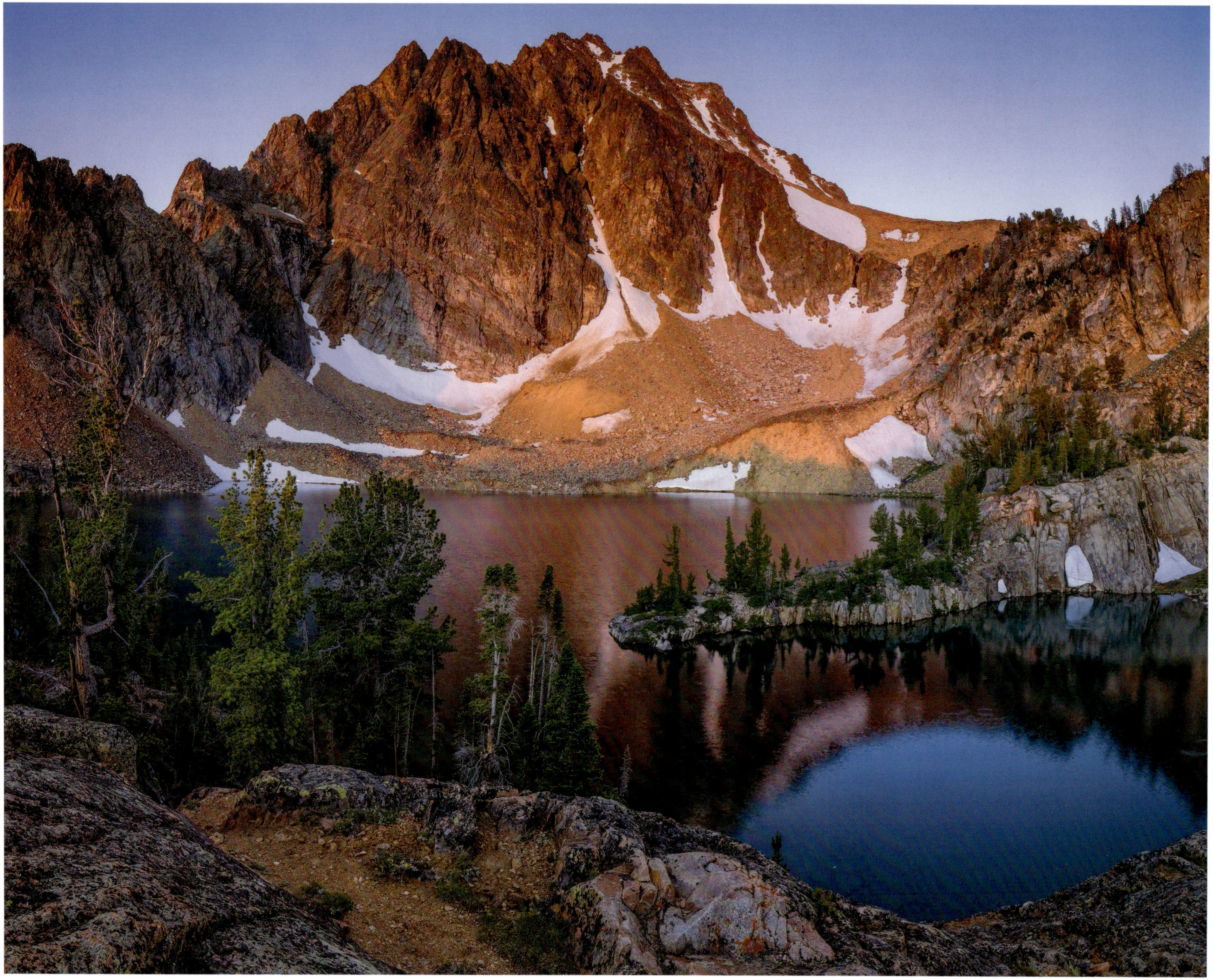

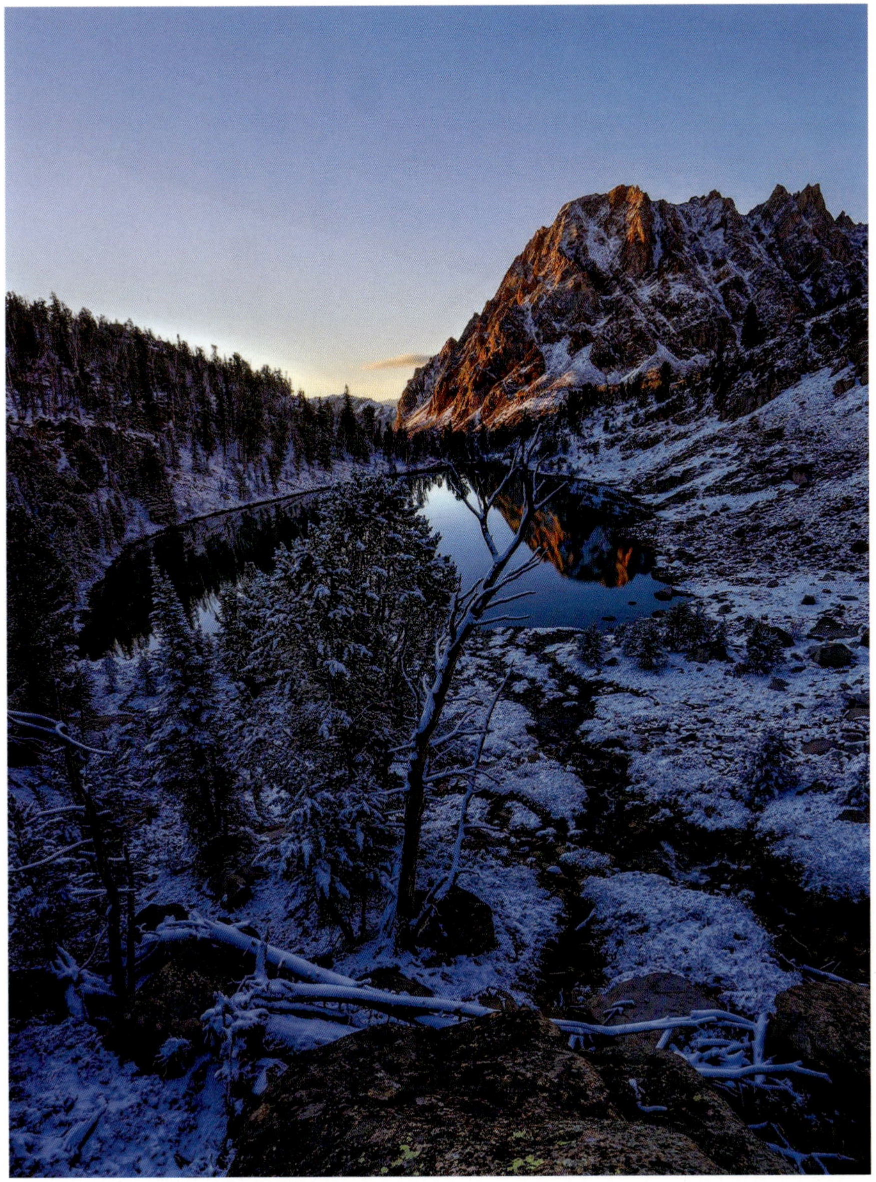

Scree Lake in light summer snow reflects Meriam Peak

(Opposite) The majestic Castle Peak looms above Castle Lake

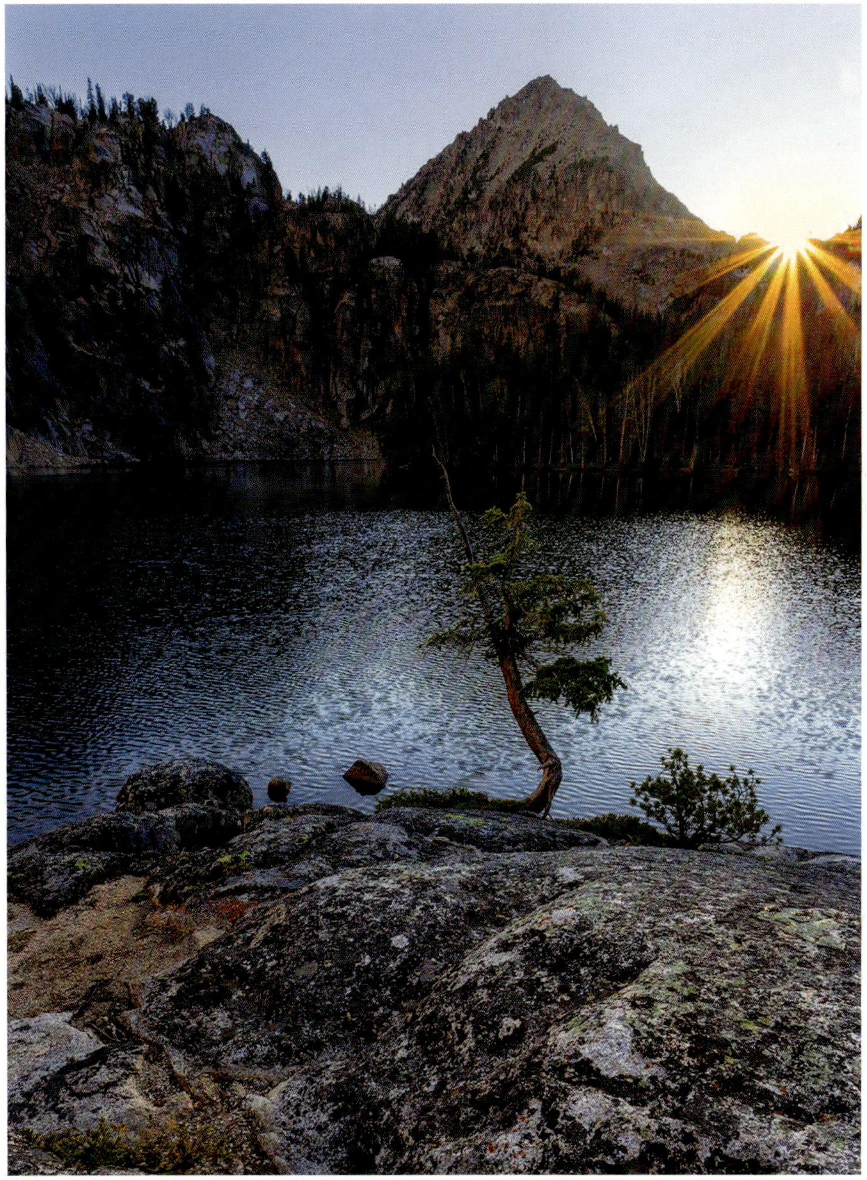

Evening sunburst - Noisy Lake

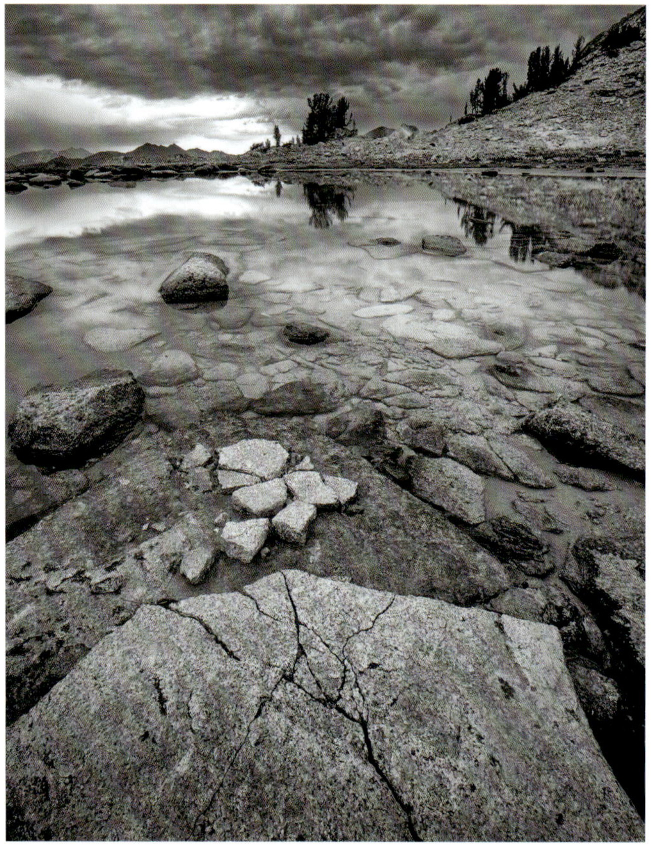

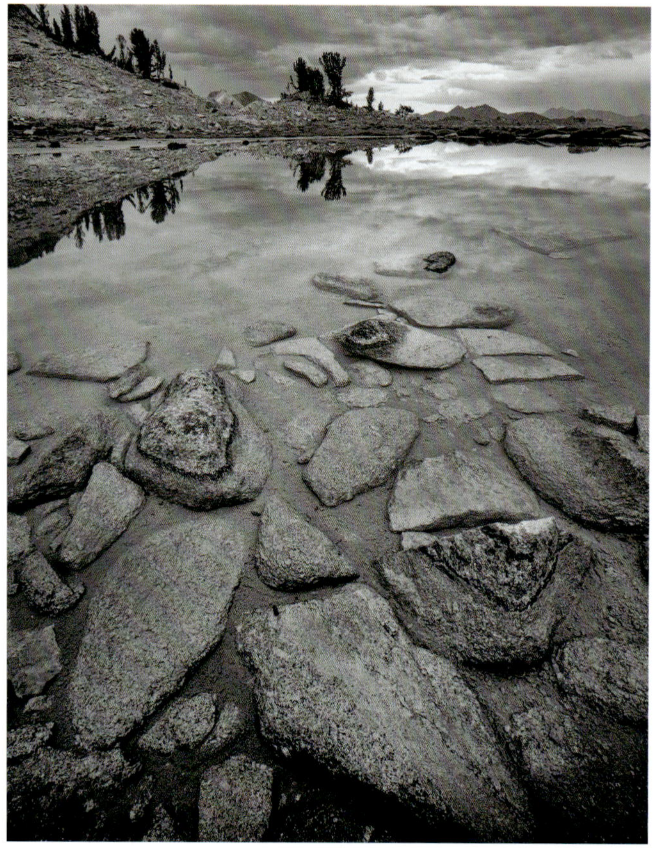

Small catch basins in the Chamberlin Basin

(Opposite) View of Castle Peak from the Upper Chamberlin Lake

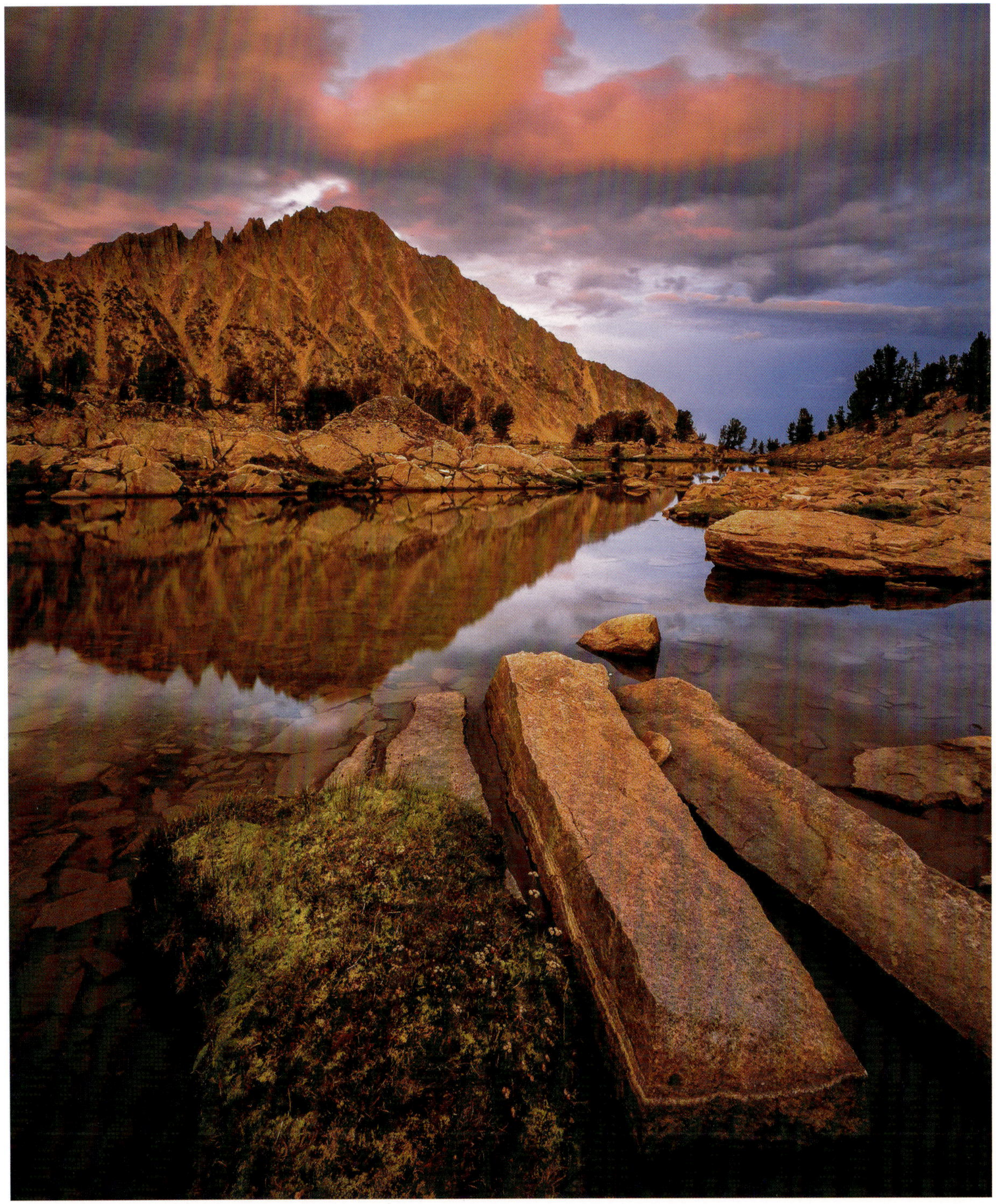

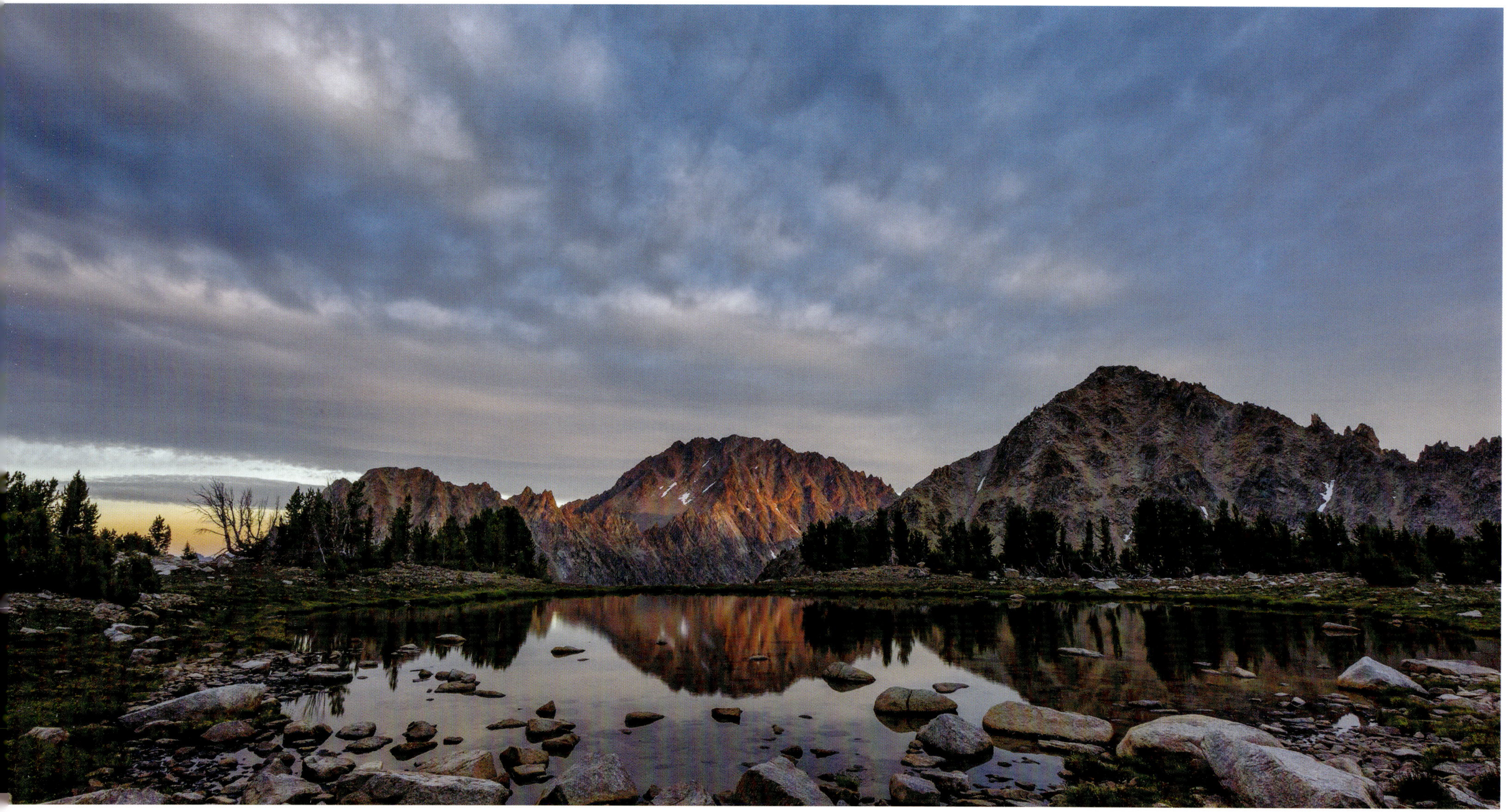

View of Castle and Meriam Peaks - Windy Devil

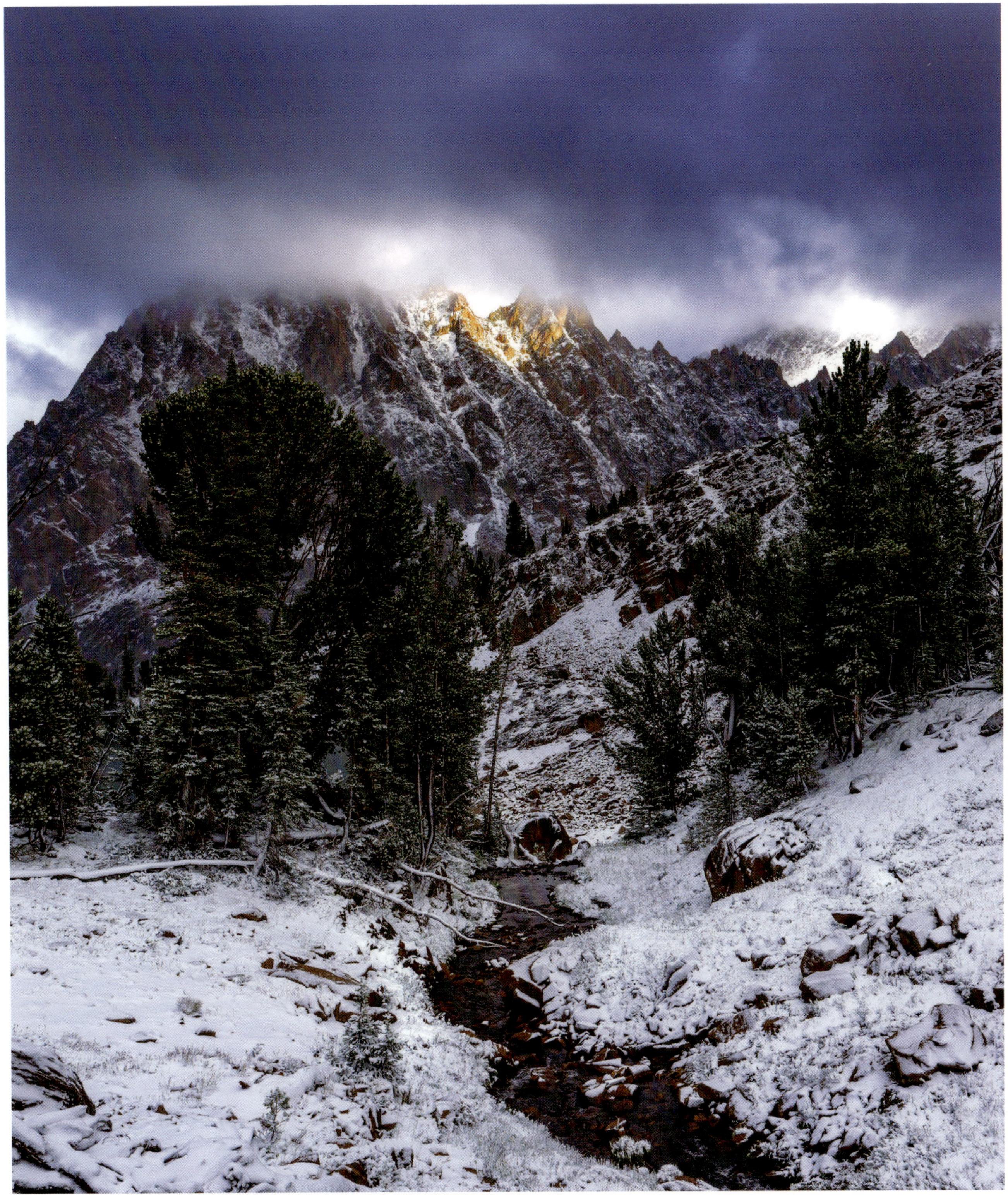

July snow on Meriam Peak

Fourth of July

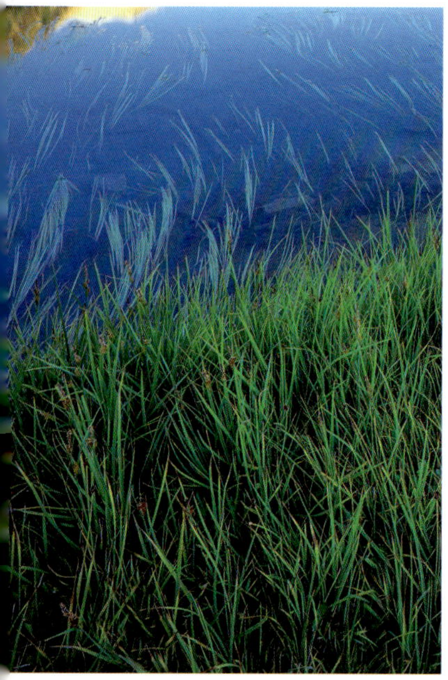

Fourth of July Creek
Fourth of July Lake
Washington Lake
Ants Basin
Born Lake
Four Lakes Basin

UP ON PATTERSON PEAK,

spears of light fall between thunderheads. Rain spatters Fourth of July Lake. In the night, snow settles high up in Ants Basin: melts. On the shoulders of the valleys, powdery pale, black knotted columns rise into green, changing as the light fades. Great clones of Aspen stands rise, whisper to earth through chains of cells, leaves which burn when the frost comes, yellow, red, clattering over the grey green hills, set against the dark pine where snowmelt and rain trickle, sliding seaward. Ancient pollen, silt of glaciers, water that's passed through trout, beaver and muskrat, rolls over moss, over lichen. Endless grains of crumbled quartz, mountains built of grains creep towed the East Fork, Warm Springs, Forth of July Creek, for the Salmon, the Snake, the Columbia, for the dark and open ocean where at last everything will rest.

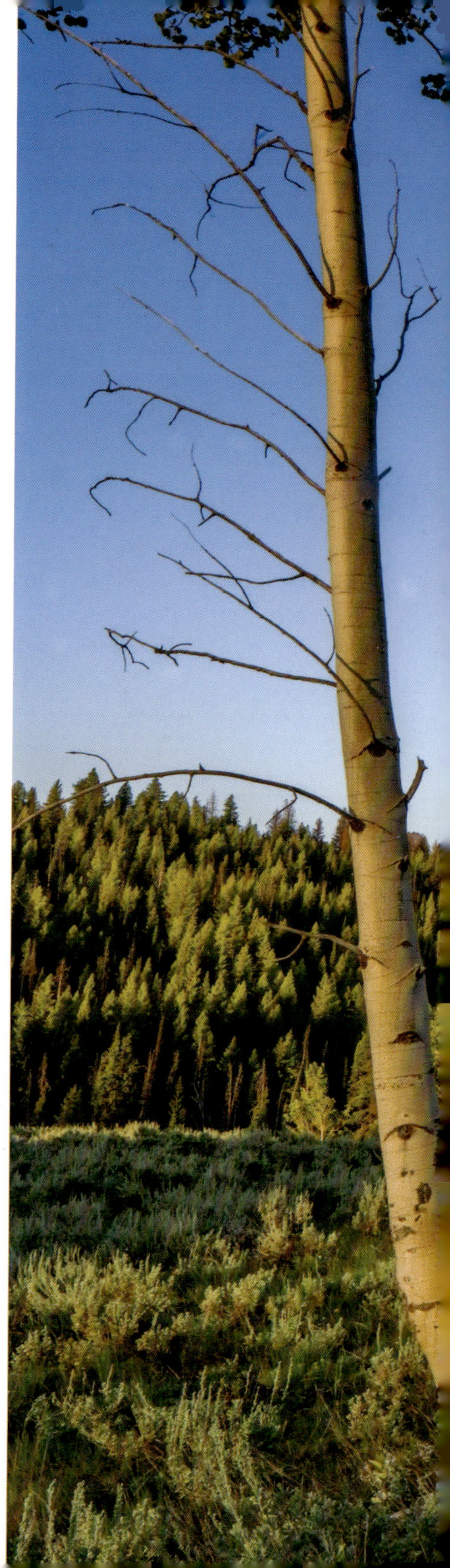

(Detail) Washington Lake - Grassy shoreline
Overlooking the Sawtooths from Fourth of July Creek

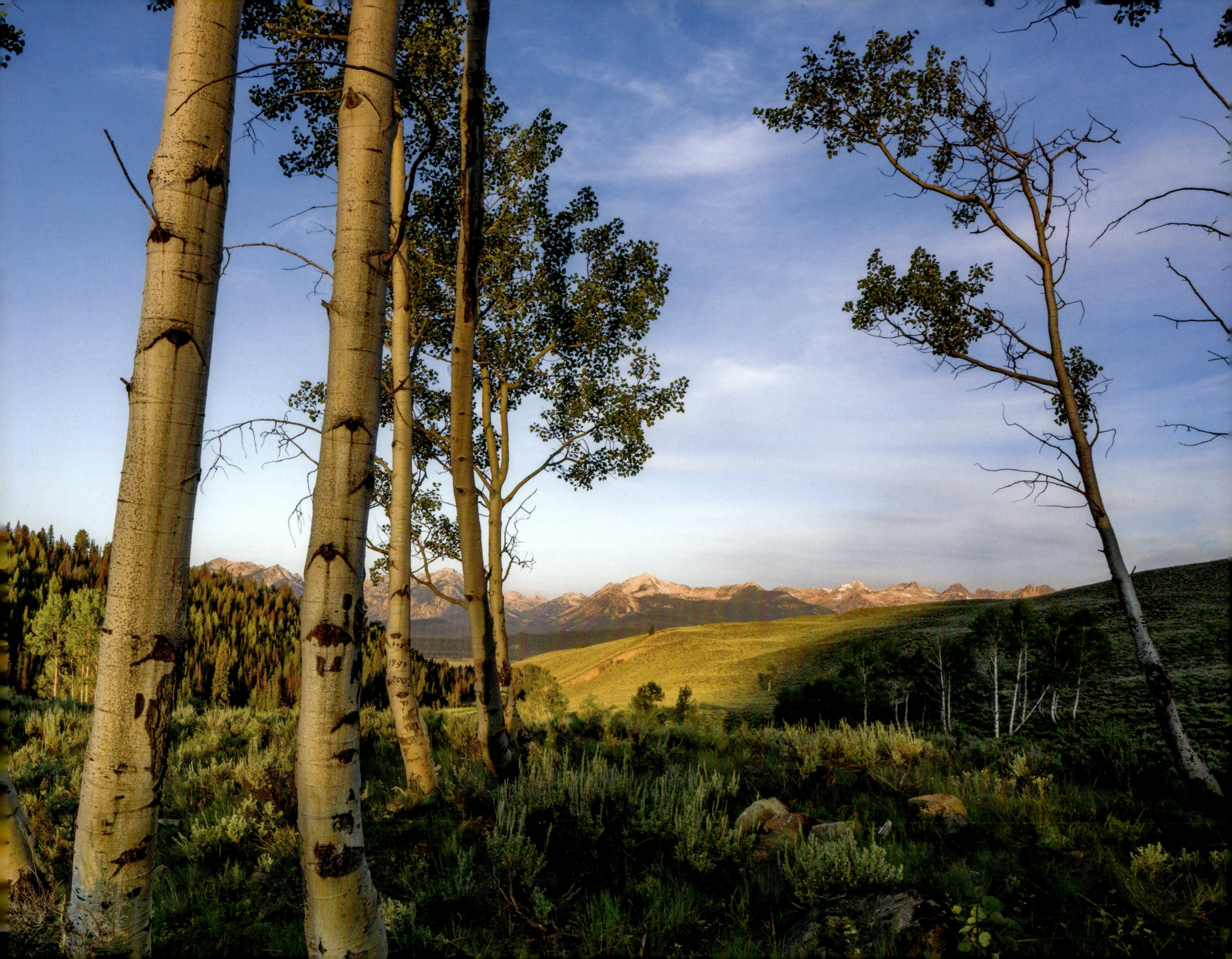

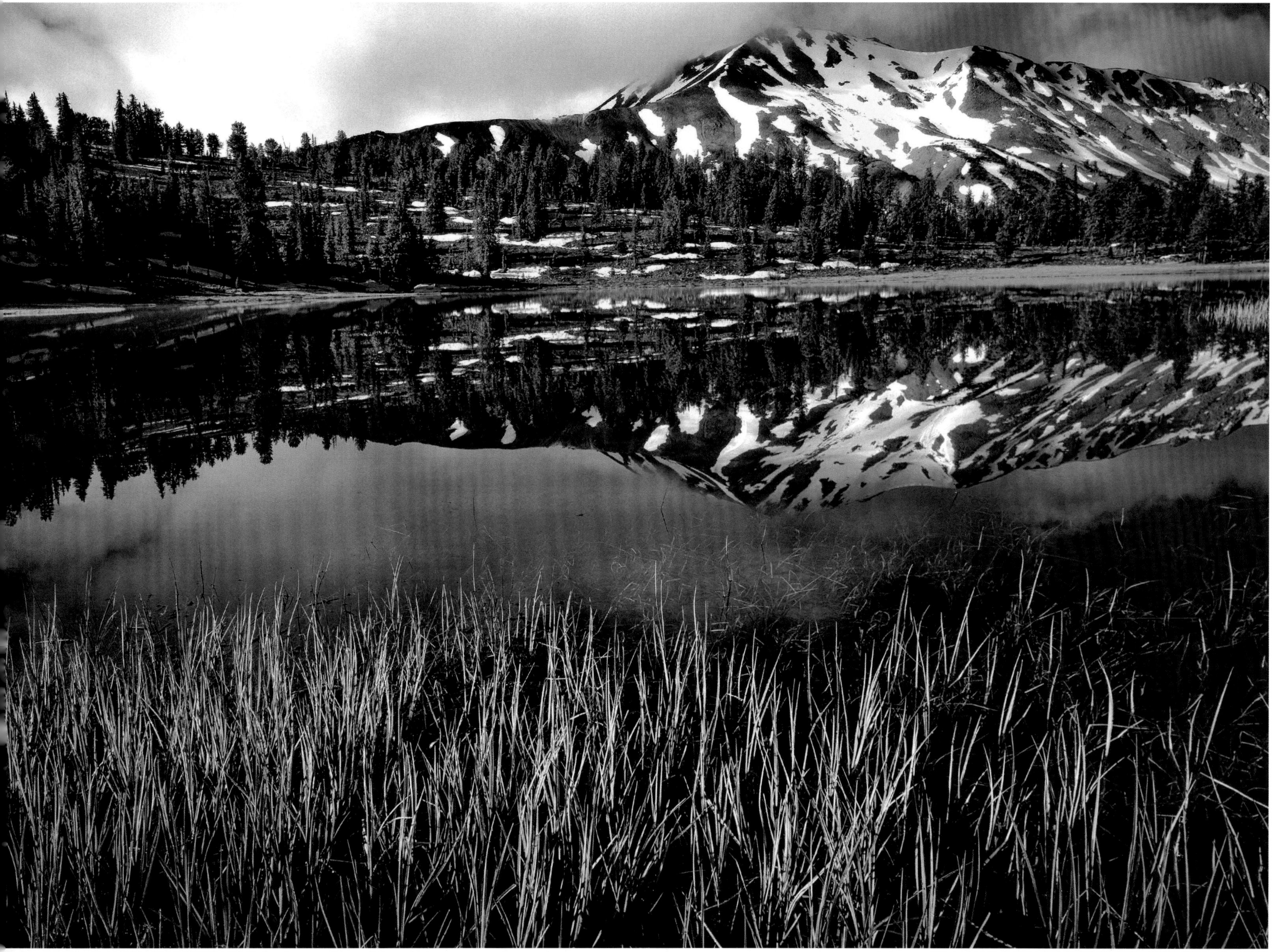

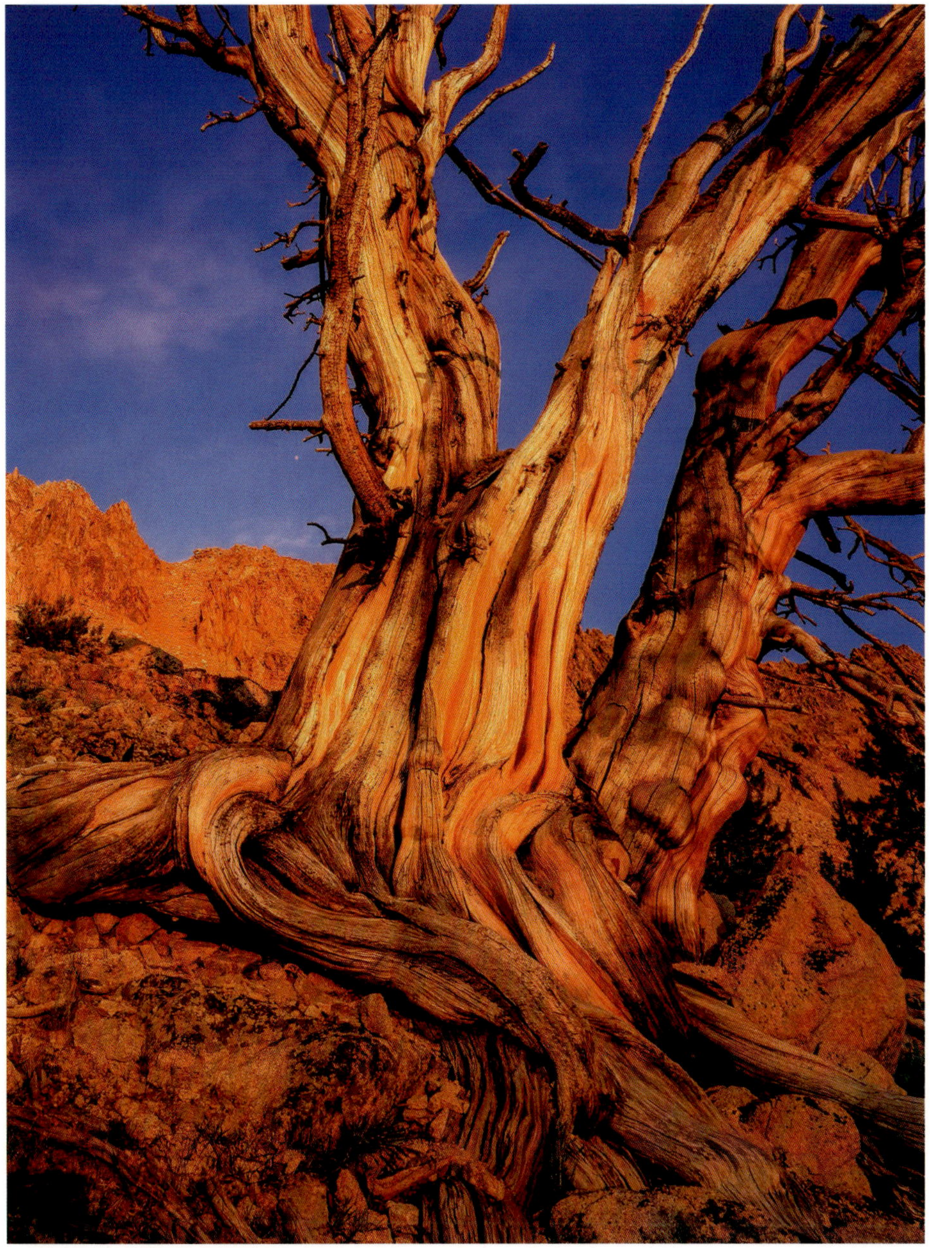

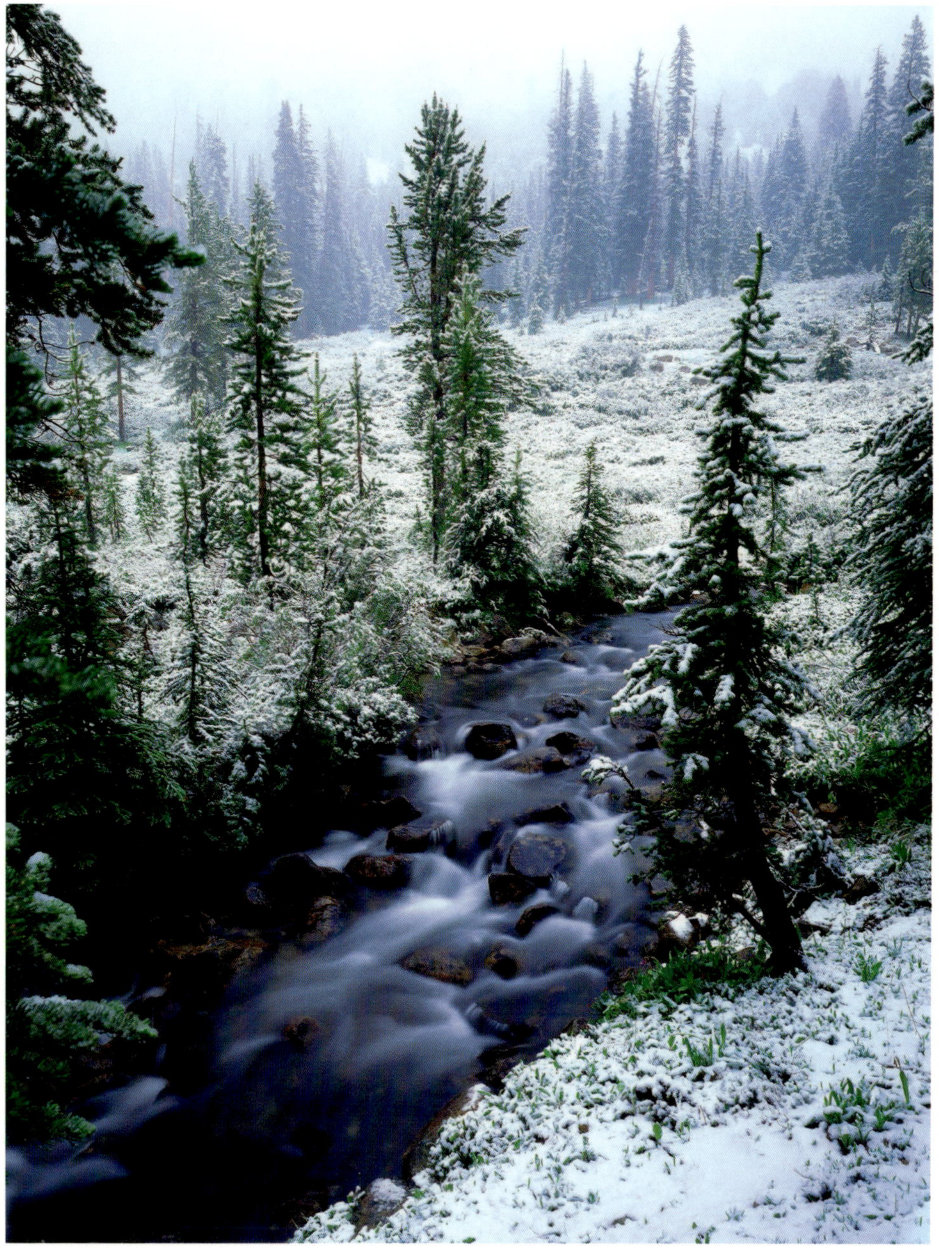

Limber pine skeleton in the headwaters of Warm Spring Creek

(Opposite) Spring - Fourth of July Lake

Early snow - Fourth of July Creek

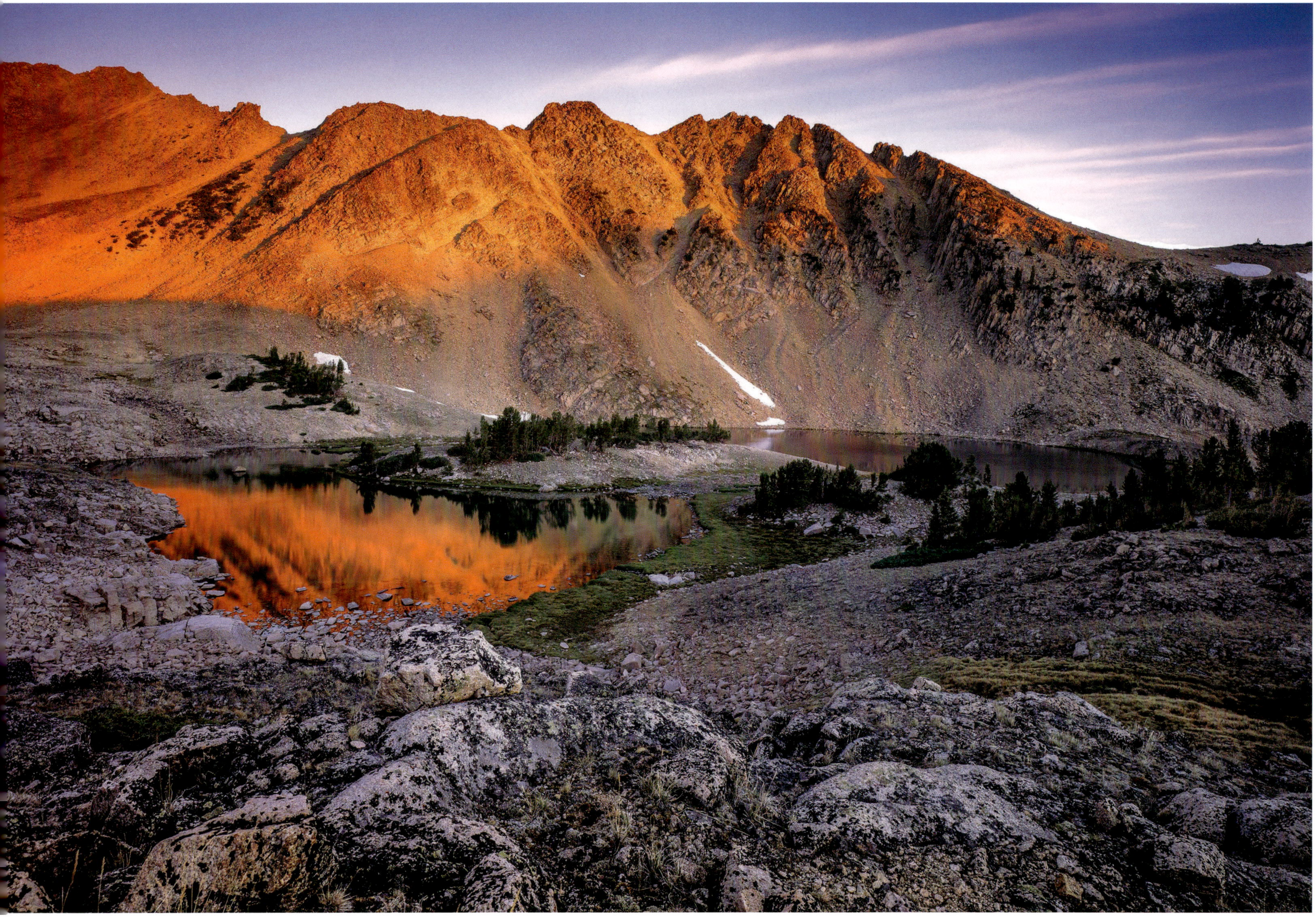

Mid summer temperatures give a brief warm up to the lakes in Four Lakes Basin

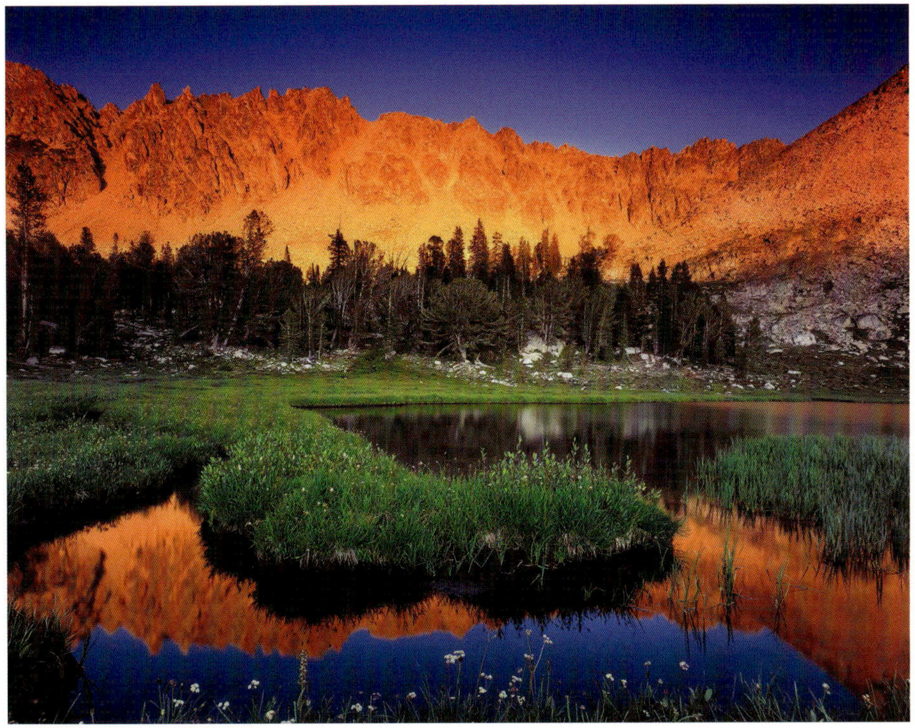

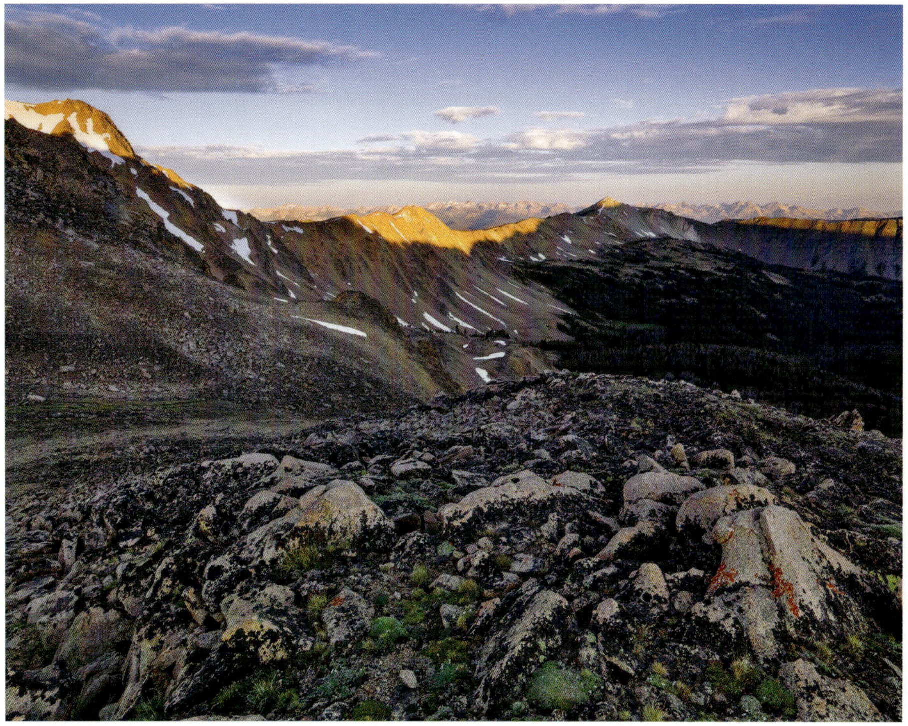

A blue bird day in the basin - Born Lake

The Sawtooths come into view high in Ants Basin

Pole Creek/Boulders

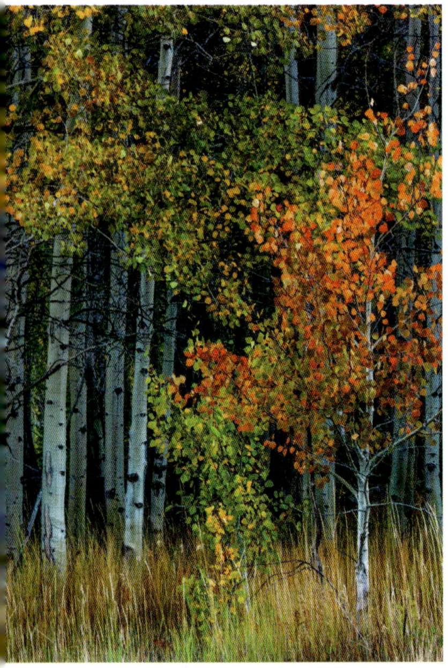

Washington Lake
Champion Lakes
Pole Creek
Boulder Mountains

LEAVING DOWN THE TRAILS IN THE LONG SAGE VALLEYS of Germania Creek or the East Fork of the Salmon where the motorbikes roar, the world begins to shift and close. You armor yourself for the sensory explosion of traffic and driving, the overload of a grocery store. And then you breathe, remembering you are still here, the Boulders still rise brown and red in the afternoon light. Heat rises off of rock and earth, the smell of sage fills your lungs. And for a second again you panic at the tininess of wilderness, at the pressures which wear at its edges and its silence. And then you breathe, for you are still here and the wild hangs above you, still rests inside, leaving you humble. It will travel the long road home with you, will rest as a source of perseverance, of certainty and a belief that, in spite of all, there is still beauty in the world and a place where you are strong.

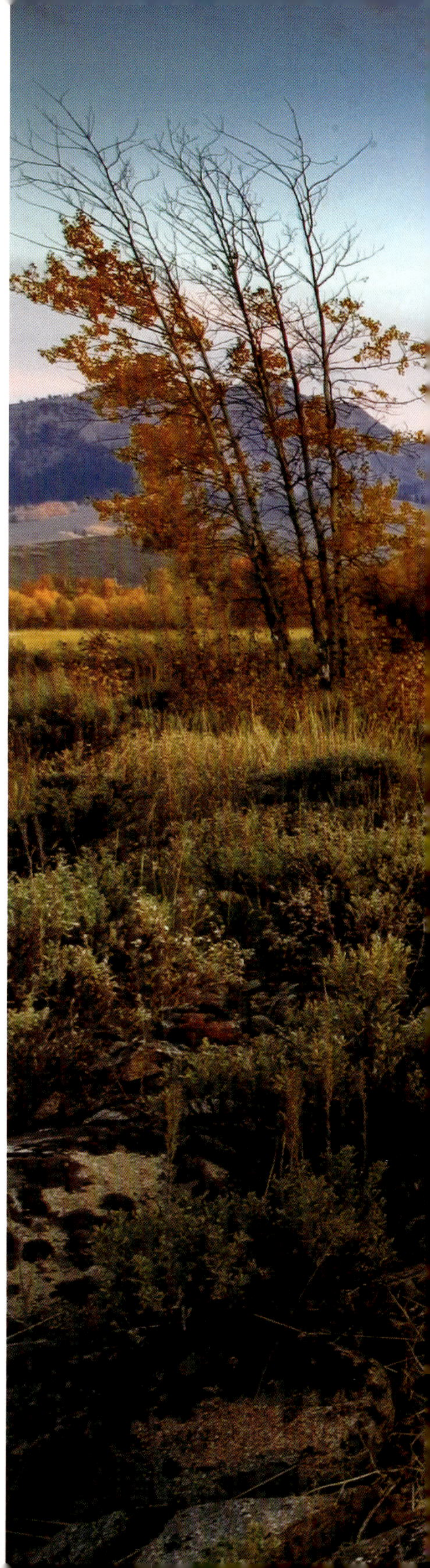

(Detail) Aspen on the trail to Horton Peak
Boulder Creek boasts some of the best fall colors in the Boulders

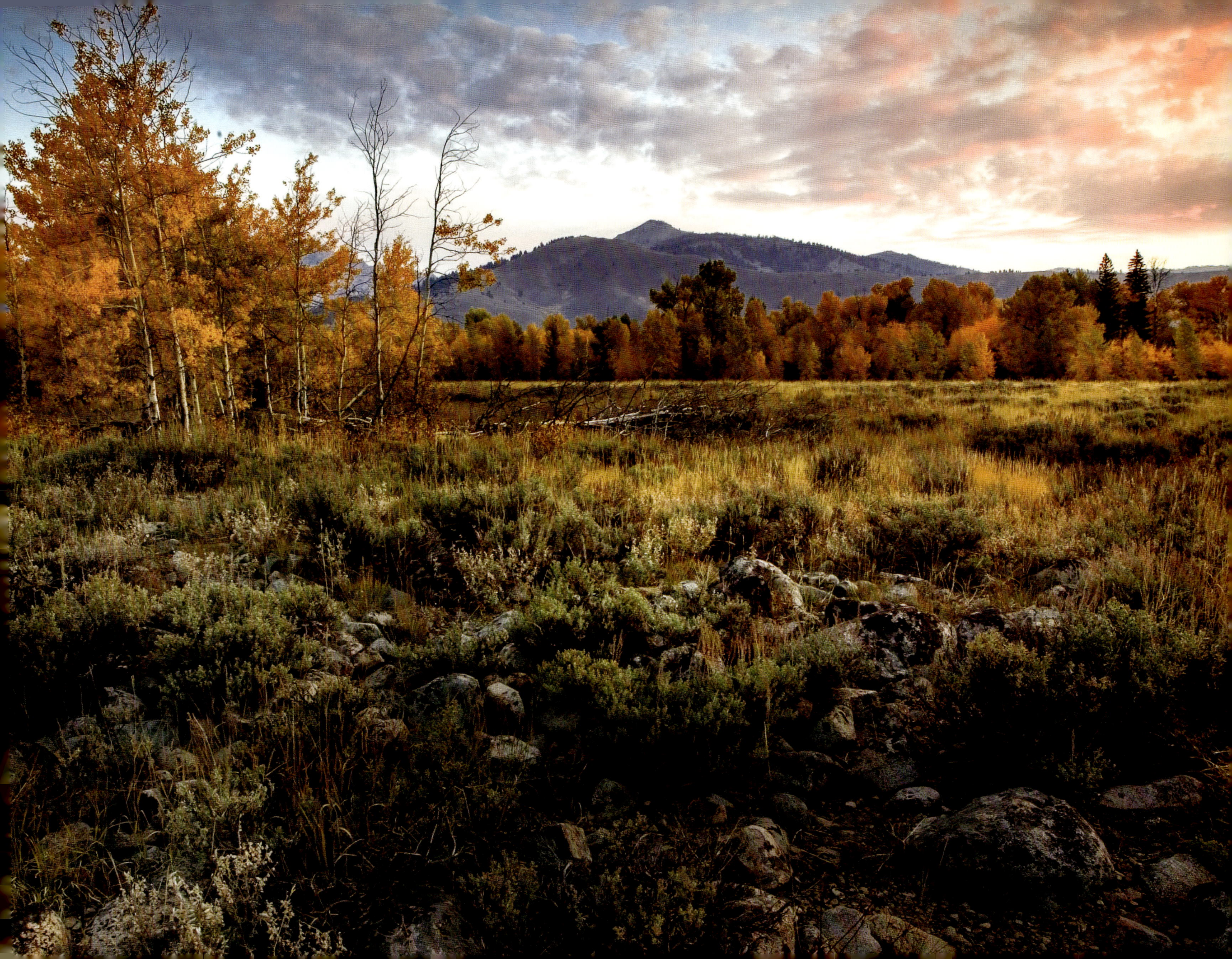

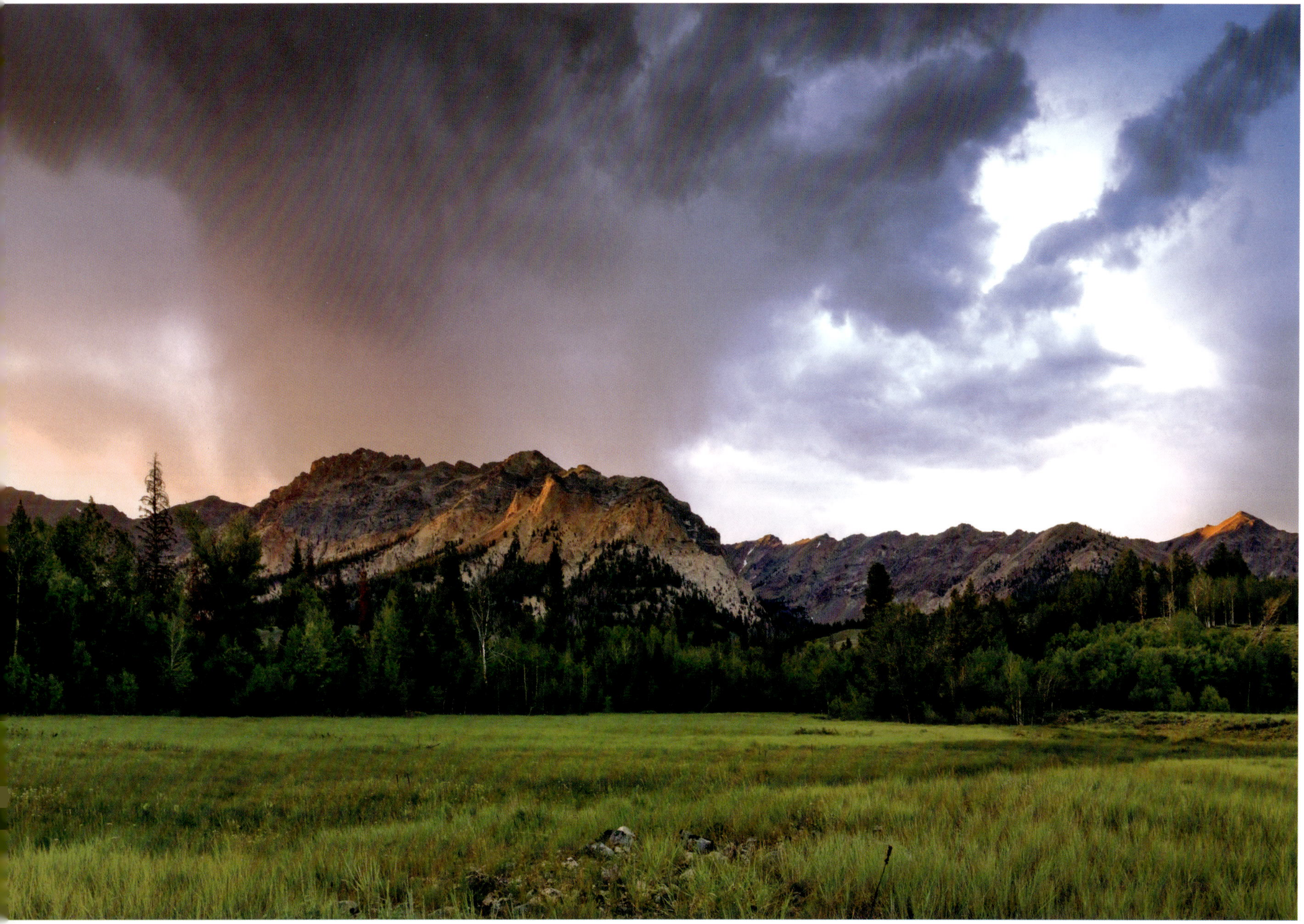

Thunderheads over Silver Peak

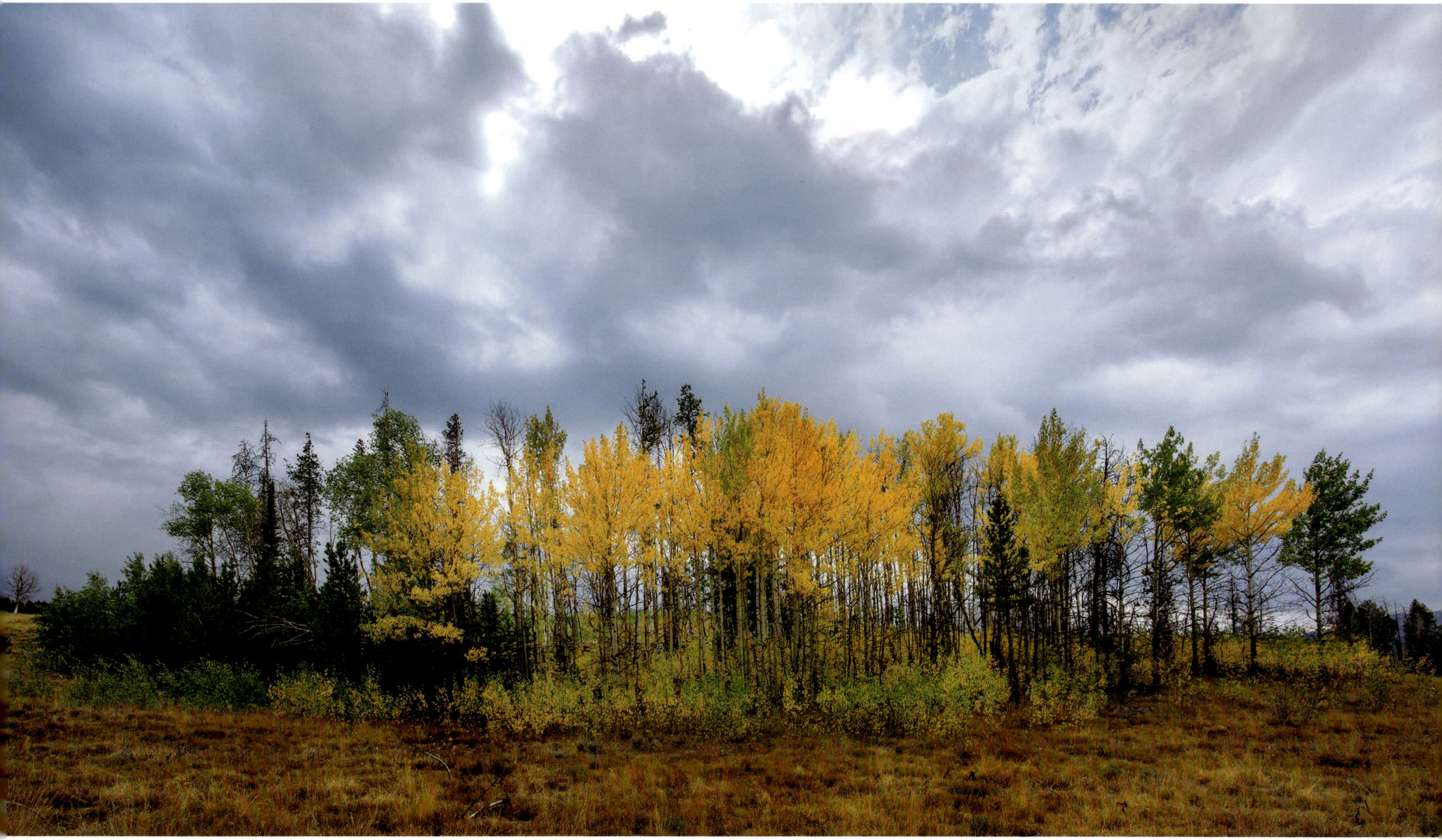

Early fall storm Pole Creek

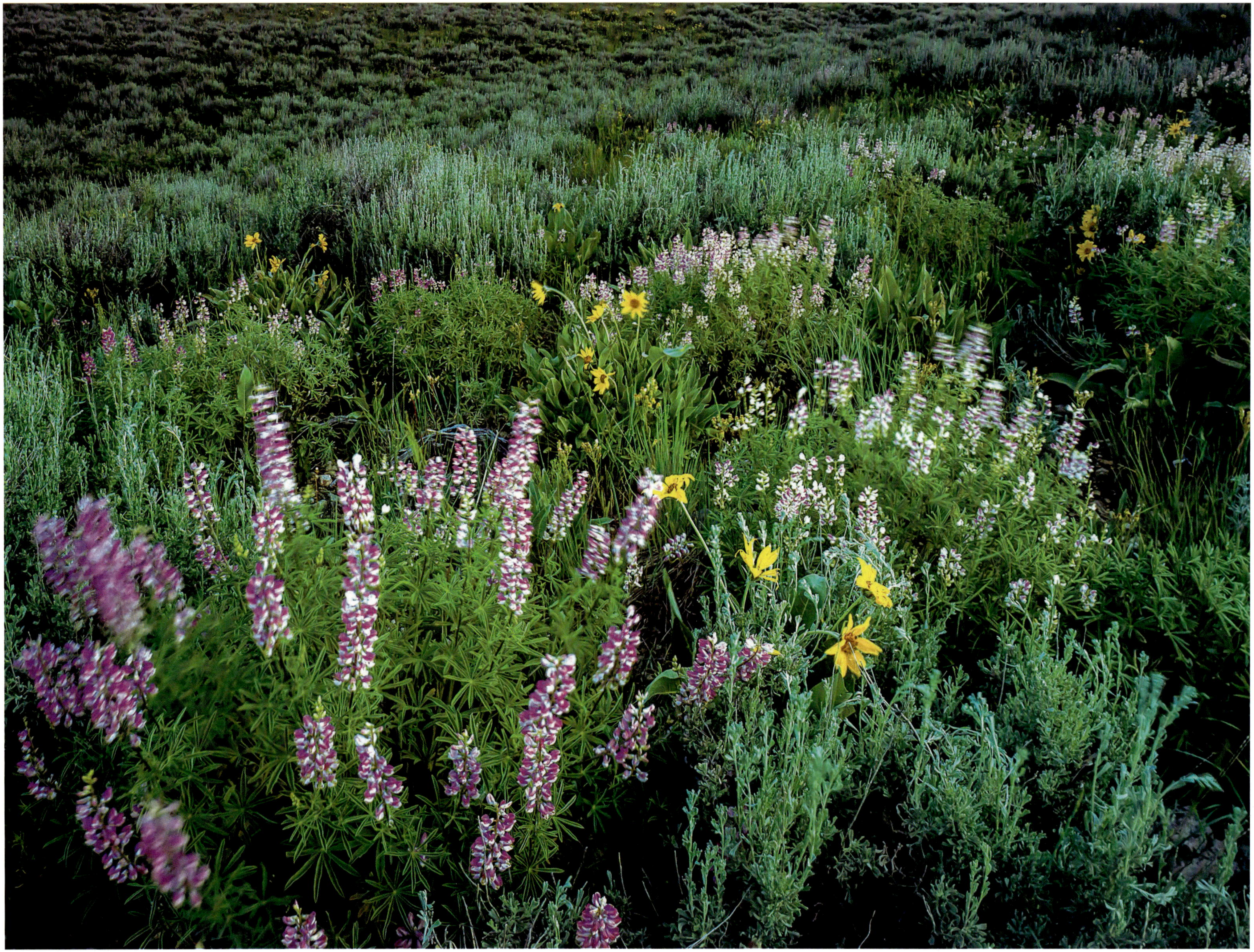

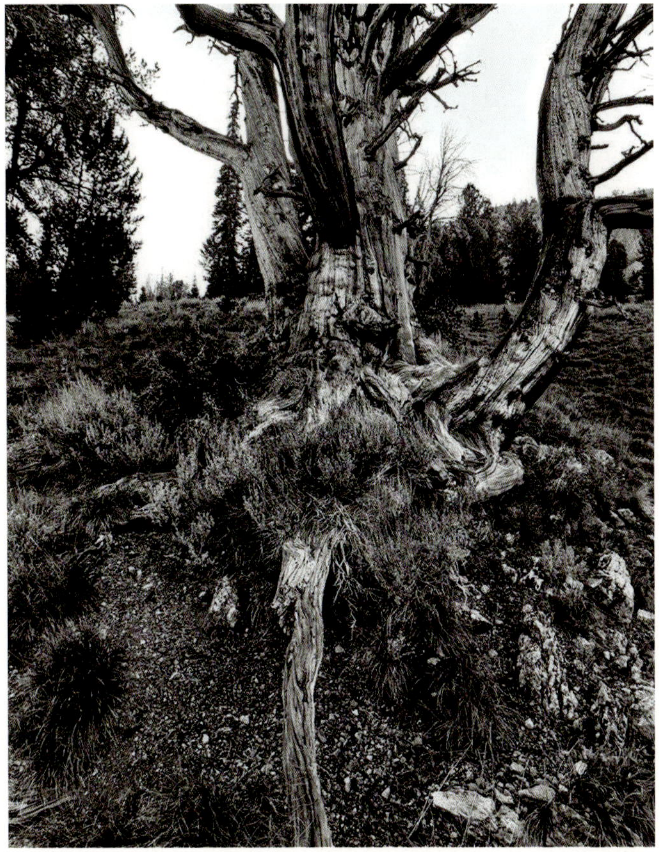

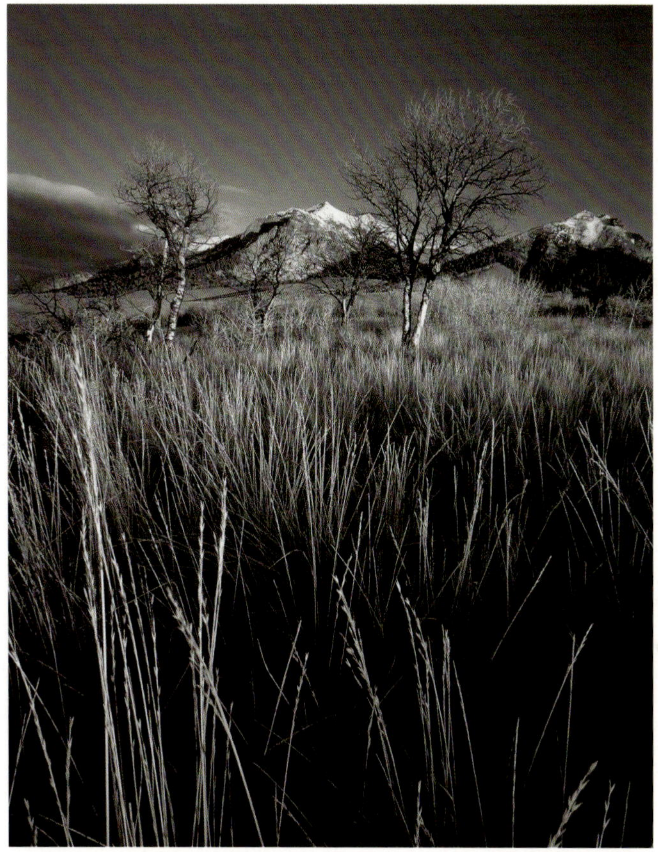

Limber pine - Champion Creek Trail

(Opposite) Boulder Range - lupine and balsam root

Boulder Peaks - Boulder Creek

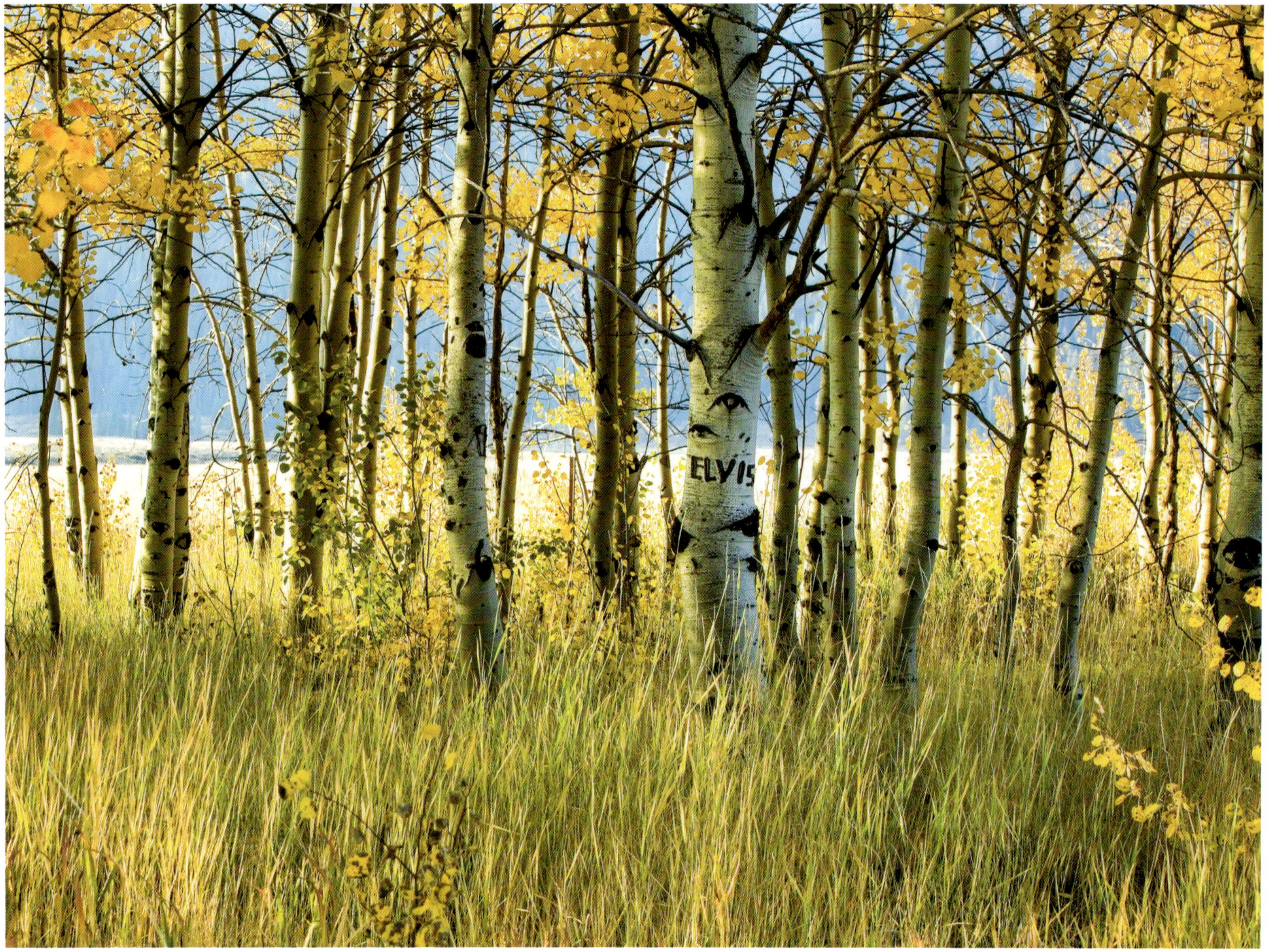

Boulder Range - Elvis Grove